# Global Leadership

## Research, Practice, and Development

Mark E. Mendenhall, Joyce S. Osland,
Allan Bird, Gary R. Oddou, and
Martha L. Maznevski

Routledge
Taylor & Francis Group

LONDON AND NEW YORK

First published 2008
by Routledge
2 Park Square, Milton Park, Abingdon, Oxon, OX14 4RN

Simultaneously published in the USA and Canada
by Routledge
270 Madison Avenue, New York, NY 10016

*Routledge is an imprint of the Taylor and Francis Group, an informa business*

© 2008 Mark E. Mendenhall, Joyce S. Osland, Allan Bird, Gary R. Oddou,
and Martha L. Maznevski

Typeset in Times New Roman and Franklin Gothic
by Keystroke, 28 High Street, Tettenhall, Wolverhampton
Printed and bound in Great Britain by
MPG Books Ltd, Bodmin, Cornwall

*British Library Cataloguing in Publication Data*
A catalogue record for this book is available from the British Library

*Library of Congress Cataloging in Publication Data*
Global leadership : research, practice, and development / Mark E. Mendenhall
... [et al.].
p. cm. – (Routledge global human resource management series)
"Simultaneously published in the USA and Canada by Routledge."
ISBN-13: 978–0–415–40523–2 (hardback)
ISBN-13: 978–0–415–40524–9 (softback)
1. Leadership. 2. Executives–Training of. 3. International business
enterprises–Personnel management. I. Mendenhall, Mark E., 1956–
HD57.7.G6527 2007
658.4′092–dc22
2007028642


ISBN10: 0–415–40524–6 (pbk)
ISBN10: 0–415–40523–8 (hbk)


ISBN13: 978–0–415–40524–9 (pbk)
ISBN13: 978–0–415–40523–2 (hbk)

# Global Leadership: Research, Practice, and Development

Global leadership is an emerging field that seeks to understand and explain the impact of globalization processes on leadership. This is the first book to review the theoretical, empirical, and conceptual literature on this important subject, and to analyze what this body of knowledge means for managers who lead in a global business context.

Accessible to both student and practitioner alike, the book explains how changes in the global context have created a demand for a distinctive set of qualities for effective leaders. The volume seeks to define the skill set that global organizations are now looking for, highlighting the need to establish communities across diverse groups of stakeholders and initiate change as key aspects of global leadership. The book also presents a critical analysis of the training and development of global leaders of the future.

Part of the successful *Global Human Resource Management* series, *Global Leadership: Research, Practice, and Development* provides an important overview of a key emerging area within business and management. It is essential reading for students of leadership, organizational theory, strategic management, human resource management, and for anyone working and managing in the global arena.

**Mark E. Mendenhall** holds the J. Burton Frierson Chair of Excellence in Business Leadership in the College of Business Administration at the Universty of Tennessee, Chattanooga.

**Dr. Joyce Osland** is the Lucas Endowed Professor of Global Leadership at San José State University's College of Business in San José, California (Silicon Valley).

**Allan Bird** is the Eiichi Shibusawa-Seigo Arai Professor of Japanese Studies and Director of the International Business Institute at the University of Missouri-St. Louis.

**Gary Oddou** is a professor of international management and directs the Global Business Management program at California State University, San Marcos.

**Martha L. Maznevski** is Lecturer Professor, IMD-International Institute for Management Development at the McIntire School of Commerce at the University of Virginia.

## Routledge Global Human Resource Management Series

*Edited by Randall S. Schuler, Susan E. Jackson, Paul Sparrow and Michael Poole*

**Routledge Global Human Resource Management** is an important new series that examines human resources in its global context. The series is organized into three strands: content and issues in global human resource management (HRM); specific HR functions in a global context; and comparative HRM. Authored by some of the world's leading authorities on HRM, each book in the series aims to give readers comprehensive, in-depth, and accessible texts that combine essential theory and best practice. Topics covered include cross-border alliances, global leadership, global legal systems, HRM in Asia, Africa, and the Americas, industrial relations, and global staffing.

**Managing Human Resources in Cross-Border Alliances**
*Randall S. Schuler, Susan E. Jackson, and Yadong Luo*

**Managing Human Resources in Africa**
*Edited by Ken N. Kamoche, Yaw A. Debrah, Frank M. Horwitz, and Gerry Nkombo Muuka*

**Globalizing Human Resource Management**
*Paul Sparrow, Chris Brewster, and Hilary Harris*

**Managing Human Resources in Asia-Pacific**
*Edited by Pawan S. Budhwar*

**International Human Resource Management**, 2nd edition
Policy and practice for the global enterprise
*Dennis R. Briscoe and Randall S. Schuler*

**Managing Human Resources in Latin America**
An agenda for international leaders
*Edited by Marta M. Elvira and Anabella Davila*

**Global Staffing**
*Edited by Hugh Scullion and David G. Collings*

**Managing Human Resources in Europe**
A thematic approach
*Edited by Henrik Holt Larsen and Wolfgang Mayrhofer*

**Managing Human Resources in the Middle East**
*Edited by Pawan S. Budhwar and Kamel Mellahi*

**Managing Global Legal Systems**
International employment regulation and competitive advantage
*Gary W. Florkowski*

**Global Industrial Relations**
*Edited by Michael J. Morley, Patrick Gunnigle, and David G. Collings*

**Managing Human Resources**
Current issues and perspectives
*Edited by Steve Werner*

**Global Leadership**
**Research, practice, and development**
*Mark E. Mendenhall, Joyce S. Osland, Allan Bird, Gary R. Oddou, and Martha L. Maznevski*

# Contents

# Illustrations

## Figures

## Tables

# Foreword

Global Human Resource Management is a series of books edited and authored by some of the best and most well-known researchers in the field of human resource management. This series is aimed at offering students and practitioners accessible, coordinated, and comprehensive books in global HRM. To be used individually or together, these books cover the main bases of comparative and international HRM. Taking an expert look at an increasingly important and complex area of global business, this is a groundbreaking new series that answers a real need for serious textbooks on global HRM.

Several books in this series, Global Human Resource Management, are devoted to human resource management policies and practices in multinational enterprises. For example, some books focus on specific activities of global HRM policies and practices, such as global compensation, global staffing, and global labor relations. Other books address special topics that arise in multinational enterprises across the globe, such as managing HR in cross-border alliances, developing strategies and structures, and developing the HR function in multinational enterprises. In addition to books on various HRM activities and topics in multinational enterprises, several other books in the series adopt a comparative, and within-region, approach to understanding global human resource management. These books on comparative human resource management can adopt two major approaches. One approach is to describe the HRM policies and practices found at the local level in selected countries in several regions of the world. This approach utilizes a common framework that makes it easier for the reader to systematically understand the rationale for the existence of various human resource management activities in different countries and easier to compare these activities across countries within a region. The second approach is to describe the HRM issues and topics that are most relevant to the companies in the countries of the region.

This book, *Global Leadership: Research, practice, and development*, is intended to describe many aspects of global leadership that multinational enterprises confront as they operate around the world. In this book, Mark Mendenhall, Joyce Osland, Allan Bird, Gary Oddou, and Martha Maznevski do a superb job in identifying and thoroughly describing the complexity and extensiveness of the various global leadership practices that MNEs need to be aware of and consider implementing. The topics covered include leadership competencies, leading global teams and global leadership development. The authors have also included several chapters specifically related to research and development issues regarding global leadership. They do all this in nine chapters that contain a wide variety of highly informative tables and figures. This is an extremely well written and highly valuable book for any global human resource scholar or global human resource professional.

This Routledge series, Global Human Resource Management, is intended to serve the growing market of global scholars and professionals who are seeking a deeper and broader understanding of the role and importance of human resource management in companies as they operate throughout the world. With this in mind, all the books in the series provide a thorough review of existing research and numerous examples of companies around the world.

Because a significant number of scholars and professionals throughout the world are involved in researching and practicing the topics examined in this series of books, the authorship of the books and the experiences of companies cited in the books reflect a vast global representation. The authors in the series bring with them exceptional knowledge of the human resource management topics they address, and in many cases the authors have been the pioneers for their topics. So, we feel fortunate to have the involvement of such a distinguished group of academics in this series.

The publisher and editor also have played a major role in making this series possible. Routledge has provided its global production, marketing and reputation to make this series feasible and affordable to academics and practitioners throughout the world. In addition, Routledge has provided its own highly qualified professionals to make this series a reality. In particular, we want to indicate our deep appreciation for the work of our series editor, Francesca Heslop. She has been very supportive of the series from the very beginning and has been invaluable in providing the needed support and encouragement to us and to the many authors in the series. She, along with her staff, including Simon Whitmore, Russell George, Victoria Lincoln, Jacqueline Curthoys, and Lindsie Court have helped make the process of completing this series an enjoyable one. For everything they have done, we thank them all.

Randall S. Schuler, Rutgers University and GSBA Zurich
Paul Sparrow, Lancaster University
Susan E. Jackson, Rutgers University and GSBA Zurich
Michael Poole, Cardiff University

# Preface

In 1990, C. K. Prahalad, in his article "Globalization: The intellectual and managerial challenges," presciently wrote that leaders would exist in

> a world where variety, complex interaction patterns among various subunits, host governments, customers, pressures for change and stability, and the need to re-assert individual identity in a complex web of organizational relationships are the norm. This world is one beset with ambiguity and stress. Facts, emotions, anxieties, power and dependence, competition and collaboration, individual and team efforts are all present. . . . Managers have to deal with these often conflicting demands simultaneously.
>
> (p. 30)

The reality that Prahalad foresaw has long since arrived; globalization and its demands have shifted the skill set necessary to lead in the twenty-first century. Headhunters are desperately trying to find executives with the right mix of skills, but they are rare and becoming difficult to find (McGarvey 2006: 375). But what are the skills that global leaders should possess in order to be successful, and what exactly is global leadership? Companies are grappling with these issues, and social scientists are hurriedly working to produce empirically sound insights to guide the selection, training, and ongoing development of global leaders (Mendenhall *et al.* 2003).

The combined factors of the leadership demands of globalization on firms, firms' responses to those demands, and social scientists' efforts to investigate global leadership have spawned a new subfield in international management and international human resource management: global leadership. This field began to come into existence in the mid-1980s but took hold firmly in the 1990s. Today, there are more scholars than ever investigating the dimensions of global leadership. Our hope is that this book will enable students, practitioners, and scholars to have ready access to the knowledge that the field has generated thus far, and will aid in the systematic investigation of the phenomenon in the future.

Chapter 1, "Leadership and the birth of global leadership," traces the heritage of scholarship from which the field of global leadership was built. It is important to review the roots of global leadership because some of the same challenges that exist in the general field of leadership have been inherited by the field of global leadership as well. Chapter 1 also explains why global leadership is conceptually different from general leadership and provides a definitional framework for the rest of the book.

In Chapter 2, "The multidisciplinary roots of global leadership," the authors note that in addition to the general field of leadership the field of global leadership also "owes a debt of gratitude to other fields of study that focus on bridging cultures, communicating and being effective across cultures, working overseas, and managing and leading people from other nations." The contributions of the fields of intercultural communication competence, expatriation, global management, and comparative leadership upon the global leadership literature are reviewed in this chapter. Chapter 3 then discusses and reviews the primary studies and models of global leadership that currently exist in the field.

Chapter 4 reviews the assessment tools and methods that scholars have used to measure global leadership competencies that were proposed in the research literature and derived from the content models that were discussed in Chapters 2 and 3. Current tools that are used are reviewed, as well as other assessment tools that exist and could be applied fruitfully to the study of global leadership competencies. Some scholars have approached the conceptualization of global leadership from a process rather than a content model-building perspective. Chapter 5 reviews the extant process models that have been developed to describe the process of global leadership development.

Chapter 6 shifts from models that focus on the leader as the primary component in global leadership, and focuses on principles derived from empirical research that are critical to successfully leading global teams. In Chapter 7 the focus shifts to the outcomes of global leadership development: knowledge creation and knowledge transfer. In this chapter the concept that global leaders act as repositories of knowledge, and thus become key components of a firm's human capital, is delineated.

By all accounts in the general leadership literature, one important aspect of leadership is to initiate change. A key function of global leaders is to lead global change efforts. In Chapter 8 the universal aspects of managing change, as well as the factors that seem particularly important in global change efforts, are discussed, and since innovation and change go hand in hand, how global leaders can promote and lead innovation is addressed. Chapter 9 broaches the critical human resource management issue of how to best go about training and developing global leaders. Development practices routinely used by global firms will be reviewed and critiqued, and the implications of the research findings in the field for the design of global leadership development programs will then be discussed.

# Acknowledgments

We would like to thank Francesca Heslop and her original team at Routledge for their professional and yeoman work in assisting us in the development, writing, and production of this book. We also express our thanks to Russell George and his team at Routledge who took over midway through the production process and who expertly shepherded the project to completion.

The publishers would like to thank the following for permission to reprint their material:

Blackwell Publishers for a figure from Bird, A. and Osland, J. 2004. "Global competencies: An introduction." In Henry Lane, Martha Maznevski, Mark Mendenhall and Jeanne McNett (eds.), *The Blackwell Handbook of Global Management*. Oxford: Blackwell: 57–80. Center for Creative Leadership: tables from Drath, W. H. (1998) "Approaching the future of leadership development." In C. D. McCauley, R. S. Moxley, and E. Van Velsor (eds.), *Handbook of Leadership Development*, p. 408, and Leslie, J. B., Dalton, M., Ernst, C., and Deal, J. (2002) *Managerial Effectiveness in a Global Context*. Greensboro, NC: Center for Creative Leadership, page 11. Elsevier, Inc. for a table material from D. Den Hartog, R. J. House, P.J. Hanges, S. A. Ruiz-Quintanilla, and P.W. Dorfman (1999) "Culture specific and cross-culturally generalizable implicit leadership theories: Are attributes of charismatic/transformational leadership universally endorsed?" *Leadership Quarterly*, 10(2): 219–256. Harvard Business School Press for a figure from McCall, M. W., Jr. and Hollenbeck, G. P. (2002) *Developing Global Executives: The Lessons of International Experience*. Boston, MA: Harvard Business School Press: page 173. John Wiley and Sons Ltd. for figures from Bird, A., "Careers as repositories of knowledge: A new perspective on boundaryless careers," *Journal of Organizational Behavior*, 15, 1994, 325–344 and Stephens, G. K., Bird, A., and Mendenhall, M. E. (2002) "International careers as repositories of knowledge: A new look at expatriation." D. C. Feldman (ed.) *Work Careers: A Developmental Perspective*. San Francisco: Jossey-Bass, pp. 294–320. McGraw-Hill, Inc. for a figure from Brake, T. (1997) "The Global Leader: Critical Factors for Creating the World Class Organization." Chicago: Irwin: 44. Pearson Inc. for a figure from "The many facets of leadership." Edited by Marshall Goldsmith, Vijay Govindarajan, Beverly Kaye and Albert A. Vicere (2003). Financial Times Prentice Hall, Upper Saddle River, NJ: page 218. Prentice-Hall for tables from Goldsmith, M., Greenberg, C., Robertson, A., and Hu-Chan, M. (2003) *Global leadership: The next generation*. Upper Saddle River, NJ: Prentice-Hall: 329–334 and Osland, J. S., Kolb, D., Rubin, I., and Turner, M. (2007) *Organizational Behavior: An Experiential Approach*, page 325. Taylor and Francis for table material from Kets de Vries, M. F. R., Vrignaud, P. and Florent-Treacy, E. (2004) "The global leadership life inventory: Development and psychometric properties of a 360-degree feedback instrument." *International Journal of Human Resource Management*, 15, 3: 475–492.

The authors would like to thank the following:

Thanks to Anu Sairaj, Shrutee Bhaskar, Karsten Jonsen for their meticulous work as research assistants. We appreciate the support of our chairs and deans: Richard Casavant and Larry Ettkin (University of Tennessee, Chattanooga); Nancie Fimbel, Abdel El-Shaieb, Michael Solt, and William Jiang (Chair), at San José State University; Keith Womer, Joel Glassman (Associate Chancellor), James Breaugh (Area Coordinator) at University of Missouri, St. Louis; Peter Lorange at IMD; and Dennis Guseman and Glen Brodowsky at California State University, San Marcos.

We would also like to thank the generous support of The Dixie Group, the J. Burton Frierson Chair of Business Leadership endowment, and the Frierson Leadership Institute at University of Tennessee, Chattanooga for their support of this project.

We would like to acknowledge the role f the membership of ION (International Organizations Network) in stiumlating our research. Finally, books are never created without family sacrifice and support. We dedicate this book to our family tribes:

Mark's crew: Janet, Anthony, Nicole, Alexis, and Zachary.

Joyce's crew: Asbjorn, Ellie and Katrina, Jessica, Joe, Zoe and Lucy, Michael, Anna, and TBD.

Allan's crew: Diane, Kyle, Allyson, Jared, and Cami.

Gary's crew: Jane, Melanie, Paul, Marc-Pierre, Susan, Shasta for his constant and positive support and Kara for the added dimension she has brought to my life that puts everything into perspective.

Martha's crew: Brian, Andrea, Katie, and Julianna.

The publishers have made every effort to contact authors/copyright holders of works reprinted in *Global Leadership: Research, Practice, and Development*. This has not been possible in every case, however, and we would welcome correspondence from those individuals/companies whom we have been unable to trace.

# Leadership and the birth of global leadership

## MARK E. MENDENHALL

> Leadership is one of the most observed and least understood phenomena on earth.
> (James MacGregor Burns)

The purpose of this book is to introduce research that has focused on leaders and leadership in the context of global business and globalization. However, before a proper introduction to the field of global leadership can be undertaken, it will first be necessary to review the field from which the discipline of global leadership evolved: leadership.

It was not until the beginning of the twentieth century, when scholars began applying the scientific method to social processes, that the study of leadership became widespread both in academe and in the business world (Yukl 2006: 2). Before this time period, leadership had been studied mostly via historical analysis, within military studies, and through biography (Bass 1990; Yukl 2006). The vast majority of empirical work from the 1930s to the 1970s was undertaken by North American and British scholars (Bass 1990), and the context of their study of leadership was primarily domestic in nature; that is, from the early part of the twentieth century through the 1970s the vast majority of social scientific studies of leadership, and concomitant theoretical developments in the field, were firmly housed in Anglo-North American contexts. In the 1980s, European and Japanese social scientists began making contributions to the study of leadership in English-language academic journals, which extended the reach of the influence of their findings among scholars globally (ibid.: xiv). By 1990 Bass would note that there were over 7,500 extant scholarly studies of leadership.

The empirical findings within the leadership field are complex, paradoxical, intriguing, and, at times, problematic. Various scholars have undertaken reviews and categorizations of the plethora of empirical studies that exist in the field. We have chosen to use the categorizations of the field by Bass (1990) and Yukl (2006) due to the comprehensive nature of their work and the scope of the studies that they covered in their reviews of the field.

## Approaches to the study of leadership

Scholars are not all cut from the same cloth; thus, they embark on the study of leadership from different perspectives and purposes when they ascertain what type of overall research approach they will use in their investigations of leadership. From these differing vantage points of the study of leadership have come varying approaches to the study of the phenomenon. Yukl (2006), in his review of the leadership literature domain, subsumes the complexity of these approaches into five general types: (1) the trait approach, (2) the behavior approach, (3) the power–influence approach, (4) the situational approach; and (5) the integrative approach.

## The trait approach

Early studies of leadership from the 1900s through the 1940s focused primarily on the discovery of key traits that separated leaders from their peers. The assumption was that internal traits, motives, personality characteristics, skills, and values of leaders were critical to leader emergence, and would predict who would and would not emerge as leaders. Numerous studies have been carried out using this approach, and after reviewing their findings, Bass noted that it was "reasonable to conclude that personality traits differentiate leaders from followers, successful from unsuccessful leaders, and high-level from low-level leaders" (1990: 86). The following traits were correlative to leadership emergence and managerial success (ibid.: 87):

- strong drive for responsibility and completion of tasks;
- vigor and persistence in the pursuit of goals;
- venturesomeness and originality in problem solving;
- drive to exercise initiative in social situations;
- self-confidence and a sense of personal identity;
- willingness to accept the consequences of one's decisions and actions;
- readiness to absorb interpersonal stress;
- willingness to tolerate frustration and delay;
- ability to influence other people's behavior;
- capacity to structure social interaction systems to the purpose at hand.

While these general findings correlated with leadership behavior, they were insufficient for predictive purposes; in other words, while some traits tended to correlate with leadership, they did not predict leadership behavior strongly enough to make them useful to real-world organizations. For example, an individual may score high in all or most of these traits, yet may not wind up emerging as a leader in the workplace or some other social situation. Thus, traits may be necessary but insufficient in and of themselves for leader emergence and effective leadership. Scholars realized that while traits play a role in leadership, other variables are also at play that likely influence the enactment of effective leadership (Yukl 2006: 182–183). Bass concluded that "who emerges as a leader and who is successful and effective is due to traits of consequence in the situation, some is due to situational effects, and some is due to the interaction of traits and situation" (1990: 87).

## The behavior approach

In partial reaction to the general failure of the trait approach as a singular method for understanding leadership dynamics, many scholars began instead to focus on the study of actual leadership behavior in relation to the internal mechanisms within a person that might cause leadership behavior (Bass 1990: 511). The focus of these scholars was to better understand what managers and leaders actually *do* while on the job and to ascertain which of these behaviors reflect effective versus ineffective leadership. This approach began in the 1950s and elicited hundreds of studies, and the pioneering research that emerged, especially from Ohio State University and the University of Michigan during the 1950s, had a significant impact on the field (Bass 1990: 511; Yukl 2006).

The Ohio State studies found the repertoire of managers' behaviors can be linked to one of two core dimensions: (1) "initiating structure" (task oriented) or "consideration" (people oriented). More specifically, initiating structure "shows the extent to which a leader initiates activity in the group, organizes it, and defines the way work is to be done" (Bass 1990: 512). It involves the maintenance of performance standards, meeting deadlines, decision making regarding job assignments, establishment of communication and work organization, etc. Consideration "describes the extent to which a leader exhibits concern for the welfare of the other members of the group" (ibid.: 511). It involves expressing appreciation for performance, focusing on workers' job satisfaction, paying attention to self-esteem levels of workers, making workers feel at ease, listening and acting on subordinates' suggestions, etc. (ibid.: 511).

Scholars found that there is no one specific configuration or balance of these two dimensions that predicts leadership effectiveness across social and work situations. For example, initiating structure becomes more critical to effective leadership when there is less structure within the group (Bass 1990). Additionally, interactions between these two factors (initiating structure and consideration) influence effective leadership; for example, "the initiation of structure by the leader (if structure is low) improves the subordinates' performance, which, in turn, increases the leader's subsequent consideration and reduces the leader's initiation of structure" (ibid.: 543). The studies carried out at the University of Michigan produced similar findings to those conducted at Ohio State University (Yukl 2006).

In short, while many insights were gained regarding understanding what constituted effective leadership, again these insights did not engender a significant increase in the ability to predict who would emerge as leaders among their peers (Yukl 2006: 51–54), due to the complex nature of how initiating structure and consideration dynamically related to each other and with various types of different work and social situations (Bass 1990).

## The situational approach

The 1960s and 1970s saw an increase in scholars who were interested in how the situation (the context, environment) influenced leadership effectiveness. This was in partial reaction to the results of the trait and behavioral approaches, which revealed that that the situation or context likely has an influence on effective leadership in addition to trait and behavioral tendencies. The aim of scholars using this approach has been to ascertain what contextual intervening variables exist that influence leadership outcomes. For example, in some types of organizational settings a specific trait in a person may assist them in being an effective leader, while in a completely different context that same trait may be detrimental to effective leadership outcomes. For example, would the traits and qualities that made the brusque World War II general George Patton a highly effective leader cause him to also be an effective president of a parent–teacher association in a modern neighborhood school district?

Theories developed from this approach are sometimes called "contingency theories," and they focus on delineating the relationships between person, situation, and leadership outcomes. Among others, the most prominent contingency theories developed during this time period were the Least Preferred Coworker (LPC) Model, the Path–Goal Theory of Leadership, Hersey and Blanchard's Situational Leadership Theory, and the Leader Substitutes Theory. While compelling in nature, in general these theories' predictive power turned out to be less than adequate when empirically tested (Yukl 2006: 215–239). Yukl has observed that "most contingency theories are stated so ambiguously that it is difficult to derive specific, testable propositions" from them, and that the empirical studies that have tested them have not been especially rigorous in their methodological designs (ibid.: 230). Despite the unresolved questions that surround these theories, they have provided the field with an important perspective: that the situation that leaders find themselves in does matter, and does influence leadership outcomes. Elements of situation or context that influence leadership outcome include "the makeup of the subordinates and the organizational constraints, tasks, goals, and functions in the situation" (Bass 1990: 510).

## The power–influence approach

Some scholars have always been interested in studying leadership through the lens of the concept of power and authority; that is, they focus on the influence processes that flow from leaders to subordinates, and view leadership as primarily a phenomenon of influence. Yukl observes that

> [t]his research seeks to explain leadership effectiveness in terms of the amount and type of power possessed by a leader and how power is exercised. Power is viewed as important not only for influencing subordinates, but also for influencing peers, superiors, and people outside the organization, such as clients and suppliers.
>
> (2006: 14)

This approach is quite common by scholars who employ a historical analysis approach to the study of leadership. Common areas of study within this approach are the difference between power and authority, the outcomes of influence attempts (particularly commitment, compliance, or resistance), the nature of influence processes, typologies of power, how power is acquired and lost, and the cataloging of influence tactics (ibid.: 146–177). The studies extant in this subfield exhibit a wide variety of scope in terms of approach and thus render even a summary review problematic; however, to provide a glimpse into their nature, we will share Yukl's overview of research on influence tactics and Bass's overview of sources of power.

Yukl notes that scholars have delineated eleven separate influence tactics that managers and subordinates use to exert power: rational persuasion, inspirational appeals, consultation, collaboration, apprising, ingratiation, exchange, personal appeals, coalition tactics, legitimating tactics, and pressure (2002: 167). These tactics, their directional usage, how they are used in differing sequences and combinations, and their likely effectiveness have been investigated. Though this research has provided much clarity regarding how influence is used in organizations, there is still much to be learned about the complexity in which these tactics are combined, deployed, and shifted, owing to a multitude of contingency factors. Yukl (ibid.: 169–170) concluded that

> [m]ost researchers treat each influence attempt as an isolated episode, rather than as part of a sequence of reciprocal influence processes that occur in an evolving relationship between the parties. As a result, we still have only a very limited understanding of influence processes in organizations and the implications for effective leadership.

French and Raven (1959) delineated five types or sources of power (expert, referent, reward, coercive, and legitimate), and their model became a foundation for many subsequent studies that focused on power and its relationship to leadership (Bass 1990: 231). Bass states that each of these five bases or sources of power can be summarized as follows (ibid.: 231–232):

- Expert power is based on B's perception of A's competence.
- Referent power is based on B's identification with or liking for A.
- Reward power depends on A's ability to provide rewards for B.
- Coercive power is based on B's perception that A can provide penalties for not complying with A.
- Legitimate power is based on the internalization of common norms or values.

While the above model seems straightforward, it turns out that the enactment of power between leaders and subordinates is complex and sometimes counterintuitive. For example, power of leaders can be diluted or counteracted by subordinates who possess high levels of self-confidence, self-esteem, and high levels of knowledge and competence regarding the task they are assigned to carry out (ibid.: 251). Thus, power is not a unidirectional, top-down force that flows from manager to subordinate. Bass (ibid.: 251) concluded that "the concept of power leaves unexplained much of what is involved in the leadership role," and that power "is not synonymous with leadership."

## The integrative approach

Yukl (2006: 15) terms the usage of the above four approaches in any combination within a single research study as the integrative approach to the study of leadership. Over the past ten years more scholars have begun to turn to this approach to the study of leadership, but it is still the exception in the field (Yukl 2002: 13). I also include within the integrative approach the recent application of nonlinear dynamics and system theory to the study of leadership. These approaches attempt to study leadership as a holistic phenomenon, assuming mutually causal relationships between all the relevant variables at play (Wheatley 2006). This approach is problematic, as measuring such complexity in real time is virtually impossible, even with the increased capability of present computer processing and software capabilities. However, attempting to get at the complexity by using different approaches in the same study has been viewed increasingly by some scholars as the best overall way to study leadership and management processes (ibid.).

\* \* \*

Within each approach to the study of leadership described above, scholars have developed different types of theories to guide their study of leadership. These theoretical developments, as we shall see, have had an impact of how global leadership has been studied as well. There are three categorizations of leadership theories made by Yukl (2006: 18–19): (1) leader-versus follower-centered theories, (2) descriptive versus prescriptive theories, and (3) universal versus contingency theories.

## Leader versus follower-centered theories

As the terminology of this categorization suggests, some scholars have focused mostly on developing theories that describe and delineate behaviors associated with leaders as opposed to their followers. This tendency has been quite common in studies associated with the trait and behavior and power–influence approaches discussed above. The tendency to focus almost solely on the leader as the center of theory building has been strong in the field, and even those working from a contingency approach have featured leader more than follower dimensions in their research (Yukl 2006: 18).

The tendency to focus on the leader as the primary element of leadership predated the social scientific study of leadership; historians, biographers, theologians, and military academies have taken this approach for centuries (Bass 1990: 37). This perspective of leadership in the social sciences has been dubbed "The Great Man Theory" of leadership, and any theory that purports to focus mainly on the leader, to the exclusion or downgrading of other variables that are part of the leadership process, is often termed a "Great Man" theory (Bass 1990).

## Descriptive versus prescriptive theories

A descriptive theory attempts to "explain leadership processes, describe the typical activities of leaders and explain why certain behaviors occur in particular situations" (Yukl 2006: 18). That is, descriptive theories are most concerned with mapping the behavioral terrain and tendencies within a given phenomenon in the hope that an in-depth understanding of the outward behavior of the phenomenon will yield insight for scholars and practitioners alike. Descriptive theories are particularly common within the behavior approach to the study of leadership (ibid.: 18).

Alternatively, Yukl notes that "prescriptive theories specify what leaders must do to become effective, and they identify any necessary conditions for using a particular type of behavior effectively" (2006: 18). Prescriptive theories try to get beneath why effective behaviors are triggered so that insight can be gained regarding what leads to effective leadership. Sometimes, leadership theorists combine aspects of both the descriptive and the prescriptive approaches in their theory-building efforts.

## Universal versus contingency theories

Universal theories are constructed to apply to leadership issues in and across all contexts, and can be either prescriptive or descriptive in nature; for example, "a descriptive universal theory may describe typical functions performed to some extent by all types of leaders, whereas a prescriptive universal theory may specify functions all leaders must perform to be effective" (Yukl 2006: 19). Contingency theories set forth the various conditions that can intervene in leadership attempts that can influence their success or failure and map the relationships between the variables at play in such situations. Thus, from the contingency perspective the future success of any leadership act is contingent upon the degree to which that act is congruent with the external conditions that are necessary in order for it to have its desired effect.

Contingency theories can be either prescriptive or descriptive as well; "a descriptive contingency theory may explain how leader behavior typically varies from one situation to another, whereas a prescriptive contingency theory may specify the most effective behavior in each type of situation" (Yukl 2006: 19).

## Unresolved problems in the field of leadership

The extant empirical and theoretical studies on leadership, while shedding much light on leadership, have also yielded challenges that have not yet been resolved by scholars working in the field. Because these challenges affect how global leadership is both studied and applied, it is necessary to review these issues before introducing the domain of global leadership.

## Problems of definition

In his review of the leadership literature, Rost (1993: 7) found that 60 percent of the studies from 1910 to 1990 contained no clear statement of definition for the phenomenon they investigated, *leadership*. The scholars simply assumed that others shared their assumptions and concept of leadership. Those scholars who did wrestle with how to define leadership for research purposes have not reached consistent agreement as to how to best define the phenomenon (Bass 1990; Rost 1993; Yukl 2006).

To study a concept like leadership scientifically, it is important to narrow one's definition of the phenomenon under study so as to be able to have a target that is manageable in terms of measurement. Broad definitions of a phenomenon require powerful, costly, complex, and sophisticated measurement instruments, owing to the necessity of having to simultaneously measure a myriad of variables that systemically interact within the phenomenon. Because it is both expensive and extremely difficult to create tools to accomplish both comprehensive and rigorous measurement of a phenomenon as complex as leadership, social scientists have focused in their research designs on more narrow aspects of leadership to study rather than the entire phenomenon. This has enabled their studies to be more rigorous in nature and more practical from a logistical and financial standpoint. This approach, however, has produced some unfortunate side effects for the field.

Because social scientists have dissected leadership into its component subprocesses in order to enhance the methodological rigor of their research design, their definitions of these component subprocesses have often been simply labeled as *leadership* when in reality their definitions reflect only parts of what constitutes leadership. As Yukl (2006) points out, social scientists have indeed tended to define leadership in terms of the portion of it that interested them as a target for their research studies, and thus "leadership has been defined in terms of traits, behaviors, influence, interaction patterns, role relationships, and occupation of an administrative position" (ibid.: 2), instead of in holistic ways. This has led to a plethora of definitions of the phenomenon of leadership and of differing conceptualizations of the nature of leadership (ibid.).

As early as 1959, Warren Bennis observed that social scientists were acting much like the proverbial blind men who each touched a different part of an elephant and then declared that the elephant was either like a wall (girth), spear (tusk), snake (trunk), tree (leg), fan (ear), or rope (tail):

> Always, it seems, the concept of leadership eludes us or turns up in another form to taunt us again with its slipperiness and complexity. So we have invented an endless proliferation of terms to deal with it . . . and still the concept is not sufficiently defined.
>
> (p. 259)

Ralph Stogdill in his 1974 review of the leadership literature stated that "there are almost as many definitions of leadership as there are persons who have attempted to define the concept" (p. 259). The situation has not changed today, over thirty years since Stogdill's observation (Bass 1990; Rost 1993; Yukl 2006).

An example of how lack of agreement over definition can cause confusion is the "leadership versus management" dichotomy. There is some disagreement in the field as to whether *leadership* is qualitatively different from the concept and practice of *management*. Warren Bennis (1989) illustrates the argument of one camp that holds that the two concepts are inherently different, and that the differences are reflected in the behavior of leaders and managers when he contends:

> The leader innovates; the manager administrates.
>
> The leader inspires; the manager controls.
>
> The leader sees the long term; the manager sees the short term.
>
> The leader asks "what?" and "why? – the manager asks "how?" and "when?"

Most scholars agree that leadership and management are different processes but that some of their dimensions are shared or overlap somewhat, and to be an effective leader one must possess skills necessary to be both a good leader and a good manager (Yukl 2006: 6–7). However, attempts at differentiating or integrating the roles, process, and relationships inherent in leadership and management systems have proven to be complex and unsuccessful, and the problem remains an important challenge in the field (Yukl 2006: 7).

Rost (1993: 6) argues that though the definitional problem in the field is bad enough, the attitude of many scholars continues to exacerbate the situation. He argues that many scholars do not see anything wrong at all with the multiplicity of definitions of leadership that exist, and that they simply "accept definitional ambiguity and confusion as something that behavioral and social scientists have to put up with and work around." This definitional permissiveness and ambiguity, it can be argued, has created a hodgepodge of empirical findings that do not make sense when compared against each other (Argyris 1979; Hosking and Morley 1988; Rost 1993). In other words, "the concept of leadership does not add up because leadership scholars and practitioners have no definition of leadership to hold on to" (Rost 1993: 8). The moral of the ancient Indian parable of 'The Blind Men and the Elephant" (see Figure 1.1), it seems, can be credibly applied to modern leadership scholars as well (Saxe 1878: 150–152).

## Problems of balkanization

John Godfrey Saxe's classic poem (Figure 1.1) applies not only to the methodological dissection of the phenomenon of leadership and the resultant problems of definition that this has caused, but to another contributing problem in the field as well: lack of multidisciplinary thinking (Rost 1993). Leaders and leadership have been a prime focus of the research of many social scientists throughout the nineteenth, twentieth, and early

| | | |
|---|---|---|
| It was six men of Indostan,<br>To learning much inclined,<br>Who went to see the Elephant<br>(Though all of them were blind),<br>That each by observation<br>Might satisfy his mind. | The Third approached the animal,<br>And happening to take<br>The squirming trunk within his hands,<br>Thus boldly up and spake:<br>"I see," – quoth he – "the Elephant<br>Is very like a snake!" | The Sixth no sooner had begun<br>About the beast to grope,<br>Then, seizing on the swinging tail<br>That fell within his scope,<br>"I see," quoth he "the Elephant<br>Is very like a rope!" |
| The First approach'd the Elephant,<br>And happening to fall<br>Against his broad and sturdy side,<br>At once began to bawl:<br>"God bless me! but the Elephant<br>Is very like a wall!" | The Fourth reached out an eager hand,<br>And felt about the knee:<br>"What most this wondrous beast is like<br>Is mighty plain," – quoth he –<br>" 'Tis clear enough the Elephant<br>Is very like a tree!" | And so these men of Indostan<br>Disputed loud and long,<br>Each in his own opinion<br>Exceeding stiff and strong,<br>Though each was partly in the right<br>And all were in the wrong! |
| The Second, feeling of the tusk,<br>Cried, – "Ho! What have we here<br>So very round and smooth and sharp?<br>To me 'tis mighty clear,<br>This wonder of an Elephant<br>Is very like a spear!" | The Fifth, who chanced to touch the ear,<br>Said – "E'en the blindest man<br>Can tell what this resembles most;<br>Deny the fact who can,<br>This marvel of an Elephant<br>Is very like a fan!" | Moral,<br>So, oft in theologic wars<br>The disputants, I ween<br>Rail on in utter ignorance<br>Of what each other mean;<br>And prate about an Elephant<br>Not one of them has seen! |

*Figure 1.1* "The blind men and the elephant"

Source: J. G. Saxe, in W. J. Linton (ed.) *Poetry of America: Selections from one hundred American poets from 1776–1876.* London: George Bell and Sons: 150–152.

twenty-first centuries, and the fields in which leadership has been studied are wide-ranging: anthropology, the arts, business, education, history, international relations, law, military, political science, psychology, religion, and sociology (Yukl 2006: 1–2). Rost (1993: 1) notes that

> [t]hese one-discipline scholars are easily recognized because they almost always put an adjective in front of the word leadership, such as business leadership, educational leadership, or political leadership; and they strongly hold the assumption that leadership as practiced in the particular profession they are studying is different from leadership as practiced in other professions.

Because leadership is studied by a variety of disciplines, each with its own preferred paradigms, worldview, and methodology, the opportunity for a broader understanding of the phenomenon exists. Unfortunately, natural bridging mechanisms do not exist between these disciplines that would allow for the dissemination and integration of scholars' findings. Interdisciplinary research is rare in academe, because it requires the learning of an entirely new scholarly paradigm, and such an endeavor is not only formidable from an intellectual standpoint but pragmatically troublesome as well. Time, effort, energy, and money that can be spent within a known research stream have to be shifted to the personal education of the scholar. Few scholars have the luxury to retrain themselves in new ways of thinking and researching, and thus the "elephant" of leadership winds up being carved up and scrutinized from many disciplines with only minor forays of attempted integration.

While there is a trend toward multidisciplinary approaches to the study of leadership by some scholars, the lion's share of leadership research is still conducted within unitary disciplines (Rost 1993). This lack of integration between academic disciplines is not unique to the field of leadership, but nevertheless the comparative paucity of multidisciplinary work in the field has no doubt restricted the development of more complex and robust models of leadership.

## The problem of Zeitgeist

In addition to the natural tendency for scholars to falsely delimit a phenomenon in order to enhance methodological rigor, Drath (1998) argued that there is another dynamic at play that influences how leadership is studied. How scholars study leadership (that is, which part of the elephant they choose to focus on) often reflects the popular views, cultural mindset, and innovative ideas regarding what constitutes *good* or *ideal* leadership during the time period in which the studies take place.

Drath (1998) contends that the influence of a given Zeitgeist on the construct of leadership causes leadership to be an evolving concept, and that leadership development methods follow the preferred ideational notion regarding leadership of a given time period. A summary of his conceptualization of the conceptual evolution of the idea of leadership is given in Figure 1.2. If one accepts Drath's perspective, leadership is an evolving phenomenon that is difficult to pin down through definition because society's view of it changes over time. It is a "complex and layered construction that has built up over the course of history. . . . This layered meaning makes it complex and hard to define, but it also makes it a versatile, useful tool that can be employed in a variety of forms" (ibid.: 409).

*Table 1.1* Evolving views of the construct of leadership

|  | *Ancient* | *Traditional* | *Modern* | *Future* |
|---|---|---|---|---|
| Idea of leadership | Domination | Influence | Common Goals | Reciprocal relations |
| Action of leadership | Commanding followers | Motivating followers | Creating inner commitment | Mutual meaning making |
| Focus of leadership development | Power of the leader | Interpersonal skills of the leaders | Self-knowledge of the leader | Interactions of the group |

Source: Drath, W. H. (1998) "Approaching the future of leadership development," In C. D. McCauley, R. S. Moxley, and E. Van Velsor (eds.) *Handbook of Leadership Development*, San Francisco/Greensboro: Jossey-Bass/Center for Creative Leadership: 408.

## Defining leader effectiveness

Another problem regarding leadership involves how effective leadership outcomes are measured. How does one know whether someone is an effective leader? Is it based on the achievement of their vision for the organization or group that they lead? If so, Gandhi would necessarily be assessed as not being an effective leader because he was not able to create a religiously or ethnically united India. Most people would hesitate to state categorically that Gandhi was not an effective leader, so if the achievement of the ultimate purpose of the leader is not a good criterion for measuring effective leadership outcomes, what is?

Traditionally, social scientists have measured leader effectiveness using a wide variety of outcome variables (Yukl 2006: 9–10), some of which are net profits, profit margin, sales increases, market share, return on investment, return on assets, productivity, attitudes of followers, commitment, absenteeism, voluntary turnover, grievances, complaints, and job transfer requests. Note that not all the variables listed are commonly included in any one empirical study; rather, the list reflects the range of variables that have commonly been used by leadership scholars.

If managers are able to increase sales and market share in their divisions, yet have fairly high levels of voluntary turnover, grievances, and complaints, are they effective leaders? And if they have low levels of voluntary turnover, grievances, and complaints, yet have declining sales and low market share, are they effective leaders? Again, the aspect of leadership effectiveness that is most salient to the researcher often drives how leadership is defined, and the interpretation of the subsequent empirical findings.

## Willingness to follow versus gaining compliance

Some definitions of leadership rely heavily on the notion that leaders must be able to influence other people to do tasks that are necessary for the survival of the group or organization. This has led to another bifurcation among scholars, however: "Do leaders have to elicit a willingness to follow them from subordinates in order to be an effective leader or is it enough to be able gain compliance from subordinates?"

How one answers this question has significant implications in terms of what variables one selects to use in a research study and how one even evaluates who is a leader and who is not. In a company, how an HR manager answers this question elicits marked differences in the design and implementation of leadership development programs.

## Conclusion

It is on the basis of scholars' assumptions and biases regarding how they view leadership that research methodologies are constructed and studies are carried out. It is no wonder, then, that research support for traditional leadership theories is mixed, at best (Yukl 2006).

It would be incorrect to infer from the discussion thus far, however, that there is complete theoretical or empirical confusion in the field of leadership. Social scientists have done a creditable job of delineating in detail many subprocesses and components of the leadership phenomenon, and much valuable information has been learned and applied to good measure by managers and organizations from the extant empirical and theoretical literature. We will now begin to introduce how the heritage of the field of leadership has influenced the development of the study and understanding of global leadership.

## Global leadership: where did it come from?

The emergence of international business as a separate field of study in the 1950s and 1960s (Toyne and Nigh 1997) led some scholars working in that area to consider how leadership operated in other cultures and the attendant implications of these cross-cultural leadership differences for international businesspeople working in multinational corporations. However, these types of studies constituted a minority of the studies conducted in the international business field. The prevailing areas of study focused on macro-level issues that related to "the firm's relationship with its external environment" (Boyacigiller and Adler 1997: 398).

In the 1960s, some scholars studying business management began to look at the challenges associated with managing human resources in multinational corporations (MNCs), and their work led to a more sophisticated understanding of the nature of national cultures and their effects upon how MNC subsidiaries should be managed on a country-by-country basis. This rubric of research was termed "comparative management" because of its focus on studying how indigenous cultures differed across dimensions of leadership, motivation, decision making, etc. These scholars also did pioneering work in extending anthropological frameworks of culture to the study of business practices (Redding 1997; Schollhammer 1969).

The 1970s saw an increase in the number of studies done on expatriate managers and the challenges associated with managing subordinates from national cultures different from one's own, in contexts outside of one's country of birth (Mendenhall and Oddou 1985). Studies of expatriate managers increased significantly in the late 1980s and throughout the 1990s, raising awareness and insight regarding the role that culture plays as a contingent variable in cross-cultural managerial and leadership effectiveness (Thomas and Lazarova 2006). Much of this research was driven in the background by the advent of globalization as a new reality in international business. Attendant with the rise of globalization in the 1990s was the prospect that

> the traditional distinction between domestic and multinational companies had started to become blurred. International competition was no longer the preserve of industrial giants.

. . . Statistics from the 1960s show that only 6 percent of the U.S. economy was exposed to international competition. By the late 1980s, the corresponding figure was over 70 percent and climbing fast.

(Evans *et al.* 2002)

In the mid-1980s, Gunnar Hedlund observed the following, presaging the current reality of global business:

A radical view concerning globality is that we are witnessing the disappearance of the international dimension of business. For commercial and practical purposes, nations do not exist and the relevant business arena becomes something like a big unified "home market."

(1986: 18)

Responding to Hedlund's prescient view above, Evans *et al.* (2002: 25) observed, "By the early 1990s, this was no longer a radical proposition." The management challenges that continually spawned out of globalization increased the need on the part of MNCs to develop executives who could manage and lead from a global perspective (Mendenhall *et al.* 2003). Suddenly, leadership was deemed to be more complex and challenging than had previously been the case, owing to the onslaught of the processes of globalization. Various scholars' surveys of the HR concerns of MNCs since the late 1990s have elicited almost identical findings: that developing global leadership and business competence in leaders is a high priority for most firms (Gregersen *et al.* 1998; Mendenhall, *et al.* 2003; Suutari, 2002). In other words, firms have begun to realize that people are the key to global success. Perhaps the concern can be summarized usefully by the following statement (Black *et al.* 199a: 1–2):

People formulate and implement strategy. . . . The strategy of a company is a function of its strategy makers. For example, whether they recognize or miss global threats or opportunities is a function of their experience and perspective. How they structure an organization for global reach and results depends on how they see the world of organizations, markets, competitors.

There is no doubt that executives face complex challenges of leadership because of the evolving globalized context in which they work, but what is it about the global context that is so challenging? "The term 'global' encompasses more than simple *geographic reach* in terms of business operations. It also includes the notion of *cultural reach* in terms of people and *intellectual reach* in the development of a global mindset" and global skills (Osland *et al.* 2006).

Lane *et al.* (2004a) argued that globalization is a term that has been used to attempt to describe what is in reality "increased complexity." They argue that there are four dimensions of complexity in the global context that together in a systemic, ongoing "combining" cause a plethora of business challenges that often are unforeseen and inherently unpredictable to executives. The first dimension, multiplicity, reflects the geometric increase in the number and type of issues that global leaders must deal with compared to domestic leaders: "Globalization is not just about 'more'; it's about 'more and different.'" Multiplicity reflects the necessity of global leaders having to deal with more and different competitors, customers, governments, stakeholders, and NGOs, in addition to multiplicity on all aspects along the value chain. Additionally, organizations must choose from an almost infinite variety of permutations of models of organizing and conducting business in their worldwide operations (ibid.).

The second aspect of the complexity inherent in globalization is the notion interdependence. Lane *et al.* (2004a: 11) note that "with fast and easy movement of capital, information, and people, distributed units are no longer isolated." Interdependencies generate complexity in that global leaders must be able to attend to, and manage, more complex systems of human and technological interaction than those faced by domestic leaders. The increase of interdependencies in economies, along all aspects of the value change – mergers and acquisitions, alliances, joint ventures, virtual teamwork, etc. – all create a higher bar for leaders in terms of performance and skill set acquisition.

Ambiguity is the third element of global complexity. Lack of information clarity, unclear cause and effect relationships, and equivocality regarding information (where multiple interpretations of the same facts are possible) exist in domestic work settings, but are increased in global work settings. Additionally, cross-cultural differences in norms in the interpretation of both qualitative and quantitative information add to the challenge of managing across borders (Lane *et al.* 2004b).

These three elements of globalization, in operation together, cause a multiplier effect that continually produces dynamic complexity in the global business realm.

And, "as if multiplicity, interdependence, and ambiguity were not enough on their own, the whole system is always in motion, always changing. And it seems to be changing at a faster rate all the time" (Lane *et al.* 2004a: 17). Flux, the ever-changing metacontext in which dynamic complexity takes place, is an environment of nonlinear, ongoing shifting in terms of system dynamics, values, organizational structure, industry trends, and sociopolitical stability.

The responses to the challenges of the complexity of globalization on the part of industry were swift: "We need executives who can handle this complexity and we need them fast." Global leadership development programs were established, and training quickly ensued. These programs were normally generated internally within companies, often with the assistance of external consultants, and were based not on empirical findings of the actual dimensions of global leadership but rather on what seemed to make sense to the designers (Von Glinow 2001).

Von Glinow (2001) noted that in the 1990s some global firms designed programs around what they traditionally viewed as the three to five core skills they associated with global executive competence, while other firms developed programs that addressed upwards of thirty or more skills that they felt were important in the development of global leaders. This hodgepodge approach led to poor results, further exacerbating the problem that firms faced: the developing of executives who could lead globally. When firms turned to academe for help, there was no response, except "We are not really sure what the dimensions of global leadership are that should act as anchors and as guides for your training curricula." Scholars began to respond to these business needs, and a field was born (Mendenhall 2006).

The field of global leadership thus began with a small cadre of scholars who were (1) determined to map the phenomenon in order to assist firms in their global leadership development efforts, and (2) eager to explore the empirical and theoretical dimensions of leadership as it applied to globalization. The field of global leadership is in its nascence, yet it has built a base of research that can offer useful direction to organizations that struggle with developing an executive cadre that is truly global in mindset and in leader-related competencies. The need for global leaders in firms has not changed; what has changed is that there is now more research than in the 1990s upon which to base global leadership development programs. The purpose of this book is to share this research and to draw from it conclusions relating to organizational practice. Before we embark on that journey, however, we must first address one more critical question: "What is the difference between global leadership and 'regular' or traditional leadership?"

## Global leadership versus traditional leadership

Some executives and managers wonder what is so special about the notion of global leadership – is it not simply sound leadership principles applied to the global context? And if so, does it really make much sense to carve out an entirely different term when a better one, *leadership*, exists? In a way, it is a similar argument to the one heretofore discussed: what is the real difference between leadership and management? In this case, the permutation is: "Are not global leadership and traditional leadership in essence the same concept?"

Some scholars working in the area of global leadership concede the point that while most – if not all – competencies associated with leadership from the traditional or domestic leadership literature are necessary to lead globally, the global context places such high demands on the deployment of those competencies that for all intents and purposes the skill level and deployment demands render the phenomenon so different in degree that it makes sense to address it as being different in kind to traditional leadership.

Specifically, the global context significantly increases for leaders the valence, intensity, and complexity of key contextual dimensions that also exist for those leading in a domestic context. It can be argued that global leadership

> differs from domestic leadership in *degree* in terms of issues related to connectedness, boundary spanning, complexity, ethical challenges, dealing with tensions and paradoxes, pattern recognition, and building learning environments, teams, and community and leading large-scale change efforts – across diverse cultures.
>
> (Osland and Bird 2006: 123)

Additionally, it can be argued that global leadership differs from domestic leadership in *kind*, owing to the nature of the outcomes the global context potentially can produce in people who must live and work in it. Living and working constantly in a global context, and experiencing the ongoing intensity of the dimensions of complexity discussed by Lane and his colleagues, can trigger a transformational experience within managers (Osland 1995). These powerful transformational or crucible experiences (Bennis and Thomas 2002; Osland 1995) have been found to produce new mental models in the individual – new worldviews, mindsets, perceptual acumen, and perspectives that simply do not exist within people who have not gone through such a series of experiences in a global context. It is this transformational process, which can only occur within someone working globally, that leads many scholars to infer that global leadership differs sufficiently in degree – or perhaps even kind – from traditional leadership to warrant studying it as a separate phenomenon (Osland *et al.* 2006)

As we move now to a more in-depth treatment of the theories, models, and findings in the field of global leadership, it is important to pause and consider what we, the co-authors of this book, mean when we use the terms "global leaders" and "global leadership." Just as in the traditional leadership literature, there is no agreed-upon definition of global leadership in the field. For the purposes of this book, we will use the following broad definition when we refer to global leaders/leadership:

> **Global leaders** are individuals who effect significant positive change in organizations by building communities through the development of trust and the arrangement of organizational structures and processes in a context involving multiple cross-boundary stakeholders, multiple sources of external cross-boundary authority, and multiple cultures under conditions of temporal, geographical and cultural complexity.

# The multidisciplinary roots
# 2 of global leadership

JOYCE S. OSLAND

So the journey is over and I am back again where I started, richer by much
experience and poorer by many exploded convictions, many perished certainties.
For convictions and certainties are too often the concomitants of ignorance. Those
who like to feel they are always right and who attach a high importance to their own
opinions should stay at home. When one is traveling, convictions are mislaid as
easily as spectacles; but unlike spectacles, they are not easily replaced.

(Aldous Huxley, *Jesting Pilate*)

The field of leadership, reviewed in the previous chapter, is not the sole contributor to
understanding global leadership. The differences in degree and kind between domestic
and global leadership are also rooted in global leadership's multidisciplinary evolution.
The study of global leadership owes a debt of gratitude to other fields of study that focus
on bridging cultures, communicating and being effective across cultures, working
overseas, and managing and leading people from other nations. We will discuss these
fields and their contribution to global leadership in the following sections: intercultural
communication competence, expatriation, global management, and comparative
leadership.

## Intercultural communication competence

As you continue reading this book, you will find numerous allusions to the importance of
communication. Intercultural communication competence (for reviews, see Dinges and
Baldwin 1996 and Deardorff 2006) has much to contribute to any field that crosses
cultural boundaries, but it is especially important for global leaders as they attempt to
understand and motivate followers, partners, and stakeholders, transmit their vision, and
receive feedback from others. Intercultural communication competence has been defined
as "the ability to effectively and appropriately execute communication behaviors that
negotiate each other's cultural identity or identities in a culturally diverse environment"
(Chen and Starosta 1999: 28). Appropriateness means taking cultural expectations and
the feelings of the other person into consideration and behaving consistently with those

expectations. Intercultural communication competence comprises knowledge, skills, attitudes, and awareness (Fantini 2000). It includes knowledge that is culture-specific (pertaining to a particular country), culture-general (pertaining to all foreign cultures), and context-specific (e.g., a business setting). Individuals who are competent also possess a good understanding of their own culture.

After reviewing the literature, Pusch (1994) concluded that intercultural competence involves the ability to manage psychological stress, communicate effectively, and establish interpersonal relationships; Paige (1993) tested and confirmed this hypothesis. According to Gudykunst (1994), the most important intercultural skills are mindfulness, cognitive flexibility, behavioral flexibility, tolerance for ambiguity, and cross-cultural empathy. Empathy is defined as "the ability to experience some aspect of reality differently from what is 'given' by one's own culture" (Bennett 1993: 53). Mindfulness is defined as the process of thinking in new categories, being open to new information, and recognizing multiple perspectives. Being mindful means switching from automatic communication routines to paying attention simultaneously to the internal assumptions, cognitions, and emotions of both oneself and the other person (Thich 1991). Thus, a related skill is the ability to see things through the eyes and mind of others, which is known as perspective taking (Tye 1990).

Paige (1993) built on these ideas to create the following description of intercultural communication competence, which includes the ability to do the job in question (technical skills) and acknowledges contextual variations (situational factors):

- knowledge of the target culture;
- personal qualities (i.e., flexibility, tolerance of ambiguity, sense of humor, openness);
- behavioral skills (communicative competence);
- self-awareness (one's values and beliefs);
- technical skills (e.g., the ability to accomplish tasks);
- situational factors (e.g., clarity of expectations, psychological pressure).

"There is no prescriptive set of characteristics that guarantees competence in all intercultural relationships and situations" because competence also depends on the "characteristics of the association" between the communicators and on the situation itself (Lustig and Koester 2003: 65). Not every relationship or every situation requires the same skill set. For example, speaking the language of the foreign culture is not a component of intercultural communication competence. However, it is appreciated in some cultures, and those who make the effort have a different relationship with host-country nationals, characterized by different communication situations.

Some scholars view intercultural communication competence as a process that begins with an ethnocentric view that is eventually transformed into intercultural communication competence (e.g., Hoopes 1979; Bennett 1993; Pedersen 1994; Fennes and Hapgood 1997). Fennes and Hapgood (1997) argue that this process includes overcoming ethnocentrism, acquiring the ability to empathize with others, and acquiring the ability both to communicate and to cooperate across cultural boundaries. The capacity to expand

and adapt one's frame of reference and match the behaviors of others is implicit in this process (Fennes and Hapgood 1997). Two of the basic tools used to understand the communication patterns of other cultures are differences in style and nonverbal communication (cf. Ting-Toomey 1999). Behavioral flexibility refers to a willingness to adopt and use different styles appropriately. Intercultural communication skills are sometimes summarized as observation, description, interpretation, and suspending evaluation (ODIS) (ibid.: 1999). Given the extent of intercultural communication in which global leaders engage, competence in this area is a necessity. To global leadership, the field of intercultural communication competence contributes these lessons – the importance of:

- learning the expectations and communication practices of other cultures;
- practicing mindfulness, empathy, perspective taking (which are all foundations for a global mindset);
- building relationships, handling stress, and switching communication styles as appropriate;
- acknowledging that different competencies and skills are required in different contexts and situations.

## Expatriation

Expatriates are employees who have been sent by their employers to reside and work outside of their home country on temporary assignment. The term includes expatriate businesspeople, diplomats, employees of international nonprofit organizations, military personnel, and missionaries, among others. While international students and people who go abroad to find work on their own are not technically categorized as expatriates, they share the experience of learning to adapt and function in another culture.

Just as immersion in a foreign country is the most efficient and effective way to learn its language, an expatriate assignment is commonly viewed as the best way to develop global leaders. When asked to name the most powerful experience in their lives for developing global leadership capabilities, 80 percent of those surveyed responded that it was living and working abroad (Gregersen et al. 1998). This belief in the crucial role of international assignments in developing global leaders prompted renewed interest in the nature of the expatriate experience, selection, adjustment, transformation, and effectiveness.

## The expatriate experience

The inherent nature of an overseas assignment makes it a valuable opportunity for personal growth (Mendenhall and Oddou 1985; Osland 1995). In addition to supplementary, more important, and broader work responsibilities, expatriates generally have more independence and potential impact on operations than they do in a domestic job (Oddou and Mendenhall 1988). The challenging nature of the experience leads many people to question their mental models and develop new ones, which contributes to a global mindset. For better or worse, expatriates are upended by concurrent changes in cultures, job context, and social support – a Petri dish for stress, accelerated learning, paradoxes, and personal transformation (Osland 1995).

Paradoxes and contradictions are an inherent part of the cross-cultural experience. Paradox can be defined as "a situation involving the presence of contradictory, mutually exclusive elements that operate equally at the same time" (Quinn and Cameron 1988). Examples of expatriate paradoxes are "seeing as valid the general stereotype about the culture but also realizing that many host-country nationals do not fit that stereotype," "feeling at ease anywhere but belonging nowhere as a result of being abroad a long time," and "possessing a great deal of power as a result of your role but downplaying it in order to gain necessary input and cooperation" (Osland 1995). Expatriates dealt with these and other paradoxes by trying to understand the "foreign" side of the paradox, determining their role in the specific situation and whether they had an ethical right to take action, weighing the contingencies, discerning critical factors for success or effectiveness, picking their battles, accepting what they could not change, and learning from the experience so they could apply it to the next paradox (Osland 2001). Wrestling with paradox helps develop behavioral flexibility, cognitive complexity, and the ability to manage uncertainty – all aspects of global leadership. The link between expatriation and global leadership development will be delineated more fully in Chapter 9.

## Expatriate selection

Despite uncertain results, some firms continue to select expatriates solely on their technical competence or their willingness to go abroad (Mendhenhall et al. 2002). Past performance in a domestic setting is not a good predictor of excellent performance overseas (Black et al. 1999b; Miller 1973). The strengths of many North American high-potentials actually translate into liabilities in the global context (Ruben 1989). The characteristics that get US high-potentials noticed – "propensity for risk-taking, a passion or commitment to seeing the organization succeed, courage to go against the grain, and a keen mind" (Spreitzer et al. 1997) – are usually found in hard-driving, self-motivated, assertive, and outwardly passionate and self-confident individuals (Mendenhall 2001a). These qualities are not universally valued and may in fact lead to failure in other countries. The same findings may apply to high-potential employees of other nationalities.

After reviewing the literature, Kealey (2003) proposed that the "model cross-cultural collaborator" possesses three categories of nontechnical skills: (1) adaptation skills (e.g., flexibility, stress tolerance), (2) cross-cultural skills (e.g., realism, cultural sensitivity), and (3) partnership skills (e.g., openness to others, professional commitment). Recent research has utilized the NEO PI-R Five-Factor Model of personality (Costa and McCrae 1992) to judge whether particular personality traits correlate with expatriate outcomes such as adjustment, effectiveness, and likelihood of completing their assignment. The results indicate that expatriates who are emotionally stable, outgoing and agreeable, open to experience (Shaffer *et al.* 2006), flexible, and not ethnocentric appear to function better than other expatriates (Caligiuri 2000; Caligiuri and DiSanto 2001). This research also indicated that selection practices should identify people who are motivated to attain assigned task goals and interact with others in the workplace and who show cultural flexibility (Shaffer *et al.* 2006; cf. Black *et al.* 1999a). Cultural flexibility is the ability to substitute activities enjoyed in one's native country with existing, and usually distinct, activities in the host country (e.g., baseball instead of cricket or vice versa).

## Expatriate adjustment

Expatriate adjustment refers to the psychological (dis)comfort or (dis)stress experienced while on assignment (Black 1988; Black *et al.* 1991). This construct has three dimensions: work adjustment (comfort with the assigned task or job), interaction adjustment (comfort interacting with host country nationals inside and outside of work), and general or cultural adjustment (e.g., general living conditions, local food, transportation, entertainment, facilities and health care services in the host country) (Black *et al.* 1991; Shaffer *et al.* 1999).

Mendenhall and his colleagues (2002) created a typology of expatriate adjustment models: (1) learning models (e.g., social information processing); (2) stress-coping models; (3) developmental models (stages of personal growth); and (4) personality-based models. These approaches may serve as examples for future models of global leadership.

> Expatriate adjustment is not a linear accumulation of knowledge. Adjusting to a new culture requires learning and internalizing new worldviews – new cognitive "software systems" – that must run simultaneously with one's own, traditional, cultural software system. Then, these separate software systems must be integrated into a new, more complex software system, one that sees more deeply into the complexities of the reality of the context in which the expatriate finds himself or herself.
>
> (Mendenhall 2001a: 7–8)

Thus, adjustment involves changes in cognition and what Osland and Bird (2000) call cultural sensemaking.

Researchers have identified the individual and external characteristics that correlate significantly with expatriate adjustment, which can also be viewed as selection criteria. The individual determinants are shown in Table 2.1. This exhibit also indicates the global leadership competencies identified in empirical research that appear to be conceptually similar to expatriate adjustment determinants. All the expatriate adjustment determinants, with the exception of extroversion, relate to a subset of global leadership competencies. This provides evidence of similarity between these two fields and explains why expatriation is included in discussions of global leadership. The overview of the global leadership literature in the next chapter indicates, however, that global leadership is more extensive and broader in scope than expatriate adjustment.

*Table 2.1* Individual determinants of expatriate adjustment and related global leadership competencies

| Expatriate adjustment determinants | Related global leadership competencies |
| --- | --- |
| Self-efficacy | Personal literacy, optimistic |
| Resilience | Resilience, resourcefulness, energy |
| Behavioral flexibility | Flexibility |
| Curiosity | Inquisitiveness, cultural interest |
| Extroversion | *No correlate* |
| Broad category width | Savvy |
| Flexible attributions | Cognitive complexity |
| Open-mindedness | Open-mindedness |
| High tolerance for ambiguity | Duality, cognitive complexity |
| Empathy/respect for others | Cultural sensitivity, social literacy |
| Nonverbal communications | Social literacy |
| Relationship skills | Social literacy, building partnerships |
| Willingness to communicate | Social literacy, constructive dialogue |

## Expatriate transformation

The developmental models of expatriate adjustment are more accurately called transformational models. Peter Adler (1975) developed a five-stage model comprising (1) contact with the other culture, (2) disintegration, (3) reintegration, (4) autonomy, and (5) independence. Pederson described the transformation that occurs during culture shock as "a series of degeneration and regeneration events of crises in a nonregular and erratic movement of change" that is both conscious and unconscious as the person tries to be more successful in the other culture (1995: 4). Osland (1995) uses the framework of the hero's journey as a metaphor for expatriate transformation.

There are many reports, both anecdotal and empirical, of ways in which expatriates change as a result of an international assignment. According to Osland (1995), they described four types of changes: positive changes in self, changed attitudes, improved work skills, and increased knowledge. The *positive changes in self* were increased tolerance, patience, confidence, respectfulness, maturity, open-mindedness, competitiveness, adaptability, independence, and sensitivity, and decreased impulsiveness. The *changed attitudes* concerned a broader perspective on the world, greater appreciation of cultural differences, increased realization of how fortunate they (in this case, Americans) were, different attitudes toward work, and a feeling that life was more interesting now than before. These attitudes are indications of greater cognitive complexity. The improved work skills they mentioned were improved interpersonal and communication skills, especially better listening skills, improved management style, a better understanding of power, the ability to do higher-quality work, and broadened exposure to business. The increased knowledge they reported had to do with a wide array of topics related to both global business and foreign countries. These findings confirm the original research by Oddou and Mendenhall (1991: 30), in which 135 expatriates were surveyed to discover the "value added" of their assignments: a wider global perspective on their firm's business operations; greater planning ability; increased ability to communicate with people of diverse backgrounds; increased ability to conceptualize and comprehend business trends and events due to their exposure to contrasting cultural, political and economic work systems; and better motivators as a result of working with culturally diverse personnel overseas. These changes have much in common with the global leadership competencies to be discussed in Chapter 3: business savvy, continuous learning, ability to manage uncertainty, cognitive complexity, behavioral flexibility, and cross-cultural skills. The particular ways expatriates change and the degree to which they are transformed varies according to the individual expatriate and the type of adventure he or she sought overseas (Osland 1995).

Repatriates, however, showed agreement in their description of the transformation process itself – a process of letting go and taking on (Osland 1995) that is summarized in Table 2.2. Many forms of transformation involve a death ("letting go") and rebirth ("taking on"). During their sojourn, expatriates let go of cultural certainty and take on the internationalized perceptions of the other culture. They learn how other countries perceive their country, perhaps in ways that are not always favorable; and they learn that other countries have advantages their own does not. Thus, they begin to see their country's flaws and develop a more cognitively complex, realistic view of it, rather than the implicit faith and pride they had previously. One expatriate reflected, "I still love my country, but I certainly have a better understanding about why other countries don't think as highly of us."

*Table 2.2* The expatriate transformation process

| Letting go | Taking on |
| --- | --- |
| Cultural certainty | Internalized perceptions of the other culture |
| Unquestioned acceptance of basic assumptions | Internalized values of the other culture |
| Personal frames of reference | New or broader schemas so that differences are accepted without a need to compare |
| Unexamined life | Constructed life |
| Accustomed role or status | Role assigned by the other culture or one's job |
| Social reinforcement knowledge | Accepting and learning the other culture's norms and behaviors |
| Accustomed habits and activities | Substituting functional equivalents |
| Known routines | Addiction to novelty and learning |

Source: Reprinted with the author's permission from Osland, J. S. (1995) *The Adventure of Working Abroad: Hero Tales from the Global Frontier*. San Francisco: Jossey-Bass: 141.

Expatriates let go of their unquestioned acceptance of basic assumptions and take on the internationalized values of the other culture. Rather than taking their own cultural values for granted, contact with the other culture leads them to question the validity of their assumptions. At the same time, they may adopt, consciously or unconsciously, the values of the other culture, a natural part of the acculturation process (Berry 1983). According to one expatriate, "I started to look at the world like the Colombians do and learned to not worry about things I cannot control." But at the same time as expatriates may be shedding some of their peripheral values, their core values (e.g., patriotism, religious values) become even stronger. As an expatriate reported, "I became more American while I was there. Even though I accepted the way things are there, it made me realize how American I really am."

Expatriates let go of their personal frames of reference and take on new or broader schemas so that differences are accepted without the need to compare them to a cultural frame of reference. At the beginning of a sojourn, people naturally make comparisons between what they observe and what they know from home, their frame of reference. Over time, that frame is expanded to include the new culture, and, eventually, well-adapted expatriates feel no need for comparisons with home-country standards. Instead, they develop new schemas to organize their perceptions. "I used to make negative comparisons between the employees here and my subordinates at home; eventually I just began to appreciate the locals for who they are and stopped making any comparisons at all. They both have strengths and weaknesses."

Expatriates let go of an unexamined life to take on a constructed life that they themselves put together piece by conscious piece. The surprises, changes, and contrasts (Louis 1980a) trigger introspection and an examination of their life in many expatriates. In some cases it is difficult to replicate the life they had prior to expatriation. Thus, expatriates, and spouses in particular, are compelled to create a new life for themselves after carefully considering what to include. As an expatriate noted, "My wife had nothing. I mean, she woke up and had no structure to her day. She really had to construct her life, and fortunately [she] did it."

Expatriates let go of their accustomed role or status and take on the role assigned by the other culture or by their job. Being a manager in a high power distance, authoritarian culture entails a higher-status position than being a manager in a low-power, egalitarian culture. Regardless of their position, they are a stranger in a foreign land and may be stereotyped in negative ways for their inability to speak the language or for their nationality. Thus, they have to learn to handle the roles assigned to them and still maintain their own sense of identity.

Expatriates let go of the social reinforcement knowledge from their own culture and take on the other culture's norms and behaviors. Beginning at a young age, people learn how to behave appropriately or to obtain desired reactions in their own culture. Some of that knowledge becomes irrelevant in another culture, and expatriates have to give up some of their own cultural scripts to adopt those of the other culture. This involves both acceptance and learning. As one expatriate commented, "I know how to get things done in my own culture, but they [tactics] don't work here and I had to figure out new tactics, whether I wanted to or not."

Expatriates let go of accustomed habits and activities to take on substitutes that are functionally equivalent. This is similar to the cultural flexibility mentioned previously. It is not possible to engage in the same activities and hobbies found at home, so many expatriates take on replacements that serve the same function. Rather than bemoan the loss of her symphony choir at home, one expatriate simply learned whatever instrument would allow her to continue playing music with others in each foreign country.

Finally, expatriates let go of their known routines and take on novelty and learning. The comfort and security of one's own culture is replaced by the uncertainty and surprises of the other culture. Well-acculturated expatriates learn to value this novelty and are energized by the endless opportunities to learn. "As one expatriate described it, living abroad is like returning to childhood when every day brings novel adventures and something new" (Osland 2001: 151). Osland (2001) identified the impetus behind expatriate transformation as their desire to become acculturated, to fit into another cultures, and to be effective at work, which leads us to the next topic, expatriate effectiveness.

## Expatriate effectiveness

Neither companies nor scholars have been completely clear or in agreement on what constitutes expatriate effectiveness (Harrison *et al.* 2004). "Corporations have defined it as accomplishment of assignment objectives, attrition rates or increased revenues, but few have systems in place to track these outcomes and attribute them to individual assignees" (Shaffer *et al.* 2006). Scholars have measured effectiveness in terms of adjustment (Black 1988; Black *et al.* 1991), the strength of their plans or decisions to go home early without completing their assignment (withdrawal cognitions) (Black and Gregersen 1990; Naumann 1992; Takeuchi *et al.* 2002), and job performance (Arthur and Bennett 1997). The core aspects of job performance for expatriates are "fulfilling specific task requirements and development and maintaining relationships with host country nationals" (Harrison and Shaffer 2005: 1455). These two facets are similar to research on domestic job performance, but there is much more uncertainty about what tactics are needed to achieve work goals and develop social relationships with strangers in an unfamiliar culture.

## Results of expatriation

Caligiuri and DiSanto (2001) studied what companies hoped to accomplish via expatriation. They asked several focus groups consisting of a total of thirty-six global HR managers and fourteen line managers in a global business unit this question: "What is your organization hoping to develop in employees sent on global assignments?" Content analysis on the answers yielded eight developmental goals of global competence, which were subsequently categorized as knowledge-, ability-, or personality-related. In addition to reducing ethnocentrism, the other goals involved increasing:

- the ability to transact business in another country;
- the ability to change leadership style according to the situation;
- knowledge of the company's worldwide business structure;
- knowledge of international business issues;
- the network of professional contacts worldwide;
- openness;
- flexibility.

The researchers then surveyed three groups in three different firms as to how they rated themselves on the eight categories. Group members were all current or former participants in the firms' global leadership development program: (1) "prepatriates" who were selected for the programs but who had not yet been sent abroad; (2) expatriates who were currently abroad; and (3) repatriates who had returned home after an international assignment.

The results indicate three findings. First, some personality traits, like flexibility and level of ethnocentrism, did not change as a result of a global assignment. No significant differences were revealed in these two traits, which is not surprising, since personality traits tend to be stable, enduring patterns of how individuals feel, think, and behave over time (Buss 1989; Costa and McCrae 1992). Because most global leadership models include personality traits, this finding highlights the importance of careful selection procedures. Second, knowledge can be developed as a result of global assignments, which was indicated by higher scores in reported knowledge of professional contacts worldwide and the company's worldwide business structure. Third, global assignments can sensitize individuals to the challenges of working abroad and increase their humility. Surprisingly, prepatriate scores were significantly higher than those of expatriates or repatriates for openness, ability to transact business in another country, ability to change leadership style, and knowledge of international business issues. Presumably, an international experience made expatriates and repatriates aware of what they do not know (Caligiuri and DiSanto 2001). To use the conscious competence learning model (Howell and Fleishman 1982), prepatriates might be categorized as showing "unconscious incompetence," whereas the expatriates and repatriates may well have advanced to "conscious incompetence." This underscores the learning and cognitive change that takes place in global assignments.

The study of expatriation makes numerous contributions to the field of global leadership, including its findings on antecedents, selection, adjustment, effectiveness, expatriate transformation, and the inherent paradoxes that lead to development of a global mindset.

# Global management

While traditional expatriate managers concentrate on a single foreign country and their relationship with headquarters, global managers are responsible for understanding and operating in the worldwide business environment (Adler and Bartholomew 1992: 53). The study of global managers shares some similarity and overlap with the study of global leadership. Indeed, a major criticism directed at some of the early research on global leadership was that these roles and terms were used interchangeably (Osland *et al.* 2006). While acknowledging that global leaders both lead and manage, our definition of global leadership stipulates that "global leaders are individuals who effect significant positive change in organizations." This requirement is based on Kotter's (1990a, b) classic study of the difference between leaders and managers, which concluded that leaders, unlike managers, are change agents. There is no evidence to date that this distinction between domestic leaders and managers does not hold true in the global context. Some global managers may also be global leaders if they are change agents and build a global community with a unified purpose, but not all global managers are automatically global leaders. Titles alone do not guarantee leadership behavior. Nevertheless, there are interesting global manager research findings that may hold lessons for global leadership.

As with global leadership, the literature on global managers comprises both empirical research and the expert opinion of people who work in the area. The global manager descriptions in this paragraph fall into the latter category. Weeks (1992) described the successful international manager as someone with knowledge of the business, high degrees of tolerance and flexibility, and the ability to work with people; these characteristics appear on our list in Table 2.1 for both expatriate adjustment determinants and global leadership competencies. Given the transnational structure they deemed necessary for global organizations, Bartlett and Ghoshal (1989) contended that effective global managers require the cognitive complexity to hold the matrix of a multistructured entity in their mind and be capable of reorganizing form to follow function as dictated by changing business demands. Adler and Bartholomew (1992) recommended that global managers be "cultural synergizers," while Bartlett *et al.* (1990) referred to them as "cross-fertilizers." All these authors arrived at their conclusions after taking a serious look at globalization and what it meant for organizations and then extrapolating, relying on inductive reasoning, to determining what kind of managers were needed.

In contrast, the research that we shall now discuss is empirical in nature. We can get some sense of who global managers are from a study of Finnish global managers with more than one expatriate assignment (Suutari and Taka 2004). Their most typical career anchors (Schein 1996) were "managerial competence" and "pure challenge." They also included "internationalism" as one of their top career anchors, which underscores how important it is to them to work in global jobs in global settings – and how difficult it may be for them to return to purely domestic work.

Two key questions regarding global managers are "What do they actually do and is that different from what domestic managers do?" To answer the first question, scholars began by looking at the roles performed by domestic managers and Mintzberg's (1973) observation of managers as they went about their daily work. He explicated these managerial roles as being monitor, spokesperson, leader, liaison, decision maker, innovator, and negotiator. Mintzberg noted, however, that not all managers perform the same roles in the same manner because there are four sets of variables that determine how they do their work: environment (differences in milieu, industry, and organization), job (difference in job level and function), person (differences in manager personality and style characteristics), and situation (differences in temporal and contextual features).

Not all scholars accept a universal theory of management or Mintzberg's managerial roles. Some research indicates that roles vary depending on national culture and the level of industrialization (Lubatkin *et al.* 1997a, b). An environmental difference noted in a study of Central American managers seemed to necessitate an additional managerial role. Observations of managers confirmed that they performed the roles identified by Mintzberg, but they also carried out a protector role with the government (Osland 1991). This role involved keeping close tabs on potential governmental actions that would impact their business, trying to ward off detrimental legislation or regulations, and trying to craft special arrangements that would protect their firm from damage or risk even if the government did take action. Lobbyists and government liaisons might be more likely to perform this role in larger countries, but the social networks of the Central American

*Table 2.3* Global managerial roles

*Informational roles*

| | | |
|---|---|---|
| 1 | Monitor | Scan environments, monitor units, probe and seek information, act as corporate nerve center of incoming information |
| 2 | Spokesperson | Communicate and disseminate information with multiple levels of the internal and extra-organizational system, advocate and represent the organization |

*Interpersonal roles*

| | | |
|---|---|---|
| 3 | Leader | Motivate, coach, build teams, maintain corporate climate and culture, and supervise the work of others |
| 4 | Liaison | Network, coordinate, link entities, and span organizational boundaries |

*Action roles*

| | | |
|---|---|---|
| 5 | Decision maker | Take action, troubleshoot, make decisions, and use power to get things done |
| 6 | Innovator | Try new approaches, seize opportunities, generate new ideas, and promote a vision |
| 7 | Negotiator | Make deals, translate strategy into action, negotiate contracts, manage conflict, and confront others |

Source: Printed with permission from the Center for Creative Leadership.

managers allowed them to have advance knowledge and to influence government actions in a way that was deemed different from the traditional liaison role.

A research team at the Center for Creative Leadership found significant differences in how domestic and global managers perform their roles (Dalton *et al.* 2002). They surveyed 211 managers of various nationalities who worked at four organizations (two Swiss, one Swedish, and one US). On the basis of Mintzberg's work and their research data, they developed and used seven managerial roles in their research, which appear in Table 2.3. The sample contained both global and domestic leaders, and the researchers tested a variety of factors related to managerial effectiveness (e.g., personality) and surveyed their bosses about their effectiveness. The findings indicated both similarity and difference between global and domestic leaders; the research team attributed the differences to the complexity of the global environment:

> The patterns of traits, role skills, and capabilities global managers need to be effective are similar to that of domestic managers. The bosses of global managers say emotional stability, skill in the roles of leader and decision maker, and the ability to cope with stress are key components to managerial effectiveness regardless of the job's global complexity. In addition, bosses look to conscientiousness, skill in the role of negotiator and innovator, business knowledge, international business knowledge, cultural adaptability, and the ability to take the perspective of others as significant to the effectiveness of global managers.
>
> (Leslie *et al.* 2002: 63)

Emotional stability, decision-maker and negotiator roles, and the ability to learn played a more significant role with global leaders than they did with domestic leaders. Surprisingly, previous international exposure and work did not contribute to the global managers' effectiveness, and the cosmopolitan managers were not viewed as trusted or well liked by their peers and other colleagues, according to their bosses' perceptions (ibid). As one would expect, the selection criteria utilized in this study did not stipulate leadership roles or abilities. While future research may discover that their findings also apply to global leaders, we cannot make this assumption a priori.

The shared platform between domestic and global jobs plus the additional demands placed on global managers was confirmed in another study that interviewed fifty-five CEOs from various industries in fifteen countries (McBer 1995). Participants described critical incidents that were content-analyzed to identify the factors that predicted effectiveness in global managers. Three of the competencies they identified were deemed universal and thus shared by both global and domestic managers: sharpening the focus, building commitment, and driving for success. However, they also identified three competencies that varied depending on the cultural context: business relationships, the role of action, and the style of authority.

The research of Spreitzer *et al.* (1997) was guided by their belief that critical skills for managers are learned from experience. Therefore, the ability to learn should be a selection criterion when companies hire or promote international managers. They developed an instrument for early identification of international executives, called Prospector, that included two categories of behaviors and competencies for international managers (expatriates or executives in an international job). The learning-oriented behaviors are as follows: uses feedback, seeks feedback, is cross-culturally adventurous, seeks opportunities to learn, is open to criticism, and is flexible. The competencies are as follows: sensitive to cultural differences, acts with integrity, is committed to success, has broad business knowledge, brings out the best in people, is insightful, and has the courage to take a stand, and takes risks. International managers were more likely to be described as effective if they were cross-culturally adventurous and insightful, sought opportunities to learn, and were open to criticism (ibid).

The Corporate Leadership Council (2000) surveyed some of its corporate members on issues relating to developing and retaining future global leaders. They identified the six global management skills in highest demand. These skills are intercultural adaptability, ability to develop individuals across diverse cultures, global strategic thinking, global team building, ability to start up business in new markets, and ability to interact with local political interests.

One of the most insightful studies on global managers was carried out by Wills and Barham (1994). After interviewing sixty successful senior executives from nine global firms, they argued that international executives operate from a deep holistic core competence composed of three integrated parts: cognitive complexity, emotional energy, and psychological maturity. Cognitive complexity and the ability to understand other viewpoints were demonstrated by cultural empathy, active listening, and a sense of humility. Emotional energy was manifested by emotional self-awareness, emotional resilience, risk acceptance, and the emotional support of their family. This support served as a coping mechanism as well as a source of emotional energy that could be applied at work. Finally, psychological maturity implies the presence of a strong value system that gives their lives meaning. Wills and Barham (1994) identified the following three values as central features of the psychological maturity found in international managers: curiosity to learn, living in the "here and now" by taking full advantage of the present, and personal morality. Wills and Barham did not refer to their interviewees as leaders or global leaders since the latter term was not in use when they completed this work. Since the subjects were selected by their organization's human resource managers as highly successful, and because they managed across a number of countries simultaneously, it is likely that many, if not all, of their subjects would fit today's definition of global leaders.

A comparison of global manager and global leader competencies would no doubt show areas of overlap since many of the competencies mentioned in this section appear in Table 2.2. The key lessons from the study of global managers are the significant differences between domestic and global managers in terms of how they perform their roles and the findings on characteristics related to perceived effectiveness.

# Comparative leadership

The field of comparative leadership studies the differences and similarities in the indigenous leadership styles of different countries. Leadership schemas and behaviors, as well as perceptions of what constitutes effective leadership, often vary from one culture to another. Comparative leadership studies often measure the different styles in the leadership continuum mentioned in Chapter 1 or rely on cultural value dimensions (Parsons and Shils 1951; Kluckhohn and Strodtbeck 1961; Hall and Hall 1990; Hofstede 1980b; Fiske 1992; Schwartz 1994; Trompenaars and Hampden-Turner 1993) to identify national or regional leadership styles and practices. Research discovered national differences in leadership, such as leader status, goals, role, communication, influence, decision making, and perceived effectiveness. For example, cultures characterized by large power distance tend to have autocratic leaders; therefore, the participative management techniques imported from low-power-distance cultures may not be appropriate. In a study of a Russian factory, participative management actually decreased rather than increased productivity (Welsh *et al.* 1993). Asking for advice may be interpreted as incompetence or weakness in cultures in which leaders are supposed to be omnipotent experts, at least until they have earned their followers' trust and confidence.

Despite documented national differences in leadership, recent research findings also point out commonalities. For example, a large comparative study that examined how managers handle routine work events found both cultural differences and similarities (Smith and Peterson 1988). The most extensive contribution comes from Project GLOBE, the largest comparative leadership study to date (House *et al.* 2004). A 170-member multinational research team obtained data on indigenous leadership from 17,000 managers in sixty-two countries. These managers worked in the telecommunications, food, and banking industries in their own countries. The researchers developed a new cultural framework composed of nine dimensions: performance orientation, assertiveness, future orientation, human orientation, institutional collectivism, in-group collectivism, gender egalitarianism, power distance, and uncertainty avoidance (Javidan and House 2001). Subsequently, similar responses on these dimensions were used to categorize the sixty-two countries into ten culture clusters. These clusters reported different leadership profiles: charismatic/value-based; team-oriented; participative; humane-oriented; autonomous; and self-protective. Thus, the cultural dimensions were shown to influence expectations of leaders.

Project GLOBE also found that different countries have both similar and different views on leadership. They identified a list of leader attributes that are universally acceptable, universally unacceptable, and culturally contingent (that is, they work in some cultures but not in others) (Den Hartog *et al.* 1999), shown in Table 2.4. Similar business conditions and practices, technology, more well-educated employees, and the presence of multinational enterprises may be responsible for at least partial convergence on leadership views. The selection criteria for Project GLOBE did not include evidence of global leadership roles or skills, since this was not their focus. Future research could test whether or not these universal attributes are also characteristic of effective global leaders.

*Table 2.4* Project GLOBE leadership traits

| Universally acceptable traits | Universally unacceptable traits | Culturally contingent traits |
| --- | --- | --- |
| Decisive | Ruthless | Enthusiastic |
| Informed | Egocentric | Self-sacrificial |
| Honest | Asocial | Risk-taking |
| Dynamic | Non-explicit | Sincere |
| Administratively skilled | Irritable | Ambitious |
| Coordinator | Non-cooperative | Sensitive |
| Just | Loner | Self-effacing |
| Team builder | Dictatorial | Compassionate |
| Effective bargainer | | Unique |
| Dependable | | Willful |
| Win–win problem solver | | |
| Plans ahead | | |
| Intelligent | | |
| Excellence oriented | | |

Source: Based on Den Hartog, D. N., House, R. J., Hanges, P. J., Ruiz-Quintanilla, S. A., Dorfman, P. W., and Associates (1999) "Culture specific and cross-culturally generalizable implicit leadership theories: Are attributes of charismatic/transformational leadership universally endorsed?" *Leadership Quarterly*, 10(2): 219–256.

On the basis of their findings about cultural differences and diverse leadership profiles, GLOBE researchers argue that global leaders require a global mindset, tolerance of ambiguity, and cultural adaptability and flexibility (Javidan *et al.* 2006).

The major contribution of comparative management to the field of global leadership is the understanding that national leadership styles have certain aspects in common, as well as many cultural differences. Therefore, when global leaders have followers from different cultures, they have to be prepared to switch styles depending on the situation and the people involved (Gill and Booth 2003).

Thanks to the groundwork laid in the fields of intercultural communication competence, expatriation, global management, and comparative leadership, the nascent field of global leadership has strong supportive roots. Our next chapter will detail the growth of global leadership as a field of study in its own right.

# Overview of the global leadership literature

**3**

## JOYCE S. OSLAND

Your life is your message. Leadership by example is not only the most pervasive but also the most enduring form of leadership. And because the world is becoming more interconnected, standards of leadership have an impact that extends around the globe. Now, as never before, a higher standard of leadership will serve us all.

(Keshavan Nair, *A Higher Standard of Leadership: Lessons from the life of Gandhi*)

History is graced with leaders who fit our definition of global leaders – political leaders like Mahatma Gandhi, military leaders like Alexander the Great, and spiritual leaders like Mother Theresa – whose impact and followers extended far beyond the borders of their own country. Such famous figures often capture the imagination and loyalty of a broad audience, owing to the confluence of their unique vision and its relevance to the environmental context. Difficult times demand constructive leaders just as surely as destructive leaders create difficult times. Today's global leaders, however, are not necessarily famous; there are more and more of them performing less visible leadership roles in an increasingly complex, ambiguous, multicultural environment. Business CEOs with a reputation as change agents on a global scale are perhaps the first group who come to mind for business students and practitioners, but people who integrate acquired companies into large transnational firms, who command coalition forces in the military, who run global nonprofit organizations, and who lead multinational political organizations are all examples of current global leaders. Our definition of global leadership does not restrict global leaders to an organization's upper echelon; anyone who leads global change efforts in the public, private, or nonprofit sectors is a global leader.

Businesses that are extending their reach globally, taking products global, and employing a global workforce all have need of global leaders. Figuring out what global leadership looks like and how it can be developed was the impetus for much of the research we will review in this chapter.

Discussions of global leadership begin by distinguishing how their role differs from that of domestic leaders, international leaders, and global managers, which we have laid out in previous chapters. Early definitions of global leadership borrowed and extrapolated traditional, domestic leadership definitions (Yeung and Ready 1995), but scholars quickly recognized that global leadership was far more complex than domestic leadership, owing to the pressures and dynamics of global competition (Weber *et al.* 1998) that broadened the scope of the leader's work. Adler clarified the issue when she wrote:

> Global leaders, unlike domestic leaders, address people worldwide. Global leadership theory, unlike its domestic counterpart, is concerned with the interaction of people and ideas among cultures, rather than with either the efficacy of particular leadership styles within the leader's home country or with the comparison of leadership approaches among leaders from various countries – each of whose domain is limited to issues and people within their own cultural environment. A fundamental distinction is that global leadership is neither domestic nor multidomestic.
>
> (2001: 77)

## Global leadership literature review

As with the topic of global managers, prescriptions about global leaders come from a variety of sources, primarily expert opinion and empirical research. Our chronology of the literature begins with the earliest publications in the 1990s, which consisted of extrapolations from the domestic leadership literature, interviews, focus groups, or observations from the authors' consulting experiences (Kets de Vries and Mead 1992; Tichy *et al.* 1992; Rhinesmith 1993; Moran and Riesenberger 1994; Brake 1997).

Tichy and his colleagues (1992) wrote about "true globalists," as they called them, who have (1) a global mindset; (2) a set of global leadership skills and behaviors; (3) energy, skills, and talent for global networking; (4) the ability to build effective teams; (5) and global change agent skills. They believe, as we do, that the best global leadership systems develop people and the organization simultaneously. Training and developing future leaders without also carrying out organization development (OD) activities to enable the organization to function globally and take advantage of these leaders makes their potential effectiveness a greater gamble.

Kets de Vries and Mead (1992) developed a list of leadership qualities that included envisioning, strong operational codes, environmental sense making, ability to instill values, inspiring, empowering, building and maintaining organizational networks, interpersonal skills, pattern recognition and cognitive complexity, and hardiness. Moran and Riesenberger (1994) held a focus group with international managers, who suggested several competencies that were categorized as attitudes, interaction, cultural understanding, and leadership. Stephen Rhinesmith, a consultant, authored an insightful book, *A Manager's Guide to Globalization* (1993, 1996), based on his work with multinational corporations. He identified twenty-four competencies that he categorized as (1) Strategy and Structure; (2) Corporate Culture; and (3) People. More recently, Rhinesmith (2003) created a simpler model centered around global mindset, which he describes as fundamentally "making decisions with increasing reference points."

In Rhinesmith's model, global mindset has two components. The first is intellectual intelligence (which he relates to cognitive complexity). Intellectual intelligence entails both business acumen and paradox management (which is similar to the previous discussion on expatriate paradoxes). Its second component is global emotional intelligence (which he relates to cosmopolitanism). Global emotional intelligence comprises cultural self-awareness, cultural adjustment, cross-cultural understanding, and cross-cultural effectiveness. Thus, global emotional intelligence involves both self-management and cultural acumen. Intellectual and global emotional intelligence are the basis for the global behavioral skills that make up the global manager's leadership style, as is seen in the model found in Figure 3.1.

Rhinesmith believes that the paradoxes of global business are never fully resolved and put to rest. There will always be global–local tensions, for example, that must be continually balanced and managed. He suggests five steps for managing paradoxes: (1) identify the competing forces of the paradox (e.g., individual versus team; stability versus change; centralization versus decentralization; work versus family); (2) create a paradox management grid to show the positive and negative forces of the competing forces; (3) optimize, rather than maximize, your primary responsibilities by seeking win–win solutions; (4) include contradictions in your thinking by meeting with stakeholders likely to have opposing views; and (5) create paradox alarm metrics that sound when negative reactions build up (Rhinesmith 2003).

Terence Brake wrote a perceptive book, *The Global Leader: Critical Factors for Creating the World Class Organization* (1997), based on the global business literature and interviews with practitioners at leading firms. To think about the universal leadership

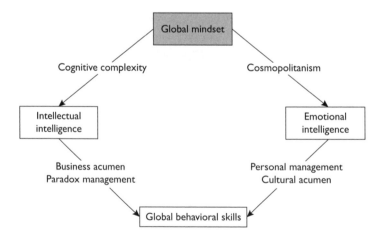

*Figure 3.1* Rhinesmith's basic components of a global mindset

Source: Reprinted with permission from Rhinesmith, S. "Basic Components of a Global Mindset." In *The Many Facets of Leadership* (2003) M. Goldsmith, V. Govindarajan, B. Kaye, and A. A. Vicere (eds.). Financial Times Prentice Hall, Upper Saddle River, NJ: 218.

process, Brake was guided by the image of Shiva, the Hindu deity who weaves together seemingly contradictory qualities and is sometimes portrayed with six faces that symbolize his many facets. Shiva has a third eye that enables him to see inward. "Shiva performs the Dance of Life that Shiva performs within a ring of fire. He is not consumed by the fire, but appears to draw on the energy of the fire for his own vitality" (ibid.: 31). He sees global leaders as working in the center of a ring of fire that is global competition. They can either embrace the fire's energy to generate higher levels of performance, or perish in the fire. The global leadership process that leads to higher performance consists of three steps (ibid.: 31–32):

1  framing the global competitive challenges as opportunities;
2  generating personal and organizational energy;
3  transforming energy into world-class performance.

Brake notes that global leaders sometimes have to unlearn what previously made their firm successful. He developed the Global Leadership Triad (Brake 1997), which consists of three sets of competencies, shown in Figure 3.2. Most of the individual competencies

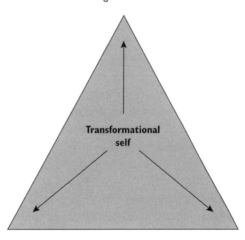

**Relationship management**
• Change agentry
• Community building
• Conflict management and negotiation
• Cross-cultural communication
• Influencing

**Transformational self**

**Business acumen**
• Depth of field
• Entrepreneurial spirit
• Professional expertise
• Stakeholder orientation
• Total organizational astuteness

**Personal effectiveness**
• Accountability
• Curiosity and learning
• Improvisation
• Maturity
• Thinking agility

*Figure 3.2* Brake's global leadership triad

Source: Reprinted with permission from Brake, T. (1997) *The Global Leader: Critical Factors for Creating the World Class Organization*. Chicago: Irwin Professional Publishing: 44.

have been discussed previously in this chapter or their meaning is obvious; definitions are provided below only for the exceptions, where Brake's meaning may vary from the reader's.

*Business acumen.* Business acumen is "the ability to pursue and apply appropriate professional knowledge and skills to achieve optimal results of the company's global stakeholders" (Brake 1997: 45). In this category, depth of knowledge refers to "demonstrating the willingness and an ability to switch perspectives between local and global/functional and cross-functional needs and opportunities" (ibid.: 45). In today's language, this would be called having a global mindset. The stakeholder orientation balances the needs of both internal (e.g., functional areas) and external groups (e.g., customers, communities). Total organizational astuteness "demonstrates insights into 'how the business works' above and beyond [the leader's] immediate area and seeks to use this knowledge to get things done within and among organizational units." Brake's (1997: 47–48) description of this competency illustrates some of the deep organizational knowledge required in global careers:

1  draws on a range of information-gathering skills to build a realistic profile of the global organization;
2  creates or utilizes multiple internal networks for sourcing business intelligence, expertise, global best practices, and resources, and for promoting coordination, and so forth;
3  recognizes key organizational constituencies and decision makers and relies on political savvy to create alliances and foster collaboration to realize global goals;
4  recognizes the assumptions and mental models entrenched in the organizational culture and articulates them when they need to be reviewed and questioned for change to take place;
5  understands and fosters the continuous review of key organizational processes, systems, standard operation procedures, working methods, and so forth;
6  demonstrates a good sense of timing in putting forward new ideas and proposals;
7  analyzes key global trends and forecasts how they will impact organizational strategy, structure, and systems.

*Relationship management.* Relationship management is "the ability to build and influence collaborative relationships in a complex and diverse global network to direct energy toward the achievement of business strategies" (Brake 1997: 48). In this category, change agentry is both the openness to new ways of doing things and the ability to motivate others to identify and implement desired changes (ibid.: 48). Community building is the willingness and ability to partner with others in interdependent relationships to accomplish business goals (ibid.: 49).

*Personal effectiveness.* Personal effectiveness is "the ability to attain increasing levels of maturity to perform at peak levels under the strenuous conditions of working in a global enterprise" (Brake 1997: 52). Brake's definition of maturity includes a sense of humor, self-confidence, and resilience, the ability to deal with crises and setbacks, and the ability to recover quickly from mistakes.

At the center of the triad is the concept of the Transformational Self, "a philosophy of possibility and personal engagement with the world – that is, a drive toward meaning and purpose through activity strengthened by reflections, personal mind management, and openness to change" (Brake 1997: 44). This is central to both domestic and global leadership, in his view.

Kanter (1997) argued that global business leaders should be cosmopolitans who can integrate and cross-fertilize knowledge and manage dispersed centers of expertise, influence, and production. In addition to creating new communication routes, they need to move capital, ideas, and people to whatever world location they are needed in. Dalton (1998: 386) wrote that global leaders should possess (1) a high level of cognitive complexity to gather and understand contradictory information from multiple sources and to make effective decisions, (2) excellent interpersonal skills that buy them time to figure out how to behave in a particular situation and country; (3) the ability to learn from experience; and (4) advanced moral reasoning to understand ethical dilemmas.

Petrick and his colleagues (1999) argued that two global leadership skills result in the corporation's reputational capital, an intangible resource for sustainable competitive advantage. The first skill is behavioral flexibility, which is defined as the ability to balance four competing values and performance criteria: (1) profitability and productivity; (2) continuity and efficiency; (3) commitment and morale; and (4) adaptability and innovation (Denison *et al.* 1995). The second skill is stewardship of sustainable development, which involves acting as a responsible steward of human and natural resources and promoting, concurrently, economic, social, biological, and ecological development (Petrick *et al.* 1999: 61). By exercising these two skills, global leaders increase their firm's reputation capital, which is a component of social capital. Social capital, rooted in trust and common norms, reduces transaction costs among cooperative partners and accelerates global prosperity (Coleman 1988; Petrick *et al.* 1999).

Other types of capital are also important for global leaders. In a conceptual article, Harvey and Novicevic argue that global assignments (i.e., expatriation and inpatriation) contribute to the development of four types of global leader capital (2004: 1177):

- human capital – the skills and competencies that leaders need to have based on expert and referent power in their organization;
- cultural capital – acceptance and social inclusiveness due to having tacit knowledge of how the organization operates;
- social capital – the standing and concurrent ability to draw on standing to accomplish tasks in an organization;
- political capital – the ability to use power or authority and gain the support of constituents in a socially effective way.

A global leader's political capital is crucial because it can be used to decrease the level of conflict among foreign subsidiaries and ensure that diverse views are represented. Politically skilled leaders also generate more support and acquiescence (ibid.).

Numerous case studies and interviews provide anecdotal descriptions of global leaders (McFarland *et al.* 1993; Maruca, 1994; Green *et al.* 2003; Marquardt and Berger, 2000; Bingham *et al.* 2000; Emerson, 2001; Wolfensohn *et al.* 2003; Millikin and Fu 2005). For example, in an interview, John Pepper, former CEO of Procter and Gamble, came up with his own list of global leader competencies: dealing with uncertainty, knowing customers, balancing tensions between global efficiency and local responsiveness, and appreciating diversity (Bingham *et al.* 2000). The *Advances in Global Leadership* volumes (Mobley *et al.* 1999; Mobley and McCall, 2001; Mobley and Dorfman, 2003; Mobley and Weldon 2006) are a source of current thinking, findings, and implications for future research. There are four published reviews of the global leadership literature (Hollenbeck, 2001; Suutari, 2002; Jokinen, 2005; and Osland *et al.* 2006).

Most empirical work on global leadership has attempted to answer these two questions: "What capabilities do global leaders need to acquire in order to be effective?" and "How can managers most effectively develop these characteristics?" The complete list of extant empirical studies on global leadership is described in Exhibit 3.3 (based on Osland *et al.* 2006). With few exceptions, the methodology most commonly utilized to study global leadership is surveys and/or interviews.

## Eight-nation competency study

Yeung and Ready (1995) produced the first empirical study, using a sample of 1,200 managers from eight nations in ten major corporations (who were not necessarily global leaders themselves). The participants were presented with a list of competencies and asked to select those items that fitted their description of global leaders. The capabilities on which they agreed were:

- being able to articulate a tangible vision, values, strategy;
- being a catalyst for strategic change;
- being a catalyst for cultural change;
- being able to empower others;
- having a results orientation;
- having a customer orientation.

This list describes a transformational leadership style and a strong performance orientation.

*Table 3.1* A chronological list of empirical research on global leadership

| Authors | Description | Method | Findings |
|---------|-------------|--------|----------|
| Yeung and Ready (1995) | Identifies leadership capabilities in a cross-national study | Surveys of 1,200 managers from 10 major global corporations and 8 countries | Capabilities: articulate vision, values, strategy; catalyst for strategic and cultural change; empower others; results and customer orientation |
| Adler (1997) | Describes women global leaders in politics and business | Archival data and interviews with women global leaders from 60 countries | Their number is increasing and they come from diverse backgrounds; are *not* selected by women-friendly countries or companies; use broad-based power rather than hierarchical power; are lateral transfers; symbolize change and unity; and leverage their increased visibility |
| Black, Morrison and Gregersen (1999) | Identifies capabilities of effective global leaders and how to develop them | Interviews of 90 senior executives and 40 nominated global leaders in 50 companies in Europe, North America, and Asia, and 108 surveys of HR executives in US firms | Capabilities: inquisitive, character, duality, savvy. Development occurs via training, transfer, travel, and multicultural teams |
| Kets de Vries and Florent-Treacy (1999) | Describes excellent global leadership | Case studies involving interviews with 3 global leaders (CEOs) | Identified best practices in leadership, structure, strategy, corporate culture |
| Rosen, Digh, Singer, Philips (2000) | Identifies leadership universals | Interviews with 75 CEOs from 28 countries; 1,058 surveys with CEOs, presidents, managing directors or chairmen; studies of national culture | Leadership universals: personal, social, business, and cultural literacies, many of which are paradoxical in nature |

*Table 3.1 Continued*

| | | | |
|---|---|---|---|
| McCall and Hollenbeck (2002) | To identify how to select and develop global executives and understand how they derail | Interviews with 101 executives from 36 countries and 16 global firms nominated as successful global executives | Competencies: open-minded and flexible; culture interest and sensitivity; able to deal with complexity; resilient, resourceful, optimistic, energetic; honesty and integrity; stable personal life; value-added technical or business skills |
| Goldsmith, Greenberg, Robertson, Hu-Chan (2003) | To identify global leadership dimensions needed in the future | Thought leader panels; focus groups with 28 CEOs, focus/dialogue groups with at least 207 current or future leaders; interviews with 202 high potential next generation leaders; 73 surveys from forum group members | Fifteen dimensions: integrity, personal mastery, constructive dialogue, shared vision, empowerment, developing people, building partnerships, sharing leadership, thinking globally, appreciating diversity, technologically savvy, customer satisfaction, anticipating opportunities, leading change, and maintaining competitive advantage |
| Bikson, Treverton, Moini, and Lindstrom (2003) | Examines impact of globalization on HR needs, global leadership competencies, and policies and practices needed to produce sufficient global leaders | Structured interviews with 135 US HR and senior managers in public, for-profit, and nonprofit sectors. Unstructured interviews with 24 experts | Insufficient future global leaders who have the required integrated skill repertoire: substantive depth in organization's primary business; managerial ability (especially teamwork and interpersonal skills); strategic international understanding; and cross-cultural experience |
| Kets de Vries, Vrignaud, and Florent-Treacy (2004) | Describes the development of 360-degree feedback instrument, GlobeInvent | Based on semi-structured interviews with a number of senior executives | Twelve dimensions/psychodynamic properties: envisioning, empowering, energizing, designing, rewarding, team building, outside orientation, global mindset, tenacity, emotional intelligence, life balance, resilience to stress |

Source: Adapted and updated from J. Osland, A. Bird, M. Mendenhall, and A. Osland (2006) "Developing Global leadership Capabilities and Global Mindset: A Review." In G. Stahl and I. Björkman (Eds.) *Handbook of Research in International Human Resource Management*. Cheltenham, UK: Edward Elgar: 205–206.

# Women global leaders

Adler (1997, 2001) noted that most leadership research has studied men. Previously, she disproved the myth that women expatriates could not succeed as well as men on overseas assignments and identified areas where they tended to perform better than men (Adler 1994). Next, she studied senior women global leaders in politics and business from sixty countries using archival data and interviews (Adler 1997). The number of women presidents and prime ministers increased rapidly from zero in the 1950s to twenty-one in the 1990s.

By contrast, research from other sources shows that the numbers for women leaders in business merely inch up annually. There are relatively few female CEOs in publicly held corporations; most female CEOs have founded their own firm or taken over family businesses. The numbers of female directors is higher in Scandinavia at 20 percent for each country in the region, but only 8.3 percent for the rest of Europe (*La Tribune* 2006). Spain is considering following Norway's mandated 40 percent female quota on public boards (ibid.). Women comprise 14.7 percent of directors in the United States (*Management Issues News* 2006). Currently, there are four female CEOs in Europe (*Management Issues News* 2006), and only ten female CEOs of US Fortune 500 firms and twenty in Fortune 1000 firms. A study of 942 companies in the Fortune 1000 revealed that nearly half had no women at all in their top executive ranks; 7.2 percent boasted more than two women executives while only 2.6 percent had more than three women. Therefore, the limited number of women in the pipeline indicates that the number of women CEOs will not be increasing rapidly in the United States in the near future (Helfat *et al.* 2006).

Adler (2001) argues for the feminization of global leadership due to the rapid increase in women political leaders and because traits and qualities generally associated with women have been linked to global leadership. For example, some research has found that women have a more participative, interactional, and relational leadership style (Fondas 1997) said to be more suited to a global setting (Hampden-Turner 1994). Adler's findings on the women global leaders were (2001: 90–96) as follows:

- *They come from diverse backgrounds.* Their route to leadership shows no predictable pattern.
- *They were* not *selected solely by women-friendly countries or companies.*
- *Their selection symbolizes hope, change and unity.* Their position as outsiders and selection against the odds implies the possibility of societal or organizational change. Violeta Chamorro of Nicaragua and Corazon Aquino of the Philippines were voted president after their husbands were assassinated. They symbolized the desire for national unity.
- *They are driven by vision, not by hierarchical status.* For instance, Dame Anita Roddick, founder and former CEO of The Body Shop, was not driven to be a CEO but to practice corporate idealism as far back as the early 1990s:

  Leaders in the business world should aspire to be true planetary citizens. They have global responsibilities since their decisions affect not just the world of business, but world problems of poverty, national security and the environment. Many, sad to say, [have] duck[ed] these responsibilities, because their vision is material rather then moral.

(Roddick 1991: 226)

- *They use broad-based popular support rather than traditional, hierarchical party or structural support.* Women political leaders gained support directly from the people, while female entrepreneurs gained support directly from the marketplace.
- *Their path to power is through lateral transfers rather than the traditional path up the hierarchy.*
- *They leverage the increased visibility they receive as women or "the first woman."* They receive more media attention than men, which they can use as a platform.

Although many of the women studied received a great deal of media attention, their intended circle of influence did not extend beyond their country or company. Not all of them were known as global change agents. But recognizing who they are, the reality of their proportional numbers, and understanding their path to power enriches our general understanding of global leadership. Adler's work is also a good reminder to scholars to ensure that their global leadership samples include gender diversity.

## The Global Explorer model

Stewart Black and his colleagues (1999b) took a qualitative, exploratory approach to determine what capabilities global leaders needed to acquire and how managers could most effectively develop them. From a sample including 50 companies in Europe, North America, and Asia, they interviewed 90 senior executives and 40 nominated global leaders; they also surveyed 108 HR managers in US firms. The result was the Global Explorer model, which consists of these global characteristics:

- *inquisitiveness* – a love of learning, being intrigued by diversity;
- *embracing duality* – uncertainty is viewed as invigorating and a natural part of global business;
- *exhibiting character* – the ability to connect emotionally with people of different backgrounds and cultures; consistently demonstrating personal integrity in a world full of ethical conflicts;
- *demonstrating savvy* – business savvy and organizational savvy.

*Inquisitiveness* is the centerpiece of the Global Explorer Model because of its fundamental importance. Whenever John Pepper of Procter and Gamble went to a new country, he visited five local families to see how they cleaned their houses, washed their clothes, and took care of their children's hygiene before going to the office (Black 2006: 184). Pepper was curious about how the local people performed the tasks related to Procter and Gamble's products. Black (2006) devised a list of recommendations for distinguishing between the inquisitive and the noninquisitive.

- *Inquisitive people seek out the new rather than the comfortable.* Inquisitive people gather information about the foreign country and business before going on trips. Once there, they take advantage of the opportunity to learn about the country, to make contacts, and to experience the novelty of a foreign culture rather than cocooning themselves in a four-star hotel and eating the same food as found at home.
- *Inquisitive people act as travelers rather than tourists.* Unlike tourists, who unquestioningly accept their own civilization, travelers constantly compare and contrast the new things and ways of doing things with what they already know. If the new way is superior, they are willing to adopt it. Kraft Foods adopted the local distribution system for ice cream in China, even though at first glance it seemed less efficient. Given the storage capacity of small stores and the narrow crowded streets, bicycles equipped with dry ice were a better solution than Kraft's usual large refrigerated trucks (Black 2006).
- *Inquisitive people question rather than confirm.* When confronted with different ways of doing business, inquisitive people are quick to ask questions that lead to new understandings rather than assuming that they already understand. Rather than simply trying to confirm what they already believe, inquisitive people are sincere about seeking new information.

Inquisitiveness is an aspect of global mindset, as is *embracing duality*. Similar to the paradoxes inherent in the expatriate experience (Osland 1995), global leaders also deal with the simultaneous existence of two contradictory conditions rooted in the global versus local tensions. For example, the corporate vice president of HR for International Flowers and Fragrances (IFF), Eric Campbell, said:

> The best local and global leaders in our company are curious enough to pay attention to the extremely subtle nuances of any locale – whether in New York or Jakarta – as well as smart enough to notice consumer similarities around the world.
>
> (Black 2006: 191)

Black (2006) has two recommendations for identifying those who can embrace duality:

- *They embrace rather than avoid ambiguity.* Ambiguity is an inherent aspect of global business. There are no easy answers to reap from the past when today's global leaders have to unravel and resolve novel, complex, rapidly changing situations. Some people complain and blame others when things are not clear and structured, while others see opportunity and challenge in ambiguity. As Black (2006: 192) concludes, "When faced with high ambiguity, high-potential global leaders have fun; low-potential leaders have anxiety attacks."
- *They act rather than freeze in the face of ambiguity.* Instead of waiting for enough information and analysis to act, people who embrace duality are willing to move forward in ambiguous situations. Businesses that wait for 100 percent certainty generally find themselves beaten by the competition. For instance, high-tech companies that wait to roll out fully debugged products can lose out to companies that have moved on to next-generation technology.

The bedrock of *exhibiting character* is integrity (Morrison 2006). "The global leader with integrity exhibits this quality by demonstrating a strong and consistent commitment to both personal and company standards" (ibid.: 166). Morrison (ibid.: 175–177) identified four distinguishing characteristics of global leaders with high ethical standards. Effective global leaders:

- like, and are interested in, people (can connect emotionally, trustworthy);
- constantly probe ethical issues;
- are committed to the company's standards and apply them wherever they are;
- know when to "hang tough" and when to be flexible on ethical issues.

According to the Global Explorer research, the recommended ways to develop these competencies are through training, international transfers in particular, travel, and having multicultural teams (Black *et al.* 1999). The Global Explorer model is parsimonious and easily grasped. The researchers used an exploratory qualitative approach, which is highly appropriate for a new field of study. They interviewed an impressive number of participants and took care to select them from numerous companies from three continents to avoid a culturally or organizationally biased view. While they combined the opinions of both global leaders and global managers, subsequent competency studies seem to confirm their findings.

# The new global leaders

Manfred Kets de Vries, a psychiatrist, began his empirical work on global leaders with Florent-Treacy by doing case studies of three global leaders who were acknowledged as highly successful global CEOs: Richard Branson at Virgin, Percy Barnevik at ABB, and David Simon at British Petroleum (Kets de Vries with Florent-Treacy 1999). They had several leadership characteristics in common. Although their communication styles were different, all three had a simple, compelling vision that they expressed with enthusiasm and self-confidence. They were accessible to followers and possessed enough empathy to allow them to "recognize and contain followers' anxieties" during the change process (Kets de Vries and Florent-Treacy 1999: 156). The three CEOs gained power by sharing it, sharing information and empowering employees. Furthermore, they surrounded themselves with colleagues who made up for their own weaknesses. The CEOs devoted energy to developing an organizational culture characterized by shared values, open communication, challenge, commitment, autonomy, innovation and learning, good corporate citizenship, and rewards for excellence. Finally, the three global leaders put in place sophisticated IT systems and decentralized, flat, networked structures that minimized bureaucracy. The result was adaptability and a strong customer orientation.

> These three leaders have focused on process: constructing the kind of high-performance learning organization that encourages individual contribution. They put a high value on

their roles as guardian of culture and teacher. As Barnevik has said, "Ninety percent of leadership is process; only 10 percent is strategy. Of that 10 percent, 2 percent is analysis and 8 percent is having the guts to make tough decisions.

(Kets de Vries and Florent-Treacy 1999: 166–167)

Perhaps for this reason, Kets de Vries with Florent-Treacy (2002) describe global leadership as a combination and expansion of both leader and manager roles. Kets de Vries continued using a clinical orientation, based on psychoanalysis, cognitive psychology, and family systems theory, to puzzle out the dynamics between leaders and followers and the "inner theater" of global leaders (Kets de Vries et al. 2004). He interviewed CEOs who participated in a leadership program at INSEAD, entitled "The Challenge of Leadership: Developing Your Emotional Intelligence," and other INSEAD participants and students (Kets de Vries and Florent-Treacy 2002; Kets de Vries et al. 2004). This convenience sample appears to be based on the assumption that all global managers and those with the title of CEO are, by definition, global leaders.

Five professors performed content analysis on the CEO interview transcripts, which yielded twelve dimensions of global leadership, shown in Table 3.2. Global leaders perform two roles at the same time: charismatic and architectural. The charismatic role includes "envisioning, empowering and energizing," originally identified by Tichy and Devanna (1986) as the role of transformational leaders attempting to make fundamental organizational change. In the charismatic role, global leaders direct, inspire and motivate followers. In the architectural role they implement processes to improve the organizational design and appropriately control and reward employee behavior (Kets de Vries and Florent-Treacy 2002).

Kets de Vries's psychoanalytical background led him to this prescription for healthy leadership: self-awareness, a well-rounded and balanced personal life, and the ability to suffer fools and laugh at oneself (Coutu 2004: 66). His dimensions of global leadership include the need to pay attention to work, career, life, and health stress issues, and to balance life's pressures appropriately.

## Global literacies

Robert Rosen, a psychologist and consultant, and his research team, Patricia Digh, Marshall Singer, and Carl Phillips (2000), interviewed seventy-five CEOs of major companies from twenty-eight countries and surveyed 1,058 respondents from eighteen countries, including CEOs, presidents, managing directors, and chairmen. The purpose of their research was (1) to define the characteristics most common to successful global leaders and their companies; (2) to identify the leadership factors most likely to predict global success in the twenty-first century; and (3) to identify the unique national contributions to leadership around the world (Rosen et al. 2000: 377). They concluded that the most successful business leaders demonstrate four universal leadership qualities called global literacies.

*Table 3.2* The global leadership life inventory dimensions

1  Articulating a compelling vision, mission, and strategy with a multicountry, multienvironment, multifunction and multigender perspective that connects employees, shareholders, suppliers and customers on a global scale

2  Giving workers at all levels a voice by empowering them through the sharing of information and the delegation of decisions to the people most competent to execute them

3  Energizing and motivating employees to actualize the organization's specific vision of the future

4  Creating the proper organizational design and control systems to make the guiding vision a reality, and using those systems to align the behavior of the employees with the organization's values and goals

5  Setting up the appropriate reward structures and giving constructive feedback to encourage the kind of behavior that is expected from employees

6  Creating team players and focusing on team effectiveness by instilling a cooperative atmosphere, building collaborative interaction, and encouraging constructive conflict

7  Making employees aware of their outside constituencies, emphasizing particularly the need to respond to the requirements of customers, suppliers, shareholders and other interest groups, such as local communities affected by the organization

8  Inculcating a global mentality in the ranks – that is, instilling values that act as a sort of glue between the regional and/or national cultures represented in the organization

9  Encouraging tenacity and courage in employees by setting a personal example in taking reasonable risks

10  Fostering trust in the organization by creating, primarily through example, an emotionally intelligent workforce whose members know themselves and know how to deal respectfully and understandingly with others

11  Articulating and modelling the need for life balance for the long-term welfare of employees

12  Paying attention to work, career, life and health stress issues, and balancing appropriately the various kinds of pressures that life brings

Source: Reprinted with permission from Kets de Vries, M. F. R., Vrignaud, P. and Florent-Treacy, E. (2004) "The global leadership life inventory: Development and psychometric properties of a 360-degree feedback instrument." *International Journal of Human Resource Management*, 15, 3: 475–492.

Personal literacy has to do with understanding and valuing oneself. In addition to self-awareness, leaders should be open, honest, and committed to learning and principles. Social literacy involves "challenging and engaging others" and hinges on the ability to form collaborative relationships and networks. Business literacy pertains to focusing and mobilizing the organization. Finally, cultural literacy involves understanding and leveraging cultural differences (Rosen *et al.* 2000: 50). Many of the components of each literacy have somewhat contradictory titles; for example, confident humility and reflective decisiveness. This was done purposely to reflect the cognitive complexity required of global leaders as they balance the complexity and tensions of today's world.

These terms reflect the need to move beyond the "either–or" thinking common in Western thought patterns to the "both–and" thinking that is more characteristic of Asian thought patterns (Nisbett 2003).

Rosen has a comprehensive view of global leaders. "Traditionally, we have asked if we have global customers or services; but in the 21st century, all markets are global and everyone needs to survive in a global marketplace. Therefore, we are all global leaders" (Rosen in Thaler-Carter 2000: 82). To transform an enterprise into a global company, Rosen *et al.* argue (2000) that you need leaders who are capable of seeing the world's challenges and opportunities, thinking with an international mindset, acting with fresh, global-centric leadership behaviors, and mobilizing a world-class team and company.

## Developing global executives

Although Morgan McCall and George Hollenbeck (2002) titled their book *Developing Global Executives: The Lessons of International Experience*, their study focused on global leaders. In fact, theirs is the only study to date whose selection criteria specifically included effectiveness. They interviewed 101 executives (92 men and 9 women) who were nominated by their companies because they were considered to be extremely successful global executives. This sample came from thirty-six countries and worked for sixteen global companies.

McCall and Hollenbeck (2002) show that there is no agreement on a universal set of global competencies because global jobs are very diverse – "there is no universal global job." They found many different paths to global leadership (ibid.: 200). Only half of these executives had backgrounds that could explain their interest in global work. Some were attracted by the travel or adventure; others simply fell into global work and went overseas at the behest of the company rather than on their own initiative. McCall and Hollenbeck noted that it is easier to be derailed in a global career than a domestic one because there are more hazards and traps. They identified a set of seven global executive competencies that allow people to work successfully across cultures (ibid.: 35):

- being open-minded and flexible in thought and tactics;
- possessing cultural interest and sensitivity;
- having the ability to deal with complexity;
- being resilient, resourceful, optimistic, and energetic;
- operating from a state of honesty and integrity;
- having a stable personal life;
- possessing value-added technical or business skills.

## Global leadership: the next generation

A team of consultants and executive coaches, Marshall Goldsmith, Cathy Greenberg, Alastair Robertson, and Maya Hu-Chan (2003), was sponsored by the Accenture Institute of Strategic Change to research the next generation of leaders. Arguing that today's leadership skills will not be sufficient for the future, owing to the changing nature of global business, they sought the opinion of both current and prospective leaders. They gathered information from future leaders from around the world in several ways: focus groups with twenty-eight CEOs, various focus groups/dialogue forums with current and future global leaders, seventy-three surveys, and over 200 interviews with high-potential leaders nominated by 120 international organizations (for-profit, governmental, multilateral, and nonprofit). More than 60 percent of those making up the interview sample were under the age of 40; more than 33 percent were still in their twenties. They began their research efforts by convening a group of thought leaders, renowned experts on domestic leadership of the future rather than specialists in comparative or global leadership. Their bibliography does not include the global leadership literature, further proof that their jumping-off point was domestic leadership. This project is more practitioner oriented and provides extensive practical advice for skill development; it is less rigorous from an academic standpoint than some of the other global leadership literature. Nevertheless, the findings are interesting and provide a slightly different perspective on global leadership.

*Table 3.3* Goldsmith, Greenberg, Robertson and Hu-Chan's next generation dimensions of global leadership

---

1  **Demonstrating integrity** – demonstrates honest, ethical behavior in all interactions, ensures high standards for ethical behavior are practiced throughout the organization, avoids political and self-serving behavior, courageously stands up for beliefs, role model for living the organization's values.

2  **Encouraging constructive dialogue** – asks for feedback on what they can improve, genuinely listens to others, accepts constructive feedback, tries to understand the other person's frame of reference, encourages others to challenge the status quo

3  **Creating a shared vision** – creates and communicates a clear vision, effectively involves people in decision making, inspires people to commit to the vision, develops an effective strategy to achieve the vision, and clearly identifies priorities

4  **Developing people** – treats people with respect and dignity, asks people what they need in order to do their work better, provides the training people need, provides effective coaching and developmental feedback in a timely manner, and recognizes achievements

5  **Building partnerships** – treats coworkers as partners rather than competitors, unites the organization into an effective team, builds partnerships across the company, and discourages destructive comments about other people or groups

6  **Sharing leadership** – willingly shares leadership with business partners, defers to those with more expertise, seeks win–win, joint outcomes, and keeps the focus on superordinate goals and the greater good

7  **Empowering people** – builds people's confidence, takes risks in letting others make decisions, provides freedom needed to do their job well, and trusts others to do their work, thereby avoiding micromanagement

8 **Thinking globally** – adaptability, gains necessary global experience, understands impact of globalization and helps others understand it, decisions include global considerations

9 **Appreciating diversity** – sees difference and diverse opinions as an advantage and helps others to perceive this, expands cultural knowledge; effectively motivates people from other cultures

10 **Developing technological savvy** – acquires necessary technological knowledge, recruits people with technological expertise, manages use of technology to increase productivity

11 **Ensuring customer satisfaction** – inspires others to achieve high levels of customer satisfaction, views business processes from ultimate customer perspective, regularly solicits customer input, consistently delivers on customer commitments, and understands competitive options available to customers

12 **Maintaining a competitive advantage** – communicates a positive, can-do sense of urgency toward getting the job done, holds others accountable for results, eliminates waste and unneeded cost, provides products and services that create a clear competitive advantage and achieve results leading to long-term shareholder value

13 **Leading change** – sees change as an opportunity, not a problem, challenges the system when needed, thrives in ambiguous situations, encourages creativity and innovation, effectively translates creative ideas into business results

14 **Achieving personal mastery** – self-awareness, emotional intelligence, self-confidence, invests in personal development, involves others to complement personal weaknesses

15 **Anticipating opportunities** – invests in learning about future trends, anticipates future opportunities, inspires a focus on future opportunities and not simply on present objectives, develops ideas to meet changing environmental needs

Source: Adapted from Goldsmith, M., Greenberg, C., Robertson, A., and Hu-Chan, M. (2003) *Global leadership: The next generation*. Upper Saddle River, NJ: Prentice Hall: 329–333.

Goldsmith and his colleagues identified fifteen dimensions of global leadership, set out in Table 3.3. They note that many aspects of leadership are universal and unlikely to change; thus, ten of their dimensions are also found in domestic leadership and were also important in the past. They predict that the following five dimensions, however, will be especially important in the future:

- thinking globally;
- appreciating cultural diversity;
- developing technological savvy;
- building partnerships and alliances;
- sharing leadership.

They place special emphasis on the last factor, shared leadership:

> Because no individual is likely to embody all of the needed and critical capabilities, and because the very nature of business organization – merged, allianced, out-sourced, and virtual – is beginning to dictate it, shared leadership is expected to gain pre-eminence as

the operating model of the future. In the future, there will be fewer "all-knowing" CEOs; instead, leadership will be widely shared in executive teams. New demands for collective responsibility and accountability for results will emerge, as will new competencies for sharing leadership. The sheer number of alliances and networks means that more than one person will lead these structures.

(Goldsmith *et al.* 2003: xxxii)

According to their survey results, the most important competencies for the future, in descending order of importance, are the following: builds effective alliances with other organizations; genuinely listens to others; creates and communicates a clear organization vision; is a role model for living the organization's values; unites the organization into an effective team; makes decisions that reflect global considerations; views the business from the ultimate customer perspective; clearly identifies priorities and focuses on a vital few; builds effective partnerships across the company; and consistently treats people with respect and dignity (Goldsmith *et al.* 2003: 321).

## The Rand study: new challenges for international leadership

A Rand study set out to answer a series of questions, including the impact of globalization trends on major public- and private-sector organizations and the kinds of competencies needed in professionals working in international organizations (Bikson *et al.* 2003). The remaining questions centered on the global talent pipeline, its future prospects, and practical methods for improving the development of global leadership capabilities. Structured interviews were done with 135 human resource managers and senior managers of seventy-five public, for-profit, and non-profit organizations. An expert panel was nominated to deal with the development policies, which will be discussed in Chapter 9.

The results pointed to some differences in the competencies valued by different sectors (e.g., substantive domain knowledge, foreign language proficiency, and competitiveness and drive). However, the participants agreed on an integrated repertoire of skills that include (Bikson *et al.* 2003):

- *Substantive depth (professional or technical knowledge) related to the organization's primary business processes.* Depth is needed for sound decision making about risks and opportunities and to gain the respect and trust of followers.
- *Managerial ability, with an emphasis on teamwork and interpersonal skills.* These skills are necessary for working with various partners and because decision making at all hierarchical levels has become more collaborative.
- *Strategic international understanding.* The leader's strategic vision for the organization is based on an understanding of both the global context and local operational realities.
- *Cross-cultural experience.* Academic instruction and language acquisition are no substitutes for real work experience in another culture.

A global leadership shortfall is predicted for the for-profit, nonprofit, and especially public sectors because they have not developed enough future leaders (Bikson *et al.* 2003). Problems in the global talent pipeline have been signaled elsewhere (Charan *et al.* 2001; Mercer Delta 2006). McKinsey and Co. (1998) started warning about the War for Talent after completing a year-long study of over seventy firms. Fred Hassan, chair and CEO of Schering-Plough, reflected on the difficulties of changing company mindsets during the Pharmacia–Upjohn merger: "My experience with that change process convinced me that identifying and developing people with global attitudes requires personal involvement from the top. The CEO has to see himself as the chief developer of talent, no matter how large the company" (Green *et al.* 2003: 41). Avon's Andrea Jung is also known as a CEO who takes the time to acquaint herself with high-potential employees and monitor their development.

## Global leader effectiveness and selection criteria

Effectiveness and selection criteria have received much less attention than global leadership competencies. Caligiuri (2004) assessed 256 of the top 300 leaders in a UK-based diversified firm with an eye to determining what personal characteristics, experience, and developmental methods relate to effectiveness in global leadership activities. Global effectiveness was gauged by self-ratings of their global activities at work, the mean of their supervisor ratings over the last six quarters, and whether or not they were designated as high-potential employees. There were five significant differences between the highly effective global leaders and others who were less effective (ibid.):

- They had significantly higher conscientiousness scores and significantly lower neuroticism scores on the "Big Five" personality test.
- They came from diverse families.
- They participated in more geographically distributed teams.
- They had long-term international assignments.
- They were mentored by people from a different culture.

Short-term global assignments were not a predictor of effectiveness. However, extensive cross-national contact on teams, long-term expatriate assignments, and cross-national mentors played an important role in developing effectiveness.

Moro Bueno and Tubbs (2004) interviewed twenty-six international leaders from various countries to discover the competencies of effective global leaders. The most frequent responses were communication skills, motivation to learn, flexibility, open-mindedness, respect for others, and sensitivity.

## Global leadership competency frameworks

Everyone agrees that more global leaders are needed; there is less consensus on what global leaders do and the competencies they should possess. The various lists of competencies contain no surprises, but they are overlapping and separated at times only by semantic differences (Jokinen 2005). There is growing consensus that global leadership consists of core characteristics, context-specific abilities, and universal leadership skills. There is less agreement on how and which competencies fit into these categories. Three attempts have been made to provide frameworks for global leadership competencies, which will now be described.

## The multidimensional construct of global leadership

Mendenhall and Osland's (2002) review of the empirical and nonempirical literature yielded fifty-six global leadership competencies, a list too large to be useful. Noting that there were numerous areas of overlap across the various lists, they concluded that global leadership is a multidimensional construct with at least six core categories of competencies: (1) cross-cultural relationship skills, (2) traits and values, (3) cognitive orientation, (4) global business expertise, (5) global organizing expertise, and (6) visioning. Their categorization of the global leadership competencies appears in Table 3.4.

## The integrated framework of global leadership

On the basis of a review of the expatriate and global leader literature, Tiina Jokinen (2005) proposes an integrated theoretical framework of global leadership that includes three types or layers of competencies: a fundamental core, mental characteristics, and behavioral skills, shown in Table 3.5. She argues that the fundamental core of global leadership consists of self-awareness, engagement in personal transformation, and inquisitiveness. These characteristics set the stage for the development of other competencies; thus, they are not end-state competencies but indicators of the potential for global leadership. The second layer in her framework consists of mental characteristics that affect the way people approach issues and therefore guide their actions. The desired mental characteristics of their model consist of optimism, self-regulation, motivation to work in an international environment, social judgment skills, empathy, cognitive skills, and the acceptance of complexity and its contradictions. The last layer is behavioral and concerns tangible skills and knowledge that lead to concrete actions and results. The behavioral level of Jokinen's framework includes social skills, networking skills, and knowledge. Jokinen notes that these competencies are continuums. She recommends, therefore, that "the emphasis shift from identifying specific lists of competencies to defining and measuring their ideal level in individuals" (ibid.: 212).

## The Pyramid model of global leadership

The Pyramid model was developed originally via a modified Delphi technique with a team of international management scholars, members of ION (International

*Table 3.4* Mendenhall and Osland's literature review results: the six dimensions of global leadership and their competencies

| Cross-cultural relationship skills | Traits | Global business expertise | Global organizing expertise | Cognitive orientation | Visioning |
|---|---|---|---|---|---|
| Close personal relationships | Inquisitiveness | Global business savvy | Team building | Environmental sense-making | Articulating a tangible vision and strategy |
| CC communication skills | | | Community building | Global mindset | Envisioning |
| "Emotionally connect" ability | Continual learner | Business acumen | Organizational and global networking | Thinking agility | Entrepreneurial spirit |
| Inspire, motivate | | Total organizational astuteness/savvy | Creating learning systems | Improvisation | Catalyst for cultural change |
| Conflict management | Accountability | Stakeholder orientation | Strong operational codes | Pattern recognition | Change agentry |
| Negotiation expertise | Integrity | Results-orientation | Global networking | Cognitive complexity | Catalyst for strategic change |
| Empowering others | Courage | | Strong customer orientation | Cosmopolitanism | |
| Managing CC ethical issues | Commitment | | | Managing uncertainty | |
| Social literacy | Hardiness | | | | |
| Cultural literacy | Maturity Tenacity Personal literacy Behavioral flexibility | | | Local *vs.* global paradoxes | |

Source: Based on Mendenhall, M., and Osland, J. "Mapping the Terrain of the Global Leadership Construct." Paper presented at the *Academy of International Business*, San Juan, Puerto Rico, June 29, 2002.

*Table 3.5* Jokinen's integrated framework of global leadership

| Layers of competencies | Competencies |
| --- | --- |
| Behavioral skills | Social skills, networking skills, and knowledge |
| Mental characteristics | Optimism, self-regulation, motivation to work in an international environment, social judgment skills, empathy, cognitive skills, and the acceptance of complexity and its contradictions |
| Fundamental core | Self-awareness, engagement in personal transformation, and inquisitiveness |

Source: Table created based on the research findings reported in Jokinen, T. (2005) "Global leadership competencies: a review and discussion," *Journal of European Industrial Training* 29(2/3): 199–216.

Organizations Network), who identified the key competencies of global managers (Bird and Osland 2004). The model, shown in Figure 3.3, was subsequently expanded and adapted for global leaders for this volume, following a review of the recent global leadership literature. The model takes the form of a pyramid to reflect the assumption that global leaders have certain threshold knowledge and traits that serve as a base for higher-level competencies. The five-level model suggests a progression that is cumulative, advancing from bottom to top. Level 1, the foundation, comprises *global knowledge*, discussed more fully in Chapter 7. Here is an example of an Indian manager-turned-entrepreneur who capitalized on the knowledge acquired in years of international work with a large high-tech firm. He saw the promise in a new invention to monitor people under anesthesia. Rather than locating all operations in one country, he organized a firm to bring together people in his extensive personal network: mathematicians in Switzerland, R&D engineers and manufacturers in India, and salespeople in Silicon Valley. His lengthy experience of working with people from different cultures made it possible for him to persuade people to join him in this venture. Because of his familiarity with technology and new products, all the IT and accounting functions are handled on the web. His experience with marketing led him to develop a marketing plan that focuses only on countries with either "lots of money" or "lots of people." Thus, his reliance on various types of global knowledge makes it possible for him to run a worldwide company successfully with a very small number of people (Bird and Osland 2004: 68–69).

Level 2 consists of four specific *threshold traits*: integrity, humility, inquisitiveness, and resilience. These are relatively stable personality traits that are difficult for some people to learn and are therefore recommended as selection criteria. Bird and Osland's selection was based on the research findings for expatriates and international managers. For example, these characteristics were included in the list Wills and Barham (1994) discovered in successful international managers: a sense of humility, emotional self-awareness and resilience, psychological maturity, curiosity to learn, and personal morality.

Without integrity, global leaders cannot earn the respect they need from people within and without their organization to be effective. In cross-cultural settings where pressures

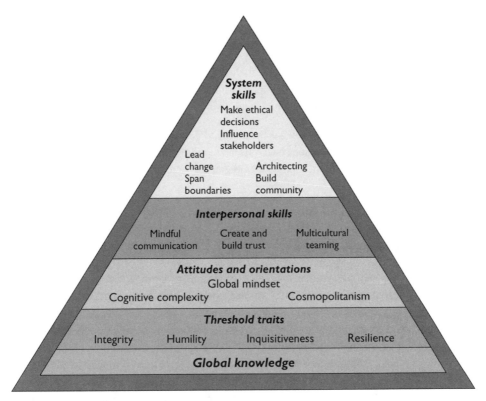

The following words appear within the pyramid image:

System skills
Make ethical decisions
Influence stakeholders
Lead change
Span boundaries
Architecting
Build community
Interpersonal skills
Mindful communication
Create and build trust
Multicultural teaming
Attitudes and orientations
Global mindset
Cognitive complexity
Cosmopolitanism
Threshold traits
Integrity
Humility
Inquisitiveness
Resilience
Global knowledge

*Figure 3.3* The Pyramid model of global leadership

Source: Adapted from Bird, A. and Osland, J. (2004). Global competencies: An introduction. In Henry Lane, Martha Maznevski, Mark Mendenhall, and Jeanne McNett (eds.), *The Blackwell handbook of global management*. Oxford: Blackwell: 57–80.

to adapt or fit in are combined with incomplete and inaccurate understandings, integrity prevents leaders from making errors in judgment that can come back to haunt them and their companies. Research has identified honesty and integrity as critical success factor for global leaders (McCall and Hollenbeck 2002; Black *et al.* 1999b).

Without humility, managers are not open to learning from other cultures or organizations and are not willing to be taught by others. It is the opposite of arrogance and ethnocentrism, which leads people to assume that they have all the answers. Carlos Ghosn, the first non-Japanese CEO of Nissan, stated, "Well, I think I am a practical person. I know I may fail at any moment. In my opinion, it was extremely helpful to be practical [at Nissan], not to be arrogant, and to realize that I could fail at any moment" (Millikin and Fu 2005: 121).

The desire to have new experiences and to learn from them is called inquisitiveness, which is described in more detail in the section that reviewed the Global Explorer model earlier in this chapter. The final trait is resilience, which refers to the optimism and persistence needed to keep moving forward despite adversity and the hardiness necessary to deal with the stresses inherent in global work. The concept of hardiness comes to us from the literature on stress and Big Five personality research. Within the Big Five, hardiness is usually referred to as emotional stability, a factor found to relate to expatriate performance (Caligiuri 2000). McCall and Hollenbeck (2002) refer to this as "resilience." Kelley and Meyers (1992) call it "emotional resilience" and characterize it in this fashion:

> The emotionally resilient person has the ability to deal with stressful feelings in a constructive way and to "bounce back" from them. Emotionally resilient people . . . have confidence in their ability to cope with ambiguity . . . and have a positive sense of humor and self-regard.

We can see a link to emotional intelligence in this description. While it is possible for people to increase their resilience and emotional intelligence, it is simpler and a safer bet for organizations to select potential global leaders who already possess this trait.

Level 3 is composed of *attitudes and orientations*, the global mindset that influences the way global leaders perceive and interpret the world. While there is still no generally accepted definition of the global mindset construct, the most extensive effort in this direction has been made by Levy and her colleagues, who argue that global mindset is composed of two factors that we have previously mentioned in passing: cognitive complexity and cosmopolitanism (Levy *et al.* 2007). Cognitive complexity refers to a knowledge structure composed of differentiation (the number of dimensions or constructs an individual uses to describe a particular domain, such as globalization or leadership) and integration (the links or relationships the individual sees among the differentiated constructs) (Bartunek *et al.* 1983). The more cognitively complex people are, the more dimensions and relationships they perceive – in other words, the more differentiated and integrated their domains. Higher levels of cognitive complexity correlate with the ability to hold competing interpretations (ibid. 1983), balance contradictions, ambiguities, and trade-offs (Tetlock 1983), and deal with dualities or paradoxes (Evans *et al.* 2002; Levy *et al.* 2007).

Cosmopolitanism is the polar opposite of parochialism, and this construct contains two aspects related to global mindset.

> First is an orientation toward the outside and the external environment, rather than a focus on the inside, the local or the parochial. A second key aspect is the characteristic of openness, which represents not only being interested in others but willing to engage and be open to exploring the alternative systems of meanings held by outsiders and to learn from them.
>
> (Levy *et al.* 2007)

A global mindset makes it possible for leaders to see beyond the narrow confines of their own culture.

Knowledge, personality traits, and attitudes become valuable only when they are translated into action. Thus, Level 4 focuses on the *interpersonal skills* that global leaders need to cross cultures: mindful communication, creating and building trust, and the ability to work in multicultural teams. An ongoing study of expert global leaders found that these skills were key components in their stories of critical leadership challenges (Osland *et al.* 2007a). Fred Hassan, chair and CEO of Plough-Schering, argues that doing well in business is about "getting to the hearts of people – that's something you don't learn in business school. Can you teach someone to engender trust? That separates leaders from managers" (Simons 2003).

The top of the pyramid, Level 5, contains *system skills*, which are really metaskills that encapsulate many other skills required for global work. They all require cross-cultural expertise and the ability both to adapt to cultural differences and to leverage them for competitive advantage. The central focus at this level is the ability to influence people and the systems in which they work, both inside and outside the organization.

The boundary-spanning aspect refers to the ability to communicate and serve as a liaison with different functional areas, businesses, and external organizations and indirect stakeholders. Boundary-spanning roles include representative, gatekeeper, advice broker, and trust broker (Friedman and Polodny 1992). Global leaders deal with a wide variety of stakeholders such as industry consortia, government agencies, regulators, suppliers, nongovernmental organizations (NGOs), the media, and business partners.

Global leaders have to build a community of their far-flung organizations to provide all members with a sense of membership. When J. T. Wang became president of Acer Inc. in Taiwan, he followed these guiding principles: the principle of one company, the policy of one brand, and the spirit of one team (Shih *et al.* 2006). Building a community seems to be a precursor to global change efforts (Osland 2004). Sometimes these communities are composed not only of employees but also of stakeholders and organizations within and beyond the industry.

Leading change on a global level is another metaskill found at this level. It begins with a new vision; subsequently, global leaders are catalysts for learning and change. They devote a good deal of their time to changing the mindset of their followers and to pushing strategic change. This topic will be discussed in greater depth in Chapter 8.

Another competency is called architecting, which refers to organizational design and alignment. It involves ensuring that all the various building blocks of the organization – strategy, structure, employee selection, training, retention, organizational culture, managerial style, systems such as planning, budgeting, and control and information systems, communication processes, financial reporting and accountability, performance metrics, and so forth – are coordinated and integrated to the optimal degree. Integration and coordination are enduring challenges for global firms seeking to align global strategies with local business processes and needs and to grow by acquiring foreign firms. Furthermore, the changes global leaders want to make result in the need to realign and redesign the organizational components so that they complement rather than block the change.

Nestlé was once a cautionary example of poor integration. At one point in its history it had five different email systems and twenty versions of accounting and planning software. Because each Nestlé America factory had a different code for vanilla, they paid over twenty different prices for the exact same vanilla – to the same vendor (Busco *et al.* 2006)!

It is a fairly simple matter to design processes that resolve problems like Nestlé America's, which the company did. The more difficult challenge is to change the mindset of employees so that they themselves are willing and able to forecast and fix problems at work. Architecting also includes the human side of business – the social architecture that builds motivated employees, healthy workplaces, and effective organizational cultures. As Warren Bennis commented, "The key to competitive advantage in the 1990s and beyond will be the capacity of leaders to create the social architecture that generates intellectual capital" (1997: 87). Global leaders are responsible, in the final analysis, for the design and function of the global organization itself.

The influence process is a universal aspect of leadership, but in the global leadership context it involves understanding how to influence multiple stakeholders, both individuals and organizations, from various cultures effectively. The Brazilian firm Aracruz Celulose SA, the world's largest pulp producer, has won numerous best practices awards for sustainability and management. Its internal operations are widely admired. Despite these accolades, the firm must also deal with external stakeholders who pressure the firm. As part of the landless movement in Brazil, indigenous groups claimed that the company bought their traditional lands; recently they have invaded and damaged Aracruz property. The company maintains that the Indians never lived on the land in question and relied on the judicial system who annexed the land for the Indians in 2007. In addition, Aracruz is also compelled to take into consideration the environmental activists who criticize the company for its monoculture of eucalyptus trees, its water use, and the bleaching process that produces white paper. The Brazilian Indians and environmenta lists are supported by European activists who persuaded the Swedish royal family to disinvest in Aracruz. Activists have also petitioned, unsuccessfully to date, the Norwegian parliament and Norway's Petroleum Fund to take similar steps. Aracruz has worked with these external stakeholders in the past, but their situation highlights the difficulty of finding lasting solutions to ambiguous, complex societal problems (Osland and Osland 2007).

Making ethical decisions – decisions that involve actions that conform to a high ethical standard – involves the capacity to see things from a larger perspective and think in terms of systems and of the implications of individual and organizational actions for all parties that might be affected. Decision making tends to violate ethical standards when it loses sight of the larger system and instead focuses on the narrow concerns or interests of individuals, organizations, or industries.

The graphic representation of the Pyramid model does not accurately reflect the dynamic nature of global leadership process that occurs when leaders interact with the environment. The model's contribution, however, is the identification of different building blocks of global leadership and the simplification of a complex array of competencies.

# Evaluation of global leadership research

As with most new fields of study, the quality of the research varies (Osland *et al.* 2006). Some of the research described in this chapter did not go through a peer review process and is therefore more difficult to judge in terms of rigor. Despite having made valuable contributions to date, the findings are not definitive. For example, there is no consensus on the construct definition of global leadership. In some research the onus of defining global leadership was left to interviewees ("What characteristics do global leaders have?" "Who would you nominate as global leaders?"); in other studies the definition was merely assumed ("all global managers or CEOs are global leaders"). Several studies asked global managers for their opinion about global leader capability without clarifying whether respondents were themselves global leaders. As a result, conceptual confusion persists, as do questions about whether there is a significant difference between global managers versus global leaders, or between global versus domestic leaders. The terms "global leader" and "global manager" are frequently used interchangeably in both selection and writing, which is disconcerting, given Kotter's (1990a, b) distinctions between managers and leaders.

Several of these research studies employed exploratory designs, which is appropriate in a nascent field of study. No one, however, has replicated Mintzberg's (1973) landmark observation of managerial behavior with global leaders by following them around as they do their work. Data collection to date is limited to opinion about global leaders or self-reports. There are no studies of their actual behavior. Research is in progress on the cognitive processes of expert global leaders (Osland *et al.* 2007a).

The global leadership research has, for the most part, taken a *content* approach and focused on identifying competencies. The list of fifty-six global leadership competencies contained in the literature is too extensive to be useful (Mendenhall and Osland 2002). Many of the models of global leadership contain overlapping concepts. Despite their usefulness competency studies fail to explain how global leaders interact with the environment in specific circumstances. They do not distinguish between essential and nonessential competencies or tell us when they are important. Leadership requirements can vary by level, culture, and situation, as well as by functions and operating units, so competency lists might not apply across the board (Conger and Ready 2004: 45).

The competency approach does not explain the conundrum of exemplary global leaders who succeed despite obvious weaknesses. Few leaders live up to the idealized view of leadership that competency lists portray (Conger and Ready 2004). No one was found to possess all the attributes identified in a study of the top twenty-five business leaders of our time (Pandya and Shell 2005). Instead, leaders possess some combination of competencies; we do not know which combinations are most effective in specific situations. McCall and Hollenbeck (2002) conclude that complex, high-level executive jobs are performed in various ways by executives with multiple forms of talent. Therefore, we sumise that global leaders can be effective without acquiring all competencies, but research has yet to test this hypothesis. Furthermore, the rise and fall of certain well-known global business leaders and the instances of domestic leaders who rise to the challenge of a one-time global leadership role may indicate that global leadership can be manifested in both episodic and long-term behavior (Osland *et al.* 2006).

Wills and Barham (1994) conceive of behavioral competencies and skills as merely the outside layers of what characterizes successful international executives. To focus solely on behavioral competencies would be misleading, since they believe that international executives operate from a deeper holistic core competence composed of cognitive complexity, emotional energy, and psychological maturity.

Yet another weakness is that the unique nature of leadership and what motivates it may have nothing at all to do with competencies. As Margaret Wheatley stated,

> I think we start in the wrong place if we ask, "What are the traits that I have to acquire?" The place to start is, "What are the things I care about that I'm willing to step forward to figure out how to be a leader?"
>
> (Madsen and Hammond 2005: 75)

The passion to make a difference and the willingness to allow others to participate in creating it is more likely to lead to leadership success than simply acquiring and checking off a list of skills.

In summary, "global leadership is an emerging field – reminiscent of the first stage of domestic leadership research – which also began by examining traits and subsequently evolved more complex theories" (Osland *et al.* 2006: 210). Follow-up research has yet to validate global leadership competencies. Because no relevant longitudinal research has been done, we have limited agreement and knowledge about the antecedents and outcomes of global leadership. More exploratory research on the dynamics of the factors that combine to create the phenomenon of global leadership, using multiple paradigmatic approaches, would help refine the global leadership construct. The development of more rigorous models from exploratory research would yield models that are amenable to the generation of propositions and hypotheses that in turn can be empirically tested (Mendenhall 1999). According to the most recent literature reviews (Jokinen 2005; Osland *et al.* 2006), future research is needed in numerous areas, including the following: distinguishing between the roles and behaviors of global managers and global leaders, definitively answering the questions of whether and how global leaders differ from domestic leaders, identification of global leadership behaviors, identification of thought processes and expert cognition in global leaders, development of process models that include interaction with the environment, definition of global leadership success and effectiveness, developmental models, the relevance of different types of international experience, and best-practices training methods. Several studies have pointed out the importance of a diverse family background and international exposure and cultural contact during childhood (e.g., Kets de Vries and Florent-Treacy 2002; McCall and Hollenbeck 2002; Caligiuri 2004). Since many global leadership competencies are developed in childhood and adolescence, more research is needed on the impact of childhood, family background, and early international experiences (ibid.). However, not all effective global leaders were exposed to other cultures or possess an extensive international background (Osland *et al.* 2007). For them, motivation and the ability to learn quickly may be more salient. There are different profiles of effective global leaders (McCall and Hollenbeck 2002; Osland *et al.* 2007). Given the importance of the motivation to learn in developing the necessary global leadership skills and knowledge, future research could describe more fully the role played by motivation to learn and learning (Jokinen 2005). In addition, Mendenhall and Osland (2002) argue for more exploratory empirical research, with multiple paradigmatic approaches, on the multidimensional global leadership construct: cross-cultural relationship skills, traits and values, cognitive orientation, global business expertise, global organizing expertise, and visioning. Finally, the ability to measure the level of global leadership capacity in both individuals and organizations would be very useful.

# Assessing global leadership competencies

## 4

ALLAN BIRD

A quick tour of the internet provides some insight regarding the topic of this chapter: the assessment of global leadership competencies. In just 0.06 seconds Google references 170 million websites relating to leadership. Narrow the search to "global leadership" and it takes 0.20 seconds to identify 983,000 sites. But key in "global leadership assessment," and only 64 sites surface. As we will discover as we proceed further, when it comes to assessing the competencies associated with effective global leadership, much work remains to be done.

In this chapter we will begin by discussing what "competency" means in the context of global leadership and note significant challenges in identifying and measuring it. We shall then move on to a consideration of a variety of instruments that are currently used by practitioners and scholars.

A comprehensive review of proposed competencies is beyond the scope of this chapter, which has as its central focus a review of assessment instruments. Chapters 1 and 2 both present an overview of the broader research on global leadership, much of which has taken a content view and, hence, has focused on leader characteristics that are, either implicitly or explicitly, put forward as competencies. For a more detailed review of the leadership competency literature, readers should consult Jokinen (2005) and Osland *et al.* (2006).

## Defining global leadership competency

The pioneering work on competency as a concept in the workplace was carried out by McClelland, who defined it as a set of underlying characteristics that an individual or team possesses which have been demonstrated to predict superior or effective performance in a job (1973). McClelland was particularly concerned with identifying behaviors that superior performers displayed and that average performers or underperformers did not show. Boyatzis (1982) emphasized the causal connection between capabilities a person possessed prior to performance that could be used to predict superior performance in a given situation. If we work from this conception of competency, there are three clear standards that must be met to define an individual characteristic or capacity as a competency: (1) it must exist prior to performance; (2) it must be causally linked to performance; and (3) it must be possessed by superior, but not by average or subpar, performers.

The task domain of global leadership makes it difficult to identify competencies that conform to the three standards presented above. As Osland and associates (2006) note, there is no agreed-upon definition for what constitutes global leadership. Even where it is possible to define succinctly a global leader as someone whose job responsibilities include a global scope (Black *et al.* 1999b), the range of positions to which such a definition applies makes it problematic to circumscribe a narrow range of activities or behaviors. Be that as it may, for our purposes here it may be useful to adopt Jokinen's (2005: 200) formulation as our definition of global leadership competencies:

> those universal qualities that enable individuals to perform their job outside their own national as well as organizational culture, no matter what their educational or ethnic background is, what functional area their job description represents, or what organization they come from.

As was noted in Chapter 1, assessing global leadership competencies presents several distinctive challenges. First, there may be a tendency to overspecify the number of competencies required for superior performance in a specific job (Conger and Ready 2004); for example, Morrison (2000) noted that one multinational has identified 250 competencies associated with global leadership; also, Mendenhall and Osland (2002) reviewed the academic scholarship on global leadership and came up with a list of fifty-three competencies (see Table 3.4 in Chapter 3). It is reasonable to question whether such lengthy lists are useful or practical.

A second challenge is that both practitioners and academics alike may be inclined to develop competency lists that reflect an idealized performance standard, rather than what is actually possible (Conger and Ready 2004). This may arise as a consequence of trying to envision what superior performance might look like or what behaviors might lead to it rather than focusing on what has been demonstrated to be superior performance or on what is realistic.

Third, there is a need to distinguish between competency types. In studying expatriate managers – the group single-most associated with global leadership research – Leiba-O'Sullivan (1999) proposes a distinction between stable and dynamic competencies. Stable competencies reflect aspects of personality and are relatively settled and enduring over time. They are difficult, if not impossible, to change significantly. However, they may be broadly applicable – that is, they may contribute to superior performance across a range of jobs or work situations. For example, the personality predisposition of optimism is widely accepted as contributing to superior performance across a multitude of managerial positions. By contrast, dynamic competencies are specific skills and abilities that can, to a greater or lesser degree, be taught. They are, however, often more narrowly applicable. For example, typing skills can be taught, though some people will learn how to type more accurately and more quickly than others. Moreover, the ability to type accurately and quickly is less likely to be associated with superior performance across a broad range of managerial positions or situations. The distinction between stable and dynamic competencies is sometimes framed respectively in terms of "soft" versus "hard" competencies, or "behavioral" versus "technical."

In the next section we will review several of the more widely used assessment instruments. After presenting the competencies purportedly measured by each, we will attempt to evaluate them in accordance with the three criteria noted above, namely do the competencies exist prior to performance; are they causally linked to performance; and do they distinguish between superior and non-superior performance? We shall do that by looking for empirical evidence that supports their ability to predict performance.

## Global leadership competency assessment instruments

Broadly classified, assessment instruments used in developing global leaders fall into one of three categories: cultural difference assessments, intercultural adaptability assessments, and global leadership competency assessments. We shall consider each type below, and discuss specific assessment instruments.

## Cultural difference assessments

It is appropriate to recognize that practitioners and scholars have developed a variety of assessments and survey instruments for identifying variations in national cultural values across a range of dimensions, although these are not directly focused on assessing global leader competencies. A number of the more widely used instruments (see, for example, Hampden-Turner and Trompenaars 2000; Hofstede 2001; Maznevski and DiStefano, 1995) are often construed as a form of indirect competency assessment. In a typical application along these lines, a manager's cultural profile (i.e., score or position on various cultural value dimensions) will be computed and will be used within the context of a training program to determine developmental needs. In this regard, it is appropriate to view cultural profiles as competency assessment proxies, as they are used to identify areas where the development of hard competencies is presumed to lead to superior performance.

Taras (2006b) has compiled the most comprehensive catalogue of such instruments to date. More than 100 instruments cover the gamut of work- or business-related dimensions on which cultures are likely to vary, including the common – e.g., individualism, power distance, uncertainty avoidance and universalism – and the not so common – e.g., family integrity, faith in people and upward influence. Where available, Taras (2006b) also provides the specific items in the instrument as well as Cronbach alpha and test–retest reliabilities.

It should also be noted in passing that Taras (2006a) has compiled a similarly comprehensive catalogue of surveys and instruments used to assess acculturation. Though less frequently used for global leader competency assessment, acculturation surveys are sometimes used in corporate training and development programs. This catalogue contains information on fifty assessments and also includes Cronbach alpha and test–retest reliability information where available.

## Intercultural adaptability assessments

In this subsection we will consider several instruments that have as their primary focus effective intercultural competence. Instruments that fall into this category are frequently used in conjunction with global manager development programs. Because effective interaction with culturally different others is a critical aspect of effective global leadership in most contexts, the assessment of intercultural competence is highly appropriate. At the same time, it is important to recognize that intercultural competence represents just one aspect of a global leader's competency set.

There are numerous intercultural adaptability assessments that are commercially available, but for which there is scant, if any, research literature. Stuart (2007) provides a practical, though perhaps less than critical, review of a range of instruments.

### The Cross-Cultural Adaptability Inventory

The *Cross-Cultural Adaptability Inventory* (*CCAI*) was developed by Christine Kelley and Judith Meyers (1995a) as a self-assessment tool for cross-cultural adaptability training and development. Over time it has come to be used for measuring competency acquisition, as in pre- and post-test measures in conjunction with training programs. The *CCAI* measures four dimensions: flexibility/openness, emotional resilience, perceptual acuity, and personal autonomy. After reviewing the literature and interviewing expert interculturalists, the developers originally settled on five dimensions, but dropped "positive regard" for others when their pilot studies failed to differentiate this dimension from the other four (Kelley and Meyers 1995b).

- *Flexibility/openness*. The first of the four dimensions addresses the tendency to be open to others and broad-mindedness toward people and ideas. It also reflects a willingness to be flexible and nonjudgmental in one's perspective. ($\alpha = 0.54$)
- *Emotional resilience*. The ability to navigate the unfamiliarity associated with intercultural situations while maintaining positive emotions is the focus of the second dimension. Negative emotional reactions, such as culture shocks or bumps, are frequent occurrences when working in intercultural contexts. Emotional resilience reflects an ability to cope in, as well as quickly recover from, such situations. ($\alpha = 0.80$)
- *Perceptual acuity*. Openness to new people and experiences and an ability to cope with stressful situations can be easier when an individual is able to read situations

accurately and detect and appropriately respond to verbal and nonverbal signals. The third dimension also refers to an ability to communicate effectively in such situations. ($\alpha = 0.78$)

- *Personal autonomy.* The final dimension focuses on the possession and maintenance of a strong personal identity in the face of adapting to a new cultural context that involves others whose values may different than one's own. ($\alpha = 0.67$)

The *CCAI* includes fifty items and is administered using a paper-and-pencil format. The survey is self-scored. The average respondent requires about ten minutes to complete the inventory. There is no mechanism for monitoring social response bias. Results are reported by tallying scores in four columns, with each column representing one of the dimensions. Interpretation of scores requires a facilitator/trainer.

The *CCAI* has primarily been used in studies attempting to measure the effectiveness of intercultural training programs. For example, Cornett-DeVito and McGlone (2000) used it to evaluate the effectiveness of intercultural training programs for law enforcement personnel. Similarly, Goldstein and Smith (1999) relied on it to evaluate the effectiveness of training programs for business professionals. However, in a recent factor-analytic study of the *CCAI* Davis and Finney (2006) found that inventory items did not support a four-factor structure. They conducted further exploratory factor analysis but concluded that no interpretable structure could be identified. There does not appear to be any published research demonstrating the *CCAI*'s ability to predict interculturally effective behavior in managers or in any other group.

## Intercultural Development Inventory

The *Intercultural Development Inventory* (*IDI*) was developed by Mitchell Hammer and Milton Bennett on the basis of Bennett's theory (1993), the development model of intercultural sensitivity (DMIS), which identified six stages of intercultural development and associated competencies that group into two sets: ethnocentric and ethnorelative. The ethnocentric stages, in order of development, are Denial, Defense, and Minimization. The ethnorelative stages are Acceptance, Adaptation, and Integration. The IDI measures an individual's worldview regarding cultural difference, which may be construed also as a capacity for intercultural competency. The ethnocentric stages can be interpreted as different ways of *avoiding* cultural differences, such as by denying that differences exist, defending one's culture against differences, or minimizing the extent or significance of the differences. The ethnorelative stages are ways of *seeking* cultural difference, through first accepting the importance of difference, then adjusting or adapting one's perspective to take difference into account and, finally, by integrating the concept of culture and difference into one's identity. Each of the six stages can also be broken down into substages.

- *Denial.* This stage is characterized by a condition in which one's own culture is taken to be the only culture. Though other cultures may exist, they should be avoided or isolated. People in this stage are uninterested in cultural differences, but when confronted with difference may respond viscerally, seeking to eliminate differences that intrude into their sphere of activity. The two substages of Denial are Isolation and Separation.

- *Defense*. The second ethnocentric stage reflects a worldview in which one's own culture (or an adopted culture) is experienced as the only good one. Other cultures are seen as being in opposition to one's own culture, i.e., "we" versus "them." Moreover, other cultures are viewed as inferior and one's own as superior. People in this stage may feel threatened by cultural difference. An alternative position in this stage is to view one's own culture as inferior and other cultures as superior – that is, to experience a reversal of dominant orientation in this stage. The three substages or categories of Defense are Denigration, Superiority, and Reversal.
- *Minimization*. The third stage in the ethnocentric set takes a perspective that one's own culture reflects a deeper element universal to all cultures. Consequently, differences are minimized or suppressed. People in this stage may ignore or mask over important differences. The Minimization substages are physical universalism ("cultures increasingly share so much in common") and transcendent universalism ("at heart we are all the same").
- *Acceptance*. The first ethnorelative stage adopts a worldview that sees one's own culture as just one of many complex worldviews. Although one may accept that there are differences and one's own perspective is not superior, this does not mean that a person at the Acceptance stage necessarily agrees with other worldviews. People at this stage are curious about and respectful of differences. The substages for Acceptance are Acceptance of Behaviors and Acceptance of Values.
- *Adaptation*. In this stage, acceptance of another culture yields both perception and behaviors appropriate for effective functioning in that culture as well as an ability to see the larger world in new ways. Adaptation entails intentional modification of behavior in order to interact with culturally different others. The two substages associated with this stage are Empathy and Pluralism.
- *Integration*. The ultimate intercultural development stage is Integration, the ability and inclination to move into and out of different cultural worldviews. People who reach Integration may confront issues of cultural marginality as they work to integrate these shifting worldviews into their self-identity. Integration is not the required level of intercultural competence in most situations. It is common, however, among "global nomads" and others with extensive experience working at cultural intersections. The substages of Integration are Contextual Evaluation and Constructive Marginality.

Based on the DMIS, the *IDI* was structured with five scales and ten clusters, roughly matching the stages and substages of the DMIS. The *IDI* scales comprise the *DD* (Denial/Defense) scale, the *R* (Reversal) scale, the *M* (Minimization) scale, the *AA* (Acceptance/Adaptation) scale, and the *EM* (Encapsulated Marginality) scale.

The *IDI* includes fifty items, requiring the average person to take ten to fifteen minutes to complete. The inventory is available in paper-and-pencil format and, recently, online. There are thirteen language versions: English, Spanish, French, Portuguese, Italian, German, Chinese, Japanese, Korean, Bahasa, Indonesian/Malay, Norwegian, and

Russian. Results are reported in terms of level of development for each of the six stages, with developmental level ranging from "unresolved" to "in transition" to "resolved." Ideally, respondents should receive their feedback report as part of a counseling session from an *IDI*-qualified facilitator.

Research on the validity and reliability of the *IDI* has found strong support for the internal validity and reliability of the psychometric properties of the instrument (Hammer *et al.* 2003; Paige *et al.* 2003). Studies of students (Straffon 2003) and returned Peace Corps volunteers (Kashima 2006) found the *IDI* predictive of level of intercultural sensitivity. Developers of the *IDI* also report similar findings for the IDI when it is used in business settings; however, because these results have not been made public through empirical studies published in peer-reviewed journals, it is not possible to confirm their validity.

## Multicultural Personality Questionnaire

Developed by Karen van der Zee and Jan-Pieter van Oudenhoven (2000), both of the University of Groningen, the *Multicultural Personality Questionnaire (MPQ)* measures five dimensions of personality relevant to adjustment and performance of expatriates. Dimensions are drawn from a review of earlier work on expatriate adjustment and from their own research. Moreover, the framing of dimensions is clearly in terms of the effective intercultural adjustment of expatriates.

- *Cultural Empathy*. This dimension relates to one's ability to empathize with people from a culture different from one's own. It also encompasses the ability to empathize with thoughts and behaviors of people from other cultures. ($\alpha = 0.83$)
- *Open-Mindedness*. Effective intercultural behavior is also predicated on having an attitude that is open to differing cultural norms and to people from other cultures. Open-mindedness reflects an unprejudiced approach to others. ($\alpha = 0.84$)
- *Social Initiative*. This dimension addresses the way in which people approach social situations, recognizing that empirical work has confirmed the importance of taking the initiative and being active in establishing and maintaining relationships with people, both at home and abroad. ($\alpha = 0.89$)
- *Emotional Stability*. The tendency to handle stressful situations calmly rather than with an affective response is important because novel or ambiguous situations can evoke strong emotion. ($\alpha = 0.84$)
- *Flexibility*. The fifth dimension focuses on a person's ability to adjust plans and behaviors easily. Van der Zee and van Oudenhoven (2000) stress the importance of this dimension in a new cultural environment, where one's established ways of doing things are likely to be inappropriate. ($\alpha = 0.64$)

The *MPQ* contains seventy-eight items and can be administered either online or via paper-and-pencil format. The average respondent requires ten to fifteen minutes to complete the instrument. There are English, Dutch, French, German, and Italian versions available. There does not appear to be any monitoring of social desirability response patterns. Results are reported graphically for each dimension using a bar line and a ten-point scale, with 10 being highest. One or two sentences of explanation specific to each dimension score are also provided.

The greater part of the research on the *MPQ* has been carried out with students; however, it has been used in conjunction with expatriate assessment as well (Van Oudenhoven *et al*. 2003). Two longitudinal studies (Mol *et al*. 2001; Van Oudenhoven and Van der Zee 2002) conducted with international student samples found that the *MPQ* was predictive of psychological well-being and social support. A subsequent study of expatriates in Taiwan (Van Oudenhoven *et al*. 2003) confirmed the *MPQ*'s predictive capability with regard to three facets of personal adjustment (satisfaction with life, physical health and psychological well-being), job satisfaction, and social support.

## *Intercultural Readiness Check*

The *Intercultural Readiness Check* (*IRC*) assessment, developed by Karen van der Zee and Ursula Brinkmann, is apparently an extension of the *Multicultural Personality Questionnaire*. The latter instrument was developed with a specific focus on expatriates, whereas the IRC seems aimed at application to a broader range of personnel, not just those slated for international assignment.

The original *IRC* measured six dimensions that the developers argued were relevant to multicultural success (Van der Zee and Brinkmann 2004): intercultural sensitivity ($\alpha = 0.80$), intercultural communication ($\alpha = 0.84$), intercultural relationship building ($\alpha = 0.80$), conflict management ($\alpha = 0.59$), leadership ($\alpha = 0.70$), and tolerance of ambiguity ($\alpha = 0.78$). Subsequent refinement of the instrument has settled on four dimensions. Reliability alphas on these four dimensions do not appear to have been publicized.

- *Intercultural Sensitivity*. The focus of this dimension is on the awareness and perception of culturally different communication styles, for example the ability to notice and accurately read verbal and nonverbal communication. It also measures interest in differing cultural norms and values.
- *Intercultural Communication*. This dimension measures one's ability to empathize with people who are culturally different. It is concerned not only with feelings but also with thoughts and behavior.
- *Building Commitment*. Motivating others, nurturing interaction and cooperation, and leading out while maintaining support and commitment from others is the focus of this dimension.
- *Managing Uncertainty*. Intercultural situations are characterized by uncertainty around meanings, norms, and behaviors. This dimension assesses ability to cope with intercultural situations.

The *IRC* is a sixty-item instrument and can be administered either online or via paper-and-pencil format. The average respondent requires ten to fifteen minutes to complete the instrument. There are English, Dutch, French, German, and Japanese versions. There does not appear to be any monitoring of social desirability response patterns. Results are reported using a graphical presentation and index, with additional commentary provided for each of the four dimensions.

The developers of the *IRC* provide generalized anecdotal evidence for its predictive capability relative to superior performance in jobs entailing a large intercultural component; however, statistical data supporting these claims have not been made public through empirical studies published in peer-reviewed journals. Nevertheless, the convergent validation of the *IRC* vis-à-vis the *MPQ* (Van der Zee and Brinkmann 2004) suggests a basis for assuming some measure of predictive capability and association with positive outcomes in intercultural situations.

## *Big Five personality inventories*

In the early 1960s, psychologists doing research on personality characteristics carried out a review of a number of empirical studies and found five recurring traits. In the 1980s, Costa and McCrae (1985) developed a standardized taxonomy, labeling the five factors Extraversion, Agreeableness, Conscientiousness, Neuroticism, and Openness to Experience. There are several terms that apply to this group of personality characteristics, such as the Big Five, the Five-Factor model, and the Five-Factor theory. It is also important to note that these factors – to be described in greater detail below – cover a wide range of personality characteristics. Consequently, most instruments that measure the five factors also measure a variety of facets. In the case of the *NEO PI-R*, for instance, each factor has six facets associated with it.

Whether personality traits are able to predict performance has been an ongoing debate. However, a number of meta-analytical studies have found strong support for their predictive validity. For example, Saulsman and Page (2004) undertook a review of fifteen different studies and found a distinct profile of the five factors for each of ten mental disorders listed in the *Diagnostic and Statistical Manual of Mental Disorders (DSM-IV)*. In the realm of job performance, Barrick and Mount (1991; see also Mount and Barrick 1998) completed a meta-analytic review covering 23,994 subjects from 162 samples in 117 studies and concluded that Conscientiousness consistently predicted performance across all jobs and all occupations. They also found that Extraversion was predictive of superior performance in occupations where social interactions were essential, such as sales and management.

- *Extraversion*. This factor refers to a person's orientation toward engagement with the external world. Extraverts are characterized as outgoing, people oriented, energetic, and action oriented. They are usually those who talk most in groups and are often assertive in social settings.
- *Agreeableness*. The extent to which people value social harmony and cooperation, or are concerned with getting along with others, is reflected in this factor. Optimism and a positive view of human nature and of people as basically trustworthy are also a part of this factor.

- *Conscientiousness*. This factor relates to how a person regulates and controls impulses. The inclination to act spontaneously or to delay gratification is associated with this factor. This factor also encompasses an achievement orientation.
- *Neuroticism*. This factor addresses emotional stability and focuses on whether people experience primarily negative emotions – that is, anxiety, hostility, anger or depression. An inclination to respond emotionally to situations is also an aspect of Neuroticism.
- *Openness to Experience*. Being creative, having an active imagination, and being open to people and experiences are all aspects of this factor, which is also sometimes referred to simply as Openness. An appreciation of art, intellectual curiosity, and an interest in complex or sophisticated ideas are also a part of this factor.

There are a variety of instruments that measure the Big Five personality traits, but perhaps the most widely used is the *NEO PI-R*, developed by Costa and McCrae (De Fruyt *et al.* 2004). The *NEO* contains 240 items and measures neuroticism, extraversion, openness, agreeableness, and conscientiousness, along with six facets for each of these factors. The assessment takes approximately forty-five minutes to complete and is available in a paper-and-pencil format with scantron form or via computer, though not currently online. Though numerous other language versions have been developed for research purposes, it is available in English and Spanish for commercial purposes.

Early studies examining the ability of personality traits to predict expatriate performance were generally negative (Brislin 1981; Harris 1973, 1975). More recently, however, a number of empirical studies have found support for the use of Big Five personality measures in predicting expatriate performance (Ones and Viswesvaran 1999). For example, Caligiuri (1995, 2000) found that emotional stability (Neuroticism) was predictive of expatriate adjustment. Deller (1998) found that ambition (a facet of Conscientiousness) and several facets of Openness were predictive of expatriate job performance. In a similar vein, Sinangil and Ones (1995, 1997) also found facets of Conscientiousness and Openness to be predictive of job performance. Dalton and Wilson (2000) studied expatriate managers in the Middle East and found that Agreeableness and Openness were predictive of home-country ratings of performance but not predictive of host-country ratings.

## Global leadership competency assessments

In this subsection we shall consider several instruments that adopt a broader focus and attempt to identify a variety of competencies, not just intercultural competence. As was noted for the intercultural adaptability assessments in the preceding subsection, there are numerous commercial global leadership assessments that are available but for which there is scant, if any, research literature. For that reason, they will not be considered in this section.

## The Global Competencies Inventory

Initially developed in 2000 by Allan Bird, Michael Stevens, Mark Mendenhall, and Gary Oddou, the *Global Competencies Inventory* (*GCI*) measures seventeen dimensions of personality predispositions associated with effective intercultural behavior and dynamic global managerial skill acquisition (Kozai Group 2002). The dimensions are predicated on an elaboration of the expatriate adjustment model developed by Black *et al.* (1991) and, accordingly, are grouped under three factors: Perception Management, Relationship Management and Self Management. The three factors and their associated dimensions will be presented below. Additionally, the *GCI* has been mapped on the global management competency model developed by Bird and Osland (2004).

**Perception Management**. This factor encompasses five dimensions that address how individuals mentally approach cultural differences. How individuals perceive people who are different from them affects how they think about such people and, in turn, how they think about people who are different from themselves influences their opinions, evaluations, and ultimately their behavior toward culturally different others. This factor also assesses how mentally flexible an individual is when confronted with cultural differences that are strange or new, as well as any tendency to make rapid (rather than thoughtful) judgments about those differences. It also evaluates an individual's ability to manage perceptions when faced with situations that are not immediately easy to understand because they differ from expectations. This factor also assesses an individual's natural curiosity toward foreign countries, cultures, and international events, as well as tendencies to draw sharp boundaries between things that are different.

- *Nonjudgmentalness*. This dimension considers an individual's inclination to suspend or withhold judgments about situations or persons that are new or unfamiliar. ($\alpha$ = 0.72)
- *Inquisitiveness*. This dimension assesses an individual's pursuit of understanding ideas, values, norms, situations and behaviors that are different one's own. It also addresses an individual's capacity to take advantage of learning opportunities. ($\alpha$ = 0.84)
- *Tolerance of ambiguity*. This dimension measures the extent to which someone is able to manage ambiguity as it relates to new and complex situations where there are not necessarily clear answers about what is going on or how things should be done. It also evaluates how much someone enjoys surrounding themselves with ideas or things that are new and unfamiliar, rather than feeling threatened by them. ($\alpha$ = 0.73)
- *Cosmopolitanism*. This dimension measures the level of natural interest in and curiosity about countries and cultures that are different from one's own. It also assesses the degree to which someone is interested in current world and international events and would enjoy traveling abroad. ($\alpha$ = 0.85)
- *Category Inclusiveness*. This dimension measures how likely someone is to include and accept things (including people) on the basis of their commonalities, rather than to draw lines that divide when there might be a noticeable basis for categories to differentiate things from one another. ($\alpha$ = 0.70)

**Relationship Management**. This second factor assesses a person's orientation toward developing and maintaining relationships in general; that is, how aware someone is of others around them, their interaction styles, values, and so on. It also considers one's personal level of self-awareness and awareness of how one's behaviors affect others. This factor complements the Perception Management factor because it examines how personal attitudes, values, and beliefs influence the development and management of interpersonal relationships in a cross-cultural environment. Positive relationships in an intercultural environment are essential for effective performance in the global workplace.

- *Relationship Interest*. This dimension measures the extent to which one has a genuine interest in, and awareness of, people who are from other cultures or ethnic groups. It also reflects one's desire to get to know them, their values, and why they do what they do. ($\alpha = 0.76$)
- *Interpersonal Engagement*. This dimension considers the extent to which one is likely to initiate and maintain friendships with people from other countries or cultural groups. It also measures how inclined someone is to actively seek out others who are different, as well as desire and ability to engage them in interesting conversations. ($\alpha = 0.80$)
- *Emotional Sensitivity*. This dimension measures the capacity to accurately read and comprehend the emotions of others and to understand their feelings from their perspective. It also measures how well one is able to listen genuinely and respond with empathy to the circumstances and challenges others face. ($\alpha = 0.74$)
- *Self-Awareness*. This dimension appraises the extent to which one is aware of personal values and interpersonal style, and personal strengths and weaknesses, and how one's past experiences have helped shape who one is as a person. It also measures how well someone claims to know himself or herself, how comfortable someone is with themselves, and the extent to which there is an understanding of the impact of personal values and behavior on relationships with others. ($\alpha = 0.73$)
- *Behavioral Flexibility*. This dimension measures one's tendency to regulate and adjust one's behavior to fit in, and to present oneself to others in ways that create positive impressions and facilitate the building of constructive relationships. ($\alpha = 0.72$)

**Self Management**. This third factor of the *Global Competencies Inventory* assesses the strength of sense of self-identity and ability to effectively manage thoughts, emotions and responses to stressful situations. To be effective in cross-cultural situations, one must be capable of understanding, changing, and adapting appropriately to a global work environment and to challenging cultural differences while at the same time having a clear and stable sense of who one is as a person, with an unambiguous understanding of one's most fundamental values. The ability to adapt and change within the context of a stable self-identity is critical to remaining mentally and emotionally healthy in a new culture.

- *Optimism*. This dimension measures the extent to which one maintains a positive outlook toward people, events and outcomes generally, and view challenges as learning opportunities. New intercultural environments are almost always stressful, so facing such situations with a positive naturally outlook improves one's ability to cope and adjust. ($\alpha = 0.74$)

- *Self-Confidence*. The Self-Confidence dimension assesses the level of personal belief in one's ability to achieve whatever one decides to accomplish, even if it is something that has never been tried before. ($\alpha = 0.83$)
- *Self-Identity*. This dimension considers an individual's ability to maintain personal values and beliefs regardless of the situation. A strong Self-Identity means one has strong personal values and maintains a high sense of personal integrity while at the same time being openly accepting of those who are different, without feeling personally threatened. ($\alpha = 0.73$)
- *Emotional Resilience*. This dimension measures one's level of emotional strength and ability to cope favorably with irritations, setbacks, frustrations, and failures. It also assesses capacity to recover quickly from psychologically and emotionally challenging situations. ($\alpha = 0.81$)
- *Non-stress Tendency*. This dimension measures one's innate capacity to respond with peacefulness and serenity to potentially stressful situations or circumstances, whether they are derived from different sources or from a wide range of stressors. ($\alpha = 0.81$)
- *Stress Management*. Stress Management assesses the degree to which one reports actively utilizing stress reduction strategies and techniques when faced with stressors in daily life, as well as the degree to which one is willing to employ new stress reduction techniques in the future. ($\alpha = 0.74$)
- *Interest Flexibility*. This dimension measures flexibility in identifying and adopting new interests, hobbies, and changes in one's daily routine when normal activities and other outlets are not available. Having enjoyable outlets, leisure activities, and being able to adapt one's daily routine are all important elements in the ability to deal with stress. An example of interest flexibility would be playing cricket instead of baseball in a country where cricket is more popular. ($\alpha = 0.83$)

The *GCI* contains 180 items and is administered online or via paper-and-pencil format. The average respondent requires from forty-five minutes to one hour to complete the instrument. A Social Desirability dimension ($\alpha = 0.83$) is also measured, though not explicitly reported to respondents. Administrators can use this dimension to determine whether a respondent has answered in a way designed to elicit favorable scores. Results for each of the seventeen dimensions, three factors, and an overall competency score are calculated relative to norms based on the responses of all previous respondents. Prior versions of the instrument reported results using percentile scores. The most recent version (3.0) reports scores by indicating a respondent's position in one of three competency categories (each subdivided into two classes): Low (limited or partial), Moderate (basic or good), and High (high or superior).

Longitudinal research (Furuya 2006) conducted with samples of Japanese international managers linked Overall Global Competency Scores with higher levels of "hard" global competencies acquisition. Specifically, higher GCI scores were related to higher levels of three types of skill: (1) *global business acumen*, consistent with the formulation put forward by Black *et al.* (1999b) of savvy use of extensive knowledge about business in a worldwide context; (2) *employee management skills*, which correspond closely to Bird and Osland's (2004) conceptualization of interpersonal skills – that is, mindful (intercultural) communication, creating and building trust, and teaming; and (3) *global administrative skills*, which corresponds to Bird and Osland's (2004) description of system skills of spanning boundaries, managing change through building community, and leading. Higher scores were also associated with higher levels of skill transfer upon assignment to a new position, increased motivation and work attachment, and with higher levels of general work performance.

## Global Executive Leadership Inventory

Manfred Kets de Vries and his associates developed the *Global Executive Leadership Inventory*. The instrument grew out of extensive work with executives involved in training programs at INSEAD (Kets de Vries *et al.* 2004). They concluded that most leadership inventories are carried out by means of self-assessment that suffer from an inherent subjectivity bias. They also noted that the gap between a leader's personal assessment of capabilities and the assessments of others was often significant. They settled on a 360-degree feedback approach as a means of identifying levels of competency and also of identifying awareness gaps in those competencies. Drawing on prior leadership research and on interviews with global executives, they identified two broad roles that global leaders carry out, one being primarily charismatic – inspiring, directing, motivating – and one primarily architectural – designing systems and processes to help make the organization and the people within it effective. These two broad roles were broken down into the following twelve dimensions:

- *Visioning*. This dimension addresses a leader's ability to develop and articulate a vision and accompanying strategy that encompass the firm's global needs and is accessible and can be embraced by all stakeholders, such as shareholders, employees, suppliers and customers. ($\alpha = 0.77$)
- *Empowering*. Finding ways to empower employees throughout the firm by means of information sharing and delegation of authority comprises the second dimension. ($\alpha = 0.80$)
- *Energizing*. The third leadership dimension involves the ability to energize and motivate employees to bring the firm's mission to reality. ($\alpha = 0.82$)
- *Designing and Aligning*. This dimension focuses on the ability to design organizational structures and control systems appropriate for the effective functioning of the firm at a global level consistent with the firm's mission, vision, and strategy. It also encompasses the ability to foster employee behavior consistent with organizational culture and values. ($\alpha = 0.84$)
- *Rewarding and Feedback*. Effective global leaders must also be able to establish and implement performance appraisal and reward systems that drive the right employee behaviors on a global level. ($\alpha = 0.87$)
- *Team Building*. This dimension addresses the ability to design, motivate, and focus teams to work effectively as regards time, space, and diversity. It also entails an ability to foster an organizational climate that encourages collaborative effort and the constructive use of conflict. ($\alpha = 0.85$)

- *Outside Orientation.* The seventh dimension emphasizes the ability to direct employee awareness and attention to external constituencies such as customers, suppliers, and other stakeholders, including local communities. ($\alpha = 0.82$)
- *Global Mindset.* Fostering an awareness of and knowledge of the global context in which the firm operates among employees at all levels is yet another capability that global leaders must possess. This dimension also encompasses a sensitivity to, and ability to work across, cultures. ($\alpha = 0.87$)
- *Tenacity.* Effective global leaders must also have courage and persistence in pursuing those ends that serve the firm's purposes and are consistent with firm and personal principles. Leading by example, they should also encourage others to do similarly. ($\alpha = 0.76$)
- *Emotional Intelligence.* The creation and maintenance of trust and the fostering of an emotionally intelligent organization is another capability found in effective global leaders, who know themselves and are able to work with others in a respectful and empathetic manner. ($\alpha = 0.91$)
- *Life Balance.* Global leadership extends beyond the boundaries and mission of the organization and into nonwork life. It involves the ability to maintain balance in work and personal life in order to maintain the long-term welfare of the individual. Effective leaders are able not only to model this behavior but to articulate it in a way that impacts those they work with and are responsible for. ($\alpha = 0.79$)
- *Resilience to Stress.* The final dimension addresses a leader's ability to manage the multiple types of stress – work, life, health, and career – and manage pressures such that balance can be maintained. ($\alpha = 0.84$)

The *GELI* is designed as a 360-degree feedback assessment. In order to generate effective reports, it is essential that at least two observers – a superior, coworker, direct report, or acquaintance – complete the observer's version of the instrument. Both the Leader and the Observer versions of the *GELI* contain 100 items and can be administered either online or via paper-and-pencil format. The average respondent requires from fifteen to twenty minutes to complete the instrument. Observers also have the option of providing written comments that elaborate on their survey responses. There are English, Dutch, French, German, and Italian versions available. There does not appear to be any monitoring of social desirability response patterns. The results are presented via a feedback report that presents the respondent's scores based on norms drawn from the more than 2,000 executives who initially completed the inventory during its development phase. The respondent's scores are also presented vis-à-vis observers' scores for each of the dimensions. Where sufficient numbers are available, observer scores are presented in aggregate, and by observer group, i.e., superiors, direct reports, colleagues and others. In this regard, the *GELI* presents a type of gap analysis.

Research on the internal validity of the *GELI* found support for the psychometric properties of the instrument (Kets de Vries *et al.* 2004). Developers of the *GELI* report that it is highly predictive of executive performance in organizations (Kets de Vries 2005); however, because these results have not been made public through empirical studies published in peer-reviewed journals, it is not possible to confirm their validity.

# Conclusion

It is important to keep in mind, as was pointed out in Chapter 2, that the field of global leadership is still in its infancy, with no established definition and no accompanying set of clearly defined behaviors. Given the nature of the phenomenon, it may be unrealistic to expect that definitional issues will be resolved in the near future. Nevertheless, work has already begun on several fronts to identify competencies associated with effective global leadership. With two exceptions – the *NEO PI-R* and the *CCAI* – none of the assessments considered in this chapter existed ten years ago. Indeed, several have appeared in just the past three or four years. We can anticipate that as global leadership achieves greater clarity as a concept, more assessments will likely be developed.

For the most part, the assessments considered in this chapter have demonstrated sound psychometric properties with regard to internal validity and reliability. Additionally, many also demonstrate convergent and discriminant validity. However, the critical issue is whether or not the characteristics they measure are predictive of superior global leadership performance: on that point there is a paucity of evidence, though perhaps reason to be optimistic. When they are considered in the context of performance more broadly defined than that related purely to global leadership, there is more evidence to support predictive validity claims. Keeping in mind that nearly all of these instruments were developed in the last ten years, we should anticipate that more empirical research exploring their predictive potential is either currently under way or will be shortly.

Where do we go from here? The chapter began by discussing *competency* as a concept and noted that it involved a link between a preexisting characteristic or capability and superior performance. The assessments considered here measure a variety of characteristics that could be classified as competencies, but what is sorely missing is a clearly defined set of behaviors that constitute *superior* global leadership performance. The *GELI* addresses this issue by focusing on managerial actions; however, even this instrument finds it difficult to identify the specific set of actions appropriate to a specific global leadership position.

Future work might proceed along two lines, both of which involve "flying a little closer to the ground." First, it would be useful to learn more about what effective global leaders actually do. As was noted in Chapter 2, most empirical research has asked managers what they *think* are the important or critical behaviors. This approach runs into the challenge noted at the outset of this chapter – that is, developing an *idealized* rather than a real, or practical, understanding of what global leaders do. Research that observes and measures actual performance may be more productive in establishing the behavioral standards necessary to work backward in the causal link to competencies. Second, it might be useful to search for hard competencies, identifiable skills or behaviors that contribute to high performance. Most of the assessments in this chapter focus on soft competencies – that is, characteristics of personality or worldview or attitude. This may seem appropriate, given that global leadership appears to fit into a wide variety of contexts and positions, and because soft competencies are broadly applicable. Nevertheless, focusing on specific hard skills would also be productive. For example, do global leaders who engage in more reflexive listening behaviors perform at higher levels than those that do not? Reflexive listening is a hard competency, a skill that can, to varying degrees, be measured. It is also one that might be expected to contribute to more effective intercultural communication, which in turn would contribute to other effective leader behaviors.

The critical importance of accurately assessing global leader competency is reflected in the current emphasis on global talent management that is at the heart of strategic thinking about international HRM in global companies. The potential value of further research on and development of competency assessments would be difficult to overestimate.

# 5

# Process models of global leadership development

## JOYCE S. OSLAND AND ALLAN BIRD

> If we want to understand leadership, we need to look at our own experiences. I believe that we carry within us enough experience to form our own simple, coherent approach to being a good leader. Creating and clarifying our own leadership approaches will help us (one by one and in our own ways) truly make a difference.
>
> (Margaret Wheatley)

> The next CEO of GE will not be like me. I spent my entire career in the US. The next head of General Electric will be somebody who spent time in Bombay, in Hong Kong, in Buenos Aires. We have to send our best and brightest overseas and make sure they have the training that will allow them to be the global leaders who will make GE flourish in the future.
>
> (Jack Welch, former CEO of GE)

Now that we have a better idea of what global leaders are like, the natural follow-on questions are "How did they get that way?" and "How can we develop prospective global leaders?" Carlos Ghosn (president of Nissan Motors Ltd and *Automotive News'* 2000 Industry Leader of the Year) is one of the most famous global leaders in the business world. When we look at his background, we find that he was born in Brazil and educated in France. Ghosn worked in the United States for seven years as head of Michelin and spent three years with Renault in France before becoming president and CEO of Nissan. One of the few non-Japanese CEOs of Japanese companies, Ghosn is given credit for Nissan's successful turnaround effort and cross-border alliance with Renault. Although cultural differences crippled other cross-border automotive alliances, such as Daimler-Chrysler, Ghosn sees them as opportunities. "When you have taken the time to understand [that people don't think or act the same way] . . . and when you are really motivated and mobilized by a very strong objective, then the cultural differences can become seeds for innovation as opposed to seeds for dissention" (Emerson 2001: 6). He believes that in order to call yourself "international," "you have to go to countries that have a totally different way of thinking, a totally different way of organization, and a totally different way of life" (ibid.: 7). Ghosn had an international experience early in life when he studied abroad, has lived in four continents, and clearly appreciates cultural differences. In this respect, his background is similar to that of many other global leaders.

Kets de Vries with Florent-Treacy (2002) identify the foundation for developing global leadership in their research sample as:

- family background that involved *intercultural experiences* (mixed-culture marriages, bilingual parents, exposure to other cultures);
- *early education* involving international schools, summer camps and travel;
- *later education* that included exchange programs, languages, and international MBA programs; and
- *spouse and children* who are supportive, adventurous, adaptable, and mobile.

To complement this foundation, organizations provide professional development in the form of training, transfer, teamwork, and travel. These same four development activities were suggested as the most effective ways to develop global leadership in other research (Black *et al*. 1999a). We will discuss the organizational role in development more directly in Chapter 9. In this chapter, our focus is on how global leaders develop.

While the global leadership literature provides numerous recommendations concerning global leadership development, few of these recommendations are based on empirical research (for a review of the literature on global leader development, see Suutari 2002). The exceptions include interviews with global managers and leaders asking for either recommendations or personal accounts concerning global leadership development (Black *et al*. 1999a; Kets de Vries with Florent-Treacy 2002; McCall and Hollenbeck 2002) and the sole longitudinal study of global leaders (Graen and Hui 1999). In a longitudinal study the eventual career progress of Japanese global leaders (ibid.: 1999: 17–18) was predicted by three behaviors that occurred in the first three years of their career: (1) building effective working relationships characterized by trust, respect, and obligation with immediate supervisors; (2) networking derived from their contacts at prestigious universities; and (3) doing more than was expected in the face of difficult and ambiguous performance expectations. The last element, "difficult and ambiguous performance expectations," is an example of the challenging experiences that constitute a common element in all models of global leadership development (Kets de Vries with Florent-Treacy 2002; McCall and Hollenbeck 2002; Osland *et al*. 2006). As Mary Catherine Bateson (1994) wrote, "Insight, I believe, refers to that depth of understanding that comes by setting experiences, yours and mine, familiar and exotic, new and old, side by side, learning by letting them speak to one another." We will look at three models of global leadership development in the following sections.

## The Chattanooga model of global leadership development

In 2001 a team of scholars (Allan Bird, Nakiye Boyacigiller, Paula Caligiuri, Mark Mendenhall, Edward Miller, Joyce Osland, Guenter Stahl, and Mary Ann Von Glinow) spent two days at the Frierson Leadership Institute in Chattanooga, Tennessee, reviewing their collective experience and wisdom as scholars and consultants in the area of global leadership. What emerged from that intensive effort was a framework for developing global leadership talent that came to be known as the Chattanooga model. It was a process model of global leadership based on the assumption that global leadership development in an individual was a nonlinear, emergent process, one that is moderated by a variety of key variables, across time (see Figure 5.1).

To understand how the process works, begin in the upper left-hand corner of the model. A manager enters a global or cross-cultural context, probably through an expatriate assignment, and is immersed in that environment over an extended period of time. Entering managers bring with them certain basic, core immutable personality traits, including fairly immutable competencies (ambition, desire to lead, sociability, openness, agreeableness, emotional stability, etc.) and cognitive processes (attribution flexibility, category width, tolerance for ambiguity, etc.). Also attached are managers' existing levels of self-efficacy that are brought to bear on various aspects of living and working globally. Moreover, the greater the extent to which managers perceive that they are "called" or view themselves as global citizens and view the assignment as something that fits "who they really are," the more likely they will be to develop leadership capabilities as opposed to engage in bureaucratic behaviors in the international assignment. Finally, managers enter the global context bringing with them varying existing levels of global leadership competencies.

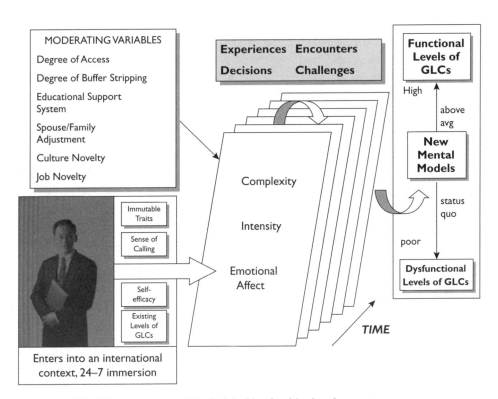

*Figure 5.1* The Chattanooga model of global leadership development

Managers enter the global context each with a unique configuration of individual variables, bringing that configuration to bear upon the multitude of daily experiences they encounter in the new milieu. The "folders" or "pages" in Figure 5.1 are representative of single experiences, interactions, and challenges the individual passes through over time. Each of these experiences differs in the degree of complexity, importance, and intensity it presents to a manager. The combination of complexity and intensity, in particular, contributes to the level of affect that the experience produces in the manager.

The recursive arrow in the model indicates that a current experience can cause, through its effect on memory, a revision or revisiting of past experiences. The development process is not based on a sequence of independent experiences; rather, each experience is tied to past experiences and constitutes a sense-making process of learning and acquiring global leadership capability. Bennis and Thomas (2002: 14) refer to this process as constituting "crucible" situations "characterized by the confluence of powerful intellectual, social, economic, or political forces" that severely test one's patience, and one's beliefs, and that produce a transformation in managers, leaving them deeply different relative to who they were prior to the crucible experience.

The specific nature of various global or cross-cultural crucible experiences is critical to the development of global leadership. If these experiences are buffered by organizational policies or by the individuals themselves, or if the degree to which access to these experiences is constrained by companies (expensive housing that separates the global manager from the society), the transforming potency of these experiences can be diluted and, ultimately, noncatalytic in effect. Additionally, other factors relating to the family and to the specific characteristics of the cultural context – that is, educational support systems, culture novelty, job novelty, and adjustment by the spouse or family – can each enhance or detract from global leadership development.

The critical factor in the global leadership development of any manager is "access to high-level challenges." Consistent access to the right sorts of challenges may produce, in some cases, solid global leadership competency development over time. But success is not guaranteed, and access may lead to failure as well. Managers may be given the right kind of experiences but find they are unable to handle them or learn from them because the challenges are overwhelming. Although the goal of challenging experiences is to help managers develop new mental leadership models, there is the possibility that the newly developed models are actually dysfunctional, reflecting a learning of the wrong lessons. An important point is that though these mental models appear at the end of the process in Figure 5.1, such models are being created over and over again, in response to each experience the individual has; thus, the developing framework is malleable, but with the potential to harden into a dysfunctional systemic framework if experiences are not handled effectively over time.

In summary, the Chattanooga model perceives the global leadership development process as emergent in nature and dynamic in process. If a manager's immutable personality traits, access to powerful challenges, etc. are consistent with what is required to work and learn in the global context, a functional global leadership process will ensue, and the manager will develop global leadership competencies. It is important to recognize, however, that other outcomes ranging from "status quo" to "dysfunctional" can result, depending on the unique processual experiences a manager receives. At any point in time, a manager's developmental trajectory can rise or fall, moderated by the unique constellation of forces that impinge upon any given experience.

Much work remains to be done in the area of global mindset and leadership development. The Chattanooga model needs to be tested, and its effectiveness and costs need to be evaluated. Moreover, the organizational aspect of development must be considered as well. Firm-specific factors such as the alignment of HRM and the organizational culture with the firm's efforts to develop global leadership and global mindset require particular attention. In addition, a systemic analysis of factors promoting or impeding global leadership is also called for.

## The Global Leadership Expertise Development model

The Global Leadership Expertise Development (GLED) model expands the Chattanooga model but focuses primarily on the development of expertise in global leaders. The argument that global leadership development is a process of personal transformation is a recurrent theme. If we presume that this thesis is cogent, it is likely that global leadership development is not a linear progression that simply adds to an existing portfolio of leadership competencies, but rather a nonlinear process whereby deep-seated change in competencies, expertise, and worldview through experiential learning occur over time (Osland *et al.* 2006). Bennis and Thomas (2002: 14) refer to the gestalt of these transformational experiences as "crucibles" – that is, situations

> characterized by the confluence of powerful intellectual, social, economic, or political forces that severely test one's patience, and one's beliefs, and that produce a transformation in the individual, leaving him/her deeply different in terms of who they were before the crucible experience.

Traditional training cannot in and of itself be the primary tool through which GL expertise and competencies are inculcated within individuals. Organizations need to ensure that prospective global leaders are exposed to transformational experiences in their developmental process.

On the basis of the research literature and the presumption that GL development is an emergent phenomenon, we offer the following process model, referred to as the GLED model (see Figure 5.2) to illustrate GL expertise development. This model is an extension of the Chattanooga model, developed by global leadership scholars at the Frierson Leadership Institute in Chattanooga, Tennessee (Osland *et al.* 2006).

The left-hand side of the GLED model contains four categories of *antecedents*: individual characteristics, cultural exposure, global education, and project novelty. The individual characteristics are associated with intercultural competence (Kozai Group 2002). Each of

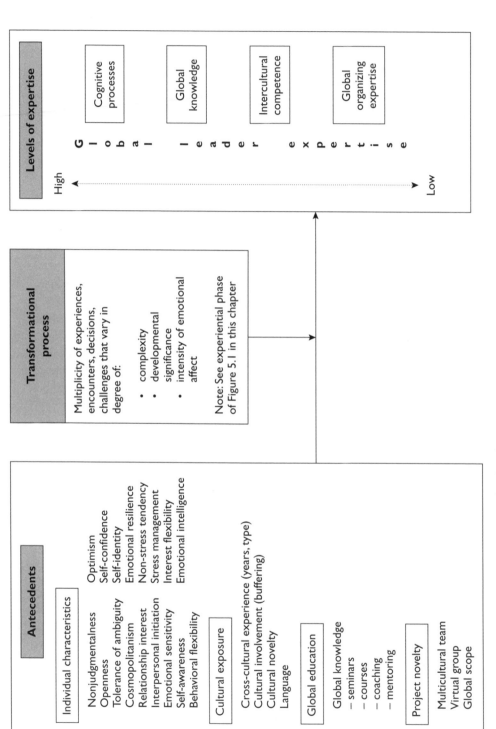

*Figure 5.2* A model of global leadership expertise development

these categories contains variables related to one or more aspects of GL development or expertise (Black *et al.* 1991; Caligiuri 2004; Kets de Vries with Florent-Treacy 2002; McCall and Hollenbeck 2002; Yamazaki and Kayes 2004).

Four dependent variables – cognitive processes (expert decision making), global knowledge (facts related to the global environment and work domain), intercultural competence (ability to work effectively across cultures), and global organizing expertise (systems thinking and architecture necessary to create and maintain global structures) – combine to determine the *level of GL expertise*. These categories are based on Mendenhall and Osland's (2002) categorization of GL competencies. GL expertise is conceptualized as a continuum. Domestic leaders or novice global leaders may manifest some degree of GL expertise as a result of their work or experience with other nationalities. Similarly, not all global leaders will be fully expert. As Dreyfus and Dreyfus (1986) note, there are several stages in the developmental journey from novice to expert. Higher measures of the antecedents are predicted to correlate with higher measures of GL expertise.

The relationship between the antecedents and outcome measures is mediated by the *transformational process*, which consists of experiences, interpersonal encounters, decision, and challenges that relate to GL expertise. Not all cross-cultural experiences develop GL expertise, so transformational experiences differ from those found in the cultural exposure category. Furthermore, not all global or cultural experiences have the same impact (McCall and Hollenbeck 2002; Osland *et al.* 2006). We predict that the transformational process will be the major cause of different levels in GL expertise leaders with global responsibilities. The transformational process refers to "crucibles" that vary in terms of their complexity, developmental significance, and intensity of emotional affect. The "folders" or "pages" in Figure 5.2 represent experiences, encounters, decisions, and challenges that individuals work through over time. Higher measures of complexity, development significance, and intensity of emotional affect result in greater likelihood of transformation, which, in turn, will result in developing a higher level of GL expertise.

A longitudinal examination of GL development would presumably reveal that dynamic individual characteristics increase as a result of transformational experiences and that current experience can cause, through memory, an updating or reliving of past experiences. Thus, GL development over time is more spiral-like and recursive than Figure 5.2 suggests (Osland *et al.* 2006). The GL development process is not based on independent experiences; rather, each experience is tied to past, multiple experiences and constitutes a sense-making process of learning and acquiring global leadership expertise (ibid.).

Both the Chattanooga model and the GLED model are conceptual in nature and have yet to be validated by empirical work with global leaders. They were designed, however, specifically for the development of global leadership and are predicated on an extensive review of the research literature.

## A model for developing global executives

Based on their interviews with global executives (who are also global leaders) who worked overseas, McCall and Hollenbeck's (2002) model focuses on the interaction and partnership between the individual and the organization. International assignments, which are viewed as the most powerful development tool in facilitating global leadership competencies (Gregersen *et al.* 1998; Hall *et al.* 2001; Mendenhall *et al.* 2001), received a great deal of attention in McCall and Hollenbeck's research and model.

Individuals cannot be forced to develop, and they do bear the ultimate responsibility for their development. Organizations, however, establish an organizational culture and policies that either enhance or impede development. Because of the experiences organizations provide, they can be the source of both intended and unintended lessons. Therefore, these authors recommend that organizations be both intentional and collaborative about development. Stated simply, this model is based on the idea that the company strategy determines what qualities are required in its leaders, and then talented people are hired and given appropriate experiences and support in order to develop those qualities.

One of their research questions involved testing whether a developmental model based on research on US executives (McCall 1998) would also apply to an internationally diverse group of global executives. They found that the earlier model was relevant for global executives, with only one adaptation, the addition of context to the experience component, which can be seen in Figure 5.1. Context, in this instance, usually relates to culture. Therefore, they concluded that "this basic process of development is the same for all executives, regardless of the countries they come from or whether the development is for global, expatriate, or local executive work" (McCall and Hollenbeck 2002: 172). Although the basic components of the model are similar for all groups, the specifics of developing global executives do differ significantly – another example of a difference of both degree and kind. "Global executive development is much more complex and unpredictable and requires a greater focus, effort, and resources concentrated over a longer period" (ibid.: 172). They justify their argument with these observations:

- The global business strategy determines, to an even greater extent, the relevant lessons leaders need to learn.
- A wider range of more difficult developmental experiences has to be available to develop a more talented cadre of executives.
- Development takes place in a more complex, multicultural global environment with more diverse executives.
- The mechanisms for development are more complicated, difficult to administer, and expensive.

## Business strategy

An organization's strategy and structure determine the number of international jobs, the types of global executives and their nationalities, and the skills the organization will

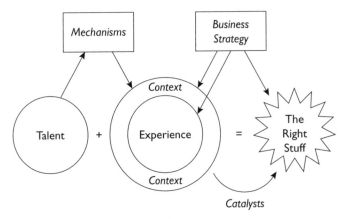

*Figure 5.3* A model for developing global executives

Source: Reprinted with permission. From McCall, M. W., Jr. and Hollenbeck, G. P. (2002) *Developing Global Executives: The Lessons of International Experience*. Boston, MA: Harvard Business School Press: 173.

need. If a firm opts to grow via acquisitions and alliances, it needs executives with experience working across company borders. If the structure is organized along strict functional lines, it will be difficult to provide executives with the necessary cross-functional experience early in their career. The choice of geographic markets, for example, can determine how many executives of what cultural mix will be needed. What type of work leaders will be expected to do and where they will do it all depends on the business strategy.

## The right stuff

In this model, "the right stuff" (Figure 5.3) refers to the end state of development, what leaders have learned. It is determined by the business strategy and therefore varies by company. McCall and Hollenbeck (2002) believe that leaders are "made" (or born, then made), because most of what they need to master can be learned, and is learned primarily from global experiences. The usual things that all executives have to know are made more difficult and subtle in a global context. There is a second category of lessons that relate specifically to the international nature of their jobs and are rooted in cultural differences and the unique demands of expatriation.

Table 5.1 lists the themes and lessons that were reported by McCall and Hollenbeck's sample when they were asked to tell about at least three experiences that had shaped them as international executives and what they had learned from those experiences. The list is not necessarily exhaustive of lessons learned; nor are these lessons universal to all global executives. They do indicate the type of lessons learned from global experiences. The authors compared these findings to the lessons learned by a sample of US executives who

*Table 5.1* The themes and lessons of international experience

**Learning to deal with cultural issues and different cultures**
1 Learning to speak a foreign language
2 Learning about specific foreign cultures and contrasts between specific cultures
3 Learning generic lessons about living and working in foreign cultures

**Learning to run a business – strategy, structure, processes; global versus local; specialized knowledge**
1 Learning strategies for doing business
2 Learning the specifics of running a business

**Learning to lead and manage others – selection, development, motivation, team building, deselection**
1 Learning how to establish credibility
2 Learning to select the right people
3 Learning to build and sustain an effective team
4 Learning to make tough calls about people
5 Learning to stay focused – keeping it simple, setting clear goals
6 Learning to keep people motivated and committed, what to delegate and what not to delegate
7 Learning to develop people and the importance of developing people

**Learning to deal with problematic relationships – headquarters, bosses, unions, government, media, politics**
1 Learning to handle immediate bosses and other superiors
2 Learning to manage the interface with headquarters and the larger organization
3 Learning to handle public appearances and the media
4 Learning to deal with governments and (external) politicians
5 Learning to deal with unions and other types of negotiations
6 Learning about internal politics

**Learning about the personal qualities required of a leader**
1 Learning to listen carefully, to ask questions, and to see the world through other people's eyes
2 Learning to be open, genuine, honest, fair; to treat other people with respect; and to trust others
3 Learning to be flexible, to adapt to changing situations, to take changing circumstances into account, to manage multiple priorities and complex relationships, and to think on one's feet
4 Learning to assess risks and take them, and to act in the face of uncertainty
5 Learning to persevere, to act with discipline, and to stay calm under tough circumstances

6 Learning to be optimistic, to believe in oneself, to trust one's instincts, to take a stand for what one believes is right, and to accept responsibility for the consequences of one's actions

**Learning about self and career**
1 Learning about likes, dislikes, strengths, weaknesses, and preferences
2 Learning what support you need from family or others, and how to manage the family under the pressure of foreign work
3 Learning to manage your own career and development

were questioned in the 1980s. Many of the same lessons emerged from both samples, indicating that, on the surface at least, there is a common skill set shared by global and domestic executives.

The comparison, however, also highlighted significant differences in lessons learned. Cultural lessons composed 15 percent of the lessons learned by global executives; this category never emerged from the domestic executives. Furthermore, global executives reported more "big picture" lessons related to the Strategies for Doing Business category, while the US executives recounted more lessons related to the Learning to Lead and Manage Others category. From this, McCall and Hollenbeck draw the conclusion that global executives have a broader perspective on the world, which is why it can be difficult for them to return to a domestic job of narrower scope once they have worked abroad. Learning to listen carefully and the importance of the family in global work were more significant to global executives than to US executives. McCall and Hollenbeck (2002) argue further that even lessons that seem similar on the surface, such as learning to be flexible, are deeper and broader when learned in the more complex and uncertain global setting. For that reason, there is no substitute for actually working in another country (ibid.: 180).

# Experience

Many of the developmental experiences that shape global leaders and executives are found in Chapter 9. The significant experiences identified in McCall and Hollenbeck's work were categorized as foundation assignments (early work experience and first managerial responsibility), major line assignments (business turnarounds, start-ups, joint ventures, alliances, mergers or acquisitions), shorter-term experiences (significant other people, special projects, consulting roles, staff advisory jobs, developmental and educational experiences, negotiations, stint at headquarters), and perspective-changing experiences (culture shock, career shifts, confrontations with reality, changes in scope or scale, mistakes and errors in judgment, family and personal challenges, crises). Exposure to significant other people was reported by the largest number of participants (32 percent). These people might have provided either positive or negative lessons.

"Especially in global work, opportunities to work in parallel with a predecessor, on-site learning (intentional or not) from a local national, and exposure to others with global careers had important influences and offered important learning opportunities" (McCall and Hollenbeck 2002: 180).

The organization cannot control all of these experiences. Nor do intentionally designed experiences always result in developmental outcomes. But individually tailoring experiences, thinking ahead about where individuals might need support, and tracking their progress provides a greater possibility that positive lessons will result. An international experience in the early years of one's career was strongly recommended by the participants. The selection of experiences, like "the right stuff," is ultimately determined by the strategy.

## Talent

There are several difficulties in assessing talent in a multicultural global organization: identifying a common standard across cultures, country differences in assessing, promoting and developing managers, wide variability in global executive jobs, and the organization's openness to promoting executives from other nationalities (McCall and Hollenbeck 2002: 185–186). In order to benefit from the diversity, these factors should be considered:

- Career histories have to be interpreted on the basis of their cultural context.
- Preexisting assets should be analyzed to assess where individuals stand now, where they could go, and which experience would contribute the most at this particular point.
- Ability to learn from experience should be evaluated, since this relates to taking advantage of the experience.
- Potential for derailment should be analyzed. "Because the traps are more numerous and deadlier in the international context, it is imperative that organizations consider the possibility of derailment when assessing talent" (McCall and Hollenbeck 2002: 187).

## Mechanisms

"Mechanisms" refers to those policies and practices that aim at "getting the right people into the right experience." McCall and Hollenbeck (2002: 189) believe that organizations have to establish and maintain five parallel processes that serve both short-term business needs and development needs:

- *Selection* refers to the organization's need to identify people who are ready to assume global positions. There has to be a system to identify and select these people when unexpected staffing needs arise.
- *Succession* involves replacement plans with lists of potential successors in case an incumbent vacates a job unexpectedly. When this is done in advance, rather than in the midst of an emergency, more thought and care can be taken.

- *Development* occurs by placing people in jobs that will expand their cultural or business skills, which is often done with people from a culturally diverse background who have a clear interest in international work.
- *Discovery* mechanisms provide parochial employees with an opportunity early in their careers to ascertain whether they might have a previously unidentified interest in international work.
- *Recovery* pertains to the organization's efforts to integrate repatriates when they return home from a global assignment.

## Catalysts

Developmental catalysts aid executives to learn from their experiences. One category of catalysts *improve information*, such as interpreting feedback or providing feedback on development as well as on performance and outcomes. A second category *provide incentives and resources*, like holding people accountable for developmental goals or promoting people who model the desired developmental behaviors. The third category of catalysts *support change* by providing emotional support or viewing change in a systems context. "While perhaps an indirect catalyst, support for the whole family [of an executive on a global assignment] turns out to be important from a learning perspective" (McCall and Hollenbeck 2002: 193).

This model's contribution lies in illustrating the strategic imperatives that drive executive development and the role played by the organization. They "globalized" a domestic model of development, and their international findings provide insight into some of the unique characteristics and challenges of developing global leaders. Given the qualitative nature of their research, future studies could generate hypotheses and test the model with quantitative measures.

## Lessons from the global leadership development models

All three models presume that the demands of global leadership in a complex, ambiguous setting will require flexibility and adaptability. Thus, the ability to learn, and learn continuously, is critical. In particular, the learning associated with challenging international assignments can result in personal transformation, a key aspect of global leadership development. Because it is "personal" and transformational, the development process for individuals is nonlinear, uncertain, and hard to predict. What companies have learned from their efforts to develop global leaders appears in Chapter 9.

# Leading global teams

**6**

MARTHA L. MAZNEVSKI

Most work in organizations today is done by teams. A team is simply a group of people working together to accomplish a task, and there are many variations on this theme. In a new product development team at Boeing or Airbus, team members represent different functions such as basic engineering and production, and work together over years in a highly interdependent way to develop and test a new product. In a sales team for Panasonic or Novartis, each salesperson has his or her own territory; team members interact with each other to share ideas and best practices and to work on a limited number of joint accounts. In a global auditing team at Ernst and Young or Deloitte Touche Tomatsu, one auditor from each subsidiary's country develops the accounts for that subsidiary and submits the accounts to a managing partner. The members of this large global audit team interact very little with each other. The managing partner then uses a small and representative "inner team" to bring together all the subsidiary accounts and create a single picture of the global client's operations.

Although teams have always been part of the organizational landscape, they have become increasingly important. Previously, the most important tool for managing people was the hierarchy (Leavitt 2003; Elliot 1989; Weber 1946, 1947): a set of nested levels of authority and responsibility. In a traditional hierarchy, organizations are divided into separate units. Each unit has a boss who divides the unit's work into several pieces, with a subordinate in charge of each piece; each of those subordinates does the same with his or her part of the organization's work, and so on. The hierarchy is a very simple way of managing people and work. Everyone's task is clearly defined, and everyone knows with whom to communicate about what.

However, hierarchies are notoriously inflexible, and in today's era of globalization they fall increasingly short. If the work requirements change – for example, if a supplier changes the specifications on a key component – hierarchies may not clarify who should adapt to the change. If the environment changes – for example, if customer demands shift from one product group to another or a new competitor arrives on the scene – hierarchies may not detect the shift soon enough, and resources are unlikely to be allocated appropriately. And if the task requires high levels of interdependence – for example, if basic development of a new drug should take into account how to manufacture the drug –

hierarchies fail miserably, as they discourage communication across separate business units or functions. The traditional hierarchy, glorified in the first half of the twentieth century, does not manage people to achieve results well in the dynamic and competitive environment of the twenty-first century.

Hierarchies must be supplemented with more informal modes of organization (for further discussions, see also Pfeffer 1995), especially teams. Teams are more dynamic and adaptable to change. They can be temporary, formed quickly to achieve a specific task then disbanded afterwards. Their membership can be fluid, including important skills as they are needed. They can coexist with other forms of organization; members of teams can, and usually do, hold other organizational roles simultaneously.

Any leader today must be both a good team member and good at leading teams. Leaders at all levels of the organization are key members of coordination teams, project teams, joint task teams, and so on. They also find themselves leading such teams at their own level and below. Helping teams perform well, whether as a member or as a designated leader, requires a sophisticated understanding of today's teams. And just as leadership itself is more complex in today's global environment than it used to be, teams themselves are also more complex.

In this chapter we begin by reviewing what we know about team effectiveness: how teams combine the efforts of individual members to create strong results. Then we identify the specific characteristics that differentiate global teams from the more mundane local variety. Next we discuss some specific issues related to global teams in the larger context. Finally, we identify the implications for leaders: what does it take to be a good leader of global teams?

## Effective teams

Although every team is a unique combination of people, tasks, processes, and environment, there are some characteristics that effective teams share no matter what their configuration. Earlier team research, mostly using laboratory studies, identified what we call here the basic conditions of team performance. More recent research, which has incorporated extensive field studies of real teams, has added insights about high-performing teams in more complex environments. Although global teams are highly complex, they are teams first. To take advantage of the opportunities offered by their global configuration, global teams must first get the basics right. To optimize performance, they can develop further characteristics and processes that manage complexity (e.g. Maznevski and Jonsen 2006). The relationship between basic conditions and high-performance characteristics is shown in Figure 6.1.

## Basic conditions of team performance

For teams to meet their basic objectives, certain conditions must be met (e.g. Govindarajan and Gupta 2001; Canney Davidson 1994; Bettenhausen 1991): the task

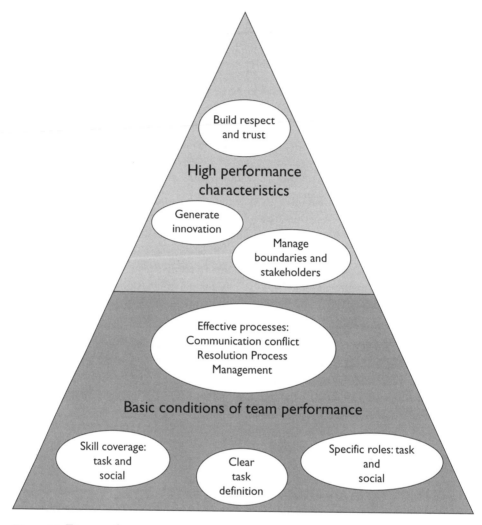

*Figure 6.1* Team performance

must be well defined; the team members must have the right combination of skills; members must develop appropriate roles; and they must engage in effective processes. Often these processes are referred to by the handy rhyme "forming, storming, norming, performing." The "forming" stage encompasses task definition and team composition; the most intense "storming" usually occurs during role assignment; "norming" is when team processes are running smoothly; and when "performing," a team puts together roles and processes to achieve performance. However, not all effective teams experience the so-called stages the same way, and it is more important to understand the underlying processes.

## Defined task and objectives

It goes *almost* without saying that team members must know clearly what their task and objectives are, in order to achieve them. Unfortunately, though, many teams do not understand their objectives well, or do not agree on them. Sometimes this is due to lack of clear communication from leaders. The leader presents a briefing or mandate that is clear to him- or herself, but is difficult or ambiguous to interpret from the point of view of the team. Often, team members have different interpretations of the task and objectives. For example, a marketing professional may think that a successful product launch is defined by high market share, while a finance professional may think it is defined by profitability; these two objectives are potentially conflicting, but many teams neglect to clarify common goals and definitions before working together.

## Team composition

It should also be obvious that teams need the right combination of skills among members. This includes the right technical skills, as well as functional and geographical knowledge. It is equally important to have a mix of skills related to managing tasks, such as planning and driving toward milestones, and social skills, such as facilitating participation and resolving conflicts. But teams frequently have significant skill overlaps and skill gaps. Teams are often composed on the basis of convenience rather than careful assignment, and sometimes the necessary skill combination is simply not available. Team members must assess the adequacy of their capabilities, and gaps should be closed by adding members or developing the skills or knowledge necessary through training or experience.

## Roles

Roles are sets of specific responsibilities within a group for interacting with others to complete the task. To be effective, teams need members to take responsibility and be accountable for different aspects of achieving results. Some roles help guide the team's processes, such as discussion facilitator, workplace organizer (e.g., for shared workspace on the network) or meeting chairperson. Others are related directly to the task itself, such as idea generator, subject expert, and decision maker. There are several classifications of roles, but research suggests that the most important thing for teams to remember is to have and reinforce both task-related roles *and* process-related or social roles (the latter are more often neglected than the former). There is also debate as to whether roles should be explicit and formally assigned, or implicit and informally emergent. In fact, teams can perform well in either case. In a team whose members are experienced in working on teams, who communicate effectively and easily with each other, and whose skill balance is appropriate for the team, roles often emerge, and team members flow easily into an effective dynamic. In this case, assigning roles formally is not necessary (although members may prefer it anyway). In a less experienced team, or one in which communication is more difficult and/or agreement on the team objectives is not clear, it is usually better to assign roles explicitly and respect their boundaries.

## Processes

A team moves from initial objectives to achievement of results by discussing, gathering information, deciding, and implementing. The three most important processes in a team to facilitate achieving results are communication, conflict management, and managing progress. All three have been studied extensively in laboratory and field settings.

Effective communication is the transmission of meaning as it was intended (Maznevski 1994). Team performance is higher to the extent that each member understands the others' perspectives and the information brought to the team, and to the extent that all members are kept informed of progress in the team in a continuous way. Team members can only act in a cooperative way if they know what they are cooperating *about* and what they are contributing *to*. To accomplish this, communication must be an active process, with extensive questioning, checking, and paraphrasing from all parties involved. Many teams find that having a member responsible for facilitating communication is extremely helpful in ensuring effective communication.

Conflict is the expression of differences in opinion or priority due to opposing needs or demands (Tjosvold 1986). The effect of conflict on a team is complex (e.g., Jehn 1994, 1995; De Dreu and Weingart 2003). Other things being equal, task-related conflict – disagreement and discussion about facts and priorities directly related to the task – tends to enhance team performance. Social or person-related conflict – disagreement and discussion about people in the team – tends to decrease team performance. It seems that teams need "the right amount" of conflict. Not having enough conflict negatively affects performance because perspectives are not questioned or improved upon. Many teams assign a formal role of "devil's advocate" to prevent such groupthink. Too much conflict decreases performance because it prevents convergence on a decision and implementation, and teams that experience too much conflict can enhance their performance by assigning someone to facilitate and even mediate such conflict. However, no research has been able to determine exactly how much is "the right amount" of conflict.

Research on managing progress has been conducted both by team researchers as "task strategy" or "task management," and within the field of operations as "project management." Teams are more likely to achieve results if they plan a clear process with activities, milestones, and deliverables, and if they track progress according to this plan, adapting it when necessary. There are many guides, software programs, and formal processes available for helping teams manage progress, depending on the task and team setting.

These four conditions – task definition, composition, roles, and processes – are necessary for performance in any team, whether it is in Brazil or China, an assembly-line team or a top management team, a short-term response team or a multi-year development team. Whenever a team is underperforming, it is useful to check these basic conditions first: they are too often taken for granted. For teams with simple, routine, or stable tasks, these four conditions are usually sufficient to predict performance. However, teams that face more challenging tasks or environments must address a further set of issues.

## Beyond the basics: achieving high performance

To perform well in more complex situations, teams must develop three characteristics in addition to the basic conditions. They must build respect and trust among members, engage in innovative and creative processes, and manage outside the team boundaries well. These aspects of team performance have been less researched than the basic conditions, partly because they are much more difficult to study. Their implementation depends on the team, and they can look quite different from one team to the next. However, when we look across quantitative, qualitative, and anecdotal studies some important patterns emerge.

### *Building respect and trust*

In a team, respecting someone is appreciating his or her contribution to the team. Such respect can come from recognizing a high level of skill or knowledge in an area one is already familiar with; for example, one engineer may recognize strong engineering expertise in another, and therefore appreciate the second engineer's contributions. Less commonly, respect can derive from acknowledging a high level of skill or knowledge in an area one is *not* familiar with. For example, a marketing professional with extensive expertise about reading the market but no engineering expertise may respect a product development engineer with such knowledge. It is more difficult for people to respect those whose expertise is different, because it is harder to understand the contribution of such expertise and to evaluate its level. Good communication and conflict resolution usually lead to the development of such respect (and vice versa) (e.g., Keller 2001).

Trust is a positive attitude about other team members, specifically a belief that a team member would make decisions, even in the absence of other team members, that would optimize the team's interests. When team members trust each other they allow themselves to be vulnerable; that is, they put themselves at risk of being hurt by the team because of their belief that team members will always try to act to help the team and its members. Respect is a prerequisite for building trust, but trust goes further. Trust is developed through a series of positive experiences, building from predictability and reliability (I respect your knowledge, and I can rely on you to do your part and to do what you committed to do) to deep-level personal trust (I can rely on you to make big decisions on my behalf). It is important to remember that trust cannot be built without taking risks; team members can only demonstrate to each other that they will act in the team's interests if other team members let them take unsupervised actions.

Respect and trust facilitate efficiency in a team (e.g., Govindarajan and Gupta 2001), increase commitment to the team and its decisions, and set the foundation for innovative processes that allow the team to build synergy beyond the individual contributions. When team members respect and trust each other, they do not second-guess each other's contributions, and they are able to act independently of each other to fulfill task requirements, including implementation. Respect and trust are particularly important when the task is impossible for team members to achieve individually, even given enough time. For example, in some manufacturing teams each person can feasibly do every part of the task, but labor is divided for the sake of efficiency. In such a team, respect and trust are less important than in a team doing a multifunctional strategy development task, in which each member must contribute something completely different, must lobby on behalf of the team with different parts of the organization, and must implement effectively in different parts of the organization. Even in teams whose tasks can be done by all members, respect and trust are important to the extent that team performance is more important than the sum of individual performances. For example, with the manufacturing team, if the team can perform much more efficiently with joint efforts and if team performance is rewarded or valued more than individual performance, then respect and trust are important for performance in this team too.

## Generating innovation

High-performing teams must go beyond communication of ideas and resolution of conflicts to generate new approaches. Innovation is developing novel solutions that create value. Although some innovations are truly big ideas and revolutionary in their field, most are the application of ideas from one situation to another that is quite different, or the novel combination of ideas to address a specific challenge. Innovation requires a combination of creativity and deep understanding of the challenge the innovation is trying to address (e.g., O'Reilly et al. 1998). Creativity is the consideration of a wide variety of alternatives and criteria for evaluating alternatives, as well as the building of novel and useful ideas that were not originally part of the consideration set.

Many group techniques combine creativity with structured problem solving to achieve high-quality innovation. All involve using ideas brought to the group only as a starting point, with team members explicitly trying to build on each other's ideas, and developing alternatives no one in the group had thought of previously. For example, Ideo, the world's most award-winning design firm, uses a process called the "Deep Dive" to create innovative solutions to design challenges: anything from developing a new toothbrush to revising the way insurance claims are processed (Kelley et al. 2001). The first step is a deep and careful examination of the challenge from all points of view, paying particular attention to features the end users need. The second step is a structured brainstorming exercise to generate as many ideas as possible. Third, the team creates prototype solutions to the challenge and tests them in a variety of contexts. From the results of the protoype, a final solution is created and implemented.

Innovative teams get the basic conditions of team performance right, and move beyond. Because innovation requires taking risks in generating new ideas and trying them out, innovative teams must have high levels of respect and trust. They also tend to use roles more fluidly than teams that are less innovative, experimenting in a trusting way with different responsibilities in the team in addition to different types of expertise. Innovative teams manage their task processes in a way that combines fluidity with discipline: they are disciplined in their understanding of the task objectives and the importance of final timelines, they are fluid and flexible in their information gathering and task management during the project itself. Finally, teams that innovate well – generate novel approaches that create good value – also manage their boundaries well, as we will examine next.

## Managing boundaries and stakeholders

For a simple, routine, stable task, a team can sometimes take the task mandate and fulfill it without looking outside the team. However, most team tasks require extensive interaction between members and various parties outside the team. Effective teams must manage these boundaries well (Ancona and Caldwell 1992). The three most important aspects of boundary management are resourcing the team, gathering information, and implementing solutions. Teams need many different types of resources, including members with particular skill sets, access to information, technology for conducting research or meeting, administrative support, travel, and so on. Usually, a large part of these resources must originate from outside the team. Furthermore, because most organizational teams' task mandates are to achieve something for the organization, the team inevitably requires information from different parts of the organization. Teams also gather information from outside the organization itself, for example by benchmarking best practices from other companies or by conducting market research. Finally, teams must hand over their output to someone outside the team, whether it is simply by creating a report for a more senior manager or by actually implementing the solution.

Boundaries and stakeholders must be managed carefully (e.g., Freeman 2004; Ancona and Caldwell 1992; Driskat and Wheeler 2003). Effective teams map out the external relationships they need, and strategically assign members to be responsible for different relationships on behalf of the team. Teams generally face two types of challenges in working with stakeholders across boundaries. First, because teams often operate outside the hierarchy, they may lack direct authority to obtain resources and information and to implement solutions. To achieve the team mandate, therefore, teams must make benefits clear from the perspective of the source: "If you provide us with this information, we will be better able to build a solution that meets your needs"; or must provide reciprocal benefit: "If you provide these resources for us, one of our team members will help you out on your next project." Because different team members typically interact with different external stakeholders at different times and places, this aspect of boundary and stakeholder management requires high levels of respect and trust among team members.

The second challenge teams typically face is interpreting and incorporating external perspectives into the team (Maznevski and Athanassiou 2006). Such perspectives rarely come in a form that is ready-made for the team's task and operations. For example, a team may have a mandate to assess the potential in a new market segment. However, because the segment is new, it is unlikely that data already exist about this segment. The team will have to derive an analysis of the potential by integrating information and opinion from many different sources. Bringing information and resources into the team from external sources shares many requirements with innovation. Team members must trust and respect each other so they can build on each other's expertise and take risks in interpreting ambiguous information in various ways. Furthermore, team members must be open-minded enough to accept different stakeholders' perspectives.

Although there is no easy formula for team performance, teams that fulfill the four basic conditions are well on their way to at least mediocre performance. Teams with more complex tasks must also pay attention to going beyond the basics with respect and trust, to create value by interacting outside the team and innovating.

## Global teams: more barriers, more opportunities

Global teams represent a subset of "teams" in general. While teams are groups of people working together to accomplish tasks, global teams are groups whose members represent different countries and/or whose tasks are multinational in nature. Everything described above with respect to teams applies to global teams, but global teams are more extreme. Global teams face higher barriers to effective performance, and it is much more difficult for global teams to achieve both the basic conditions and the characteristics of high-performing teams. On the other hand, the characteristics and contexts of global teams provide more potential for high performance and for creating an important impact within organizations. Global teams that perform well make a big difference to their companies. Two characteristics of global teams particularly differentiate them from teams in general: their composition, and their distribution. Each of these characteristics will now be described and their implications for performance discussed. The discussions are summarized in Table 6.1.

## Diverse composition

Global teams, on average, have much more diverse composition than teams in general do (Schneider and Barsoux 2003). This diverse composition has enormous implications: it provides great potential for higher performance by bringing in new perspectives and connection to external stakeholders; at the same time, it makes smooth team interactions much more difficult. Diverse teams therefore tend to perform either better or worse than homogeneous teams, depending on how they are managed (DiStefano and Maznevski 2000; Earley and Mosakowski 2000; Thomas 1999; Thomas et al. 1996). Interestingly,

*Table 6.1* Diversity and dispersion: overcome barriers to take advantage of opportunities

|  | *Barriers* | *Opportunities* |
|---|---|---|
| Diversity | Tendency towards:<br>• less effective communication<br>• increased conflict<br>• lower alignment on task | Potential for:<br>• increased creativitiy and innovation<br>• more complete and comprehensive perspectives, stakeholder coverage |
| Dispersion | Difficult to achieve and maintain basic team conditions, due to:<br>• limited communication<br>• invisible relationships<br>• logistical challenges | Potential for:<br>• more complete and comprehensive perspectives, stakeholder coverage<br>• focused, objective, balanced communication |

the most common reaction to diversity is to suppress it (e.g., Richard and Johnson 2001; Tsui and O'Reilly 1989) – that is, to focus only on similarities. This moves a team from being low-performing or value destroying, to the medium performance of homogeneous teams – an improvement, but still missing the potential offered from diversity.

Global teams are diverse in terms of nationality, but because they are generally created to address strategic tasks they are also usually diverse in terms of function, and their members often represent business units with different priorities and needs. This triple dose of diversity means that global teams cannot suppress their differences, the way more local teams often can and do. It also means that the potential for high performance is even greater than for teams with less diversity. Functional and business unit differences are evident; although they are difficult for teams to manage, they are generally clear and their effects quite rational. These differences can be dealt with using careful application of the normal group processes already described. Cultural differences, however, usually affect dynamics deep below the surface (Harrison *et al*. 1998) and must be dealt with differently.

## *Impact of cultural diversity*

People from different cultures bring different expectations to the team. We learn these expectations through years of experiences in families, schools, communities, and other cultural institutions, and, as with other aspects of culture, people tend not even to be aware that they hold these expectations. Comparative research shows us that although all cultures use teams, cultures differ from each other quite widely in terms of how they tend to work in teams. Different cultures even use different metaphors to describe teams; for example, some cultures think of teams as families, while other cultures compare business teams to sports teams.

One of the most important differences among cultures is related to how roles are defined and managed. For instance, in more hierarchical cultures, such as those of Japan and Brazil, it is generally assumed that a team must have a single leader and that the leader must have hierarchical decision-making authority within the team. If the team is not managed this way, it is believed, then it will lapse into chaos and inefficiency. In other cultures, such as those of Scandinavian countries, it is assumed that team leadership should be more emergent, fluid, and shared, with different people taking the lead at different points in the team's task. More individualistic cultures, such as those of the United States and France, tend to define specific task-related roles clearly so as to identify individual areas of accountability. In these cultures, team members are comfortable differentiating individual performance within the team, rewarding some more than others. More collective cultures, such as those of Singapore, Malaysia, and Thailand, tend to define roles more fluidly, with people contributing to the team as they can and with higher accountability for the group than for individuals. In these cultures, teams prefer to reward everyone on the team equally. These differences, of course, affect the ease with which team members from different cultures agree on roles within the team, one of the basic conditions for good team performance.

Another set of important differences among cultures is related to acceptable norms for communication and conflict resolution. In some cultures, such as in many Latin countries, it is acceptable to express one's ideas at any time, even speaking at the same time as others and with openly expressed emotion; in other cultures, such as in many East Asian countries, it is only acceptable to speak when asked a question, and it is never acceptable to speak at the same time as others – silence is preferable. In many cultures, showing excessive emotion is considered inappropriate. Some cultures, such as those in Nordic countries, show respect for each other by expressing conflict only indirectly (it is important not to hurt each other's feelings or cause others to lose face); while others, such as the Dutch, show respect by expressing disagreement openly (it is important not to waste each other's time on trivial agreement). With such widely varying norms for communication, it is difficult for culturally diverse teams to communicate effectively, to send and receive meaning as it was intended. And with such widely varying norms for showing respect in conflict resolution, it is difficult to resolve conflicts constructively.

These differences can be exacerbated by what are called fault lines (Lau and Murnighan 1998): rifts in teams that are created by alignment of different types of differences. For example, a global team may consist of two production engineers, two marketers, and two R&D scientists, from the United States, Japan, and Germany. If the engineers are from the United States, the marketers from Japan, and the scientists from Germany, then the functional and cultural divisions are aligned and there are likely to be three subgroups within the team who find it very difficult to collaborate. On the other hand, if each of the functions is represented by people from different countries, the subgroups will be less evident and differences will be easier to bridge.

Given these challenges, it is even more important for global teams to build respect and trust than it is for other teams to do so. Research shows that multicultural teams that develop a collaborative and cohesive climate do perform well, outperforming homogeneous teams (e.g., Mullen and Copper 1994; Mudrack 1989). Such respect and trust help team members appreciate that their differences are related to different ways of expressing and working together, not different objectives. But, as was noted above, it is more difficult to build respect and trust among people who are different from each other than among people who are similar to each other!

## Managing cultural diversity in teams effectively

Research in this area suggests that global teams must explicitly address and manage *both* their similarities *and* their differences; they must *both* create social cohesion *and* acknowledge and respect individual differences. Diverse teams that focus only on their differences create great rifts within the team and find it difficult to converge or align. Teams that focus only on their similarities, though, in an effort to maximize social cohesion, also underperform; they do not take advantage of their differences. Moreover, their suppressed differences eventually manifest themselves in the context of deep and personal conflicts, hurting the team and its performance.

The starting point is for team members to map out their similarities and differences, especially with respect to culture, function, or expertise, and business unit perspective. Mapping is creating a picture of the team's diversity, using charts and, where possible, data from personality or cultural dimension assessments. If done with an open mindset and motivation, this mapping process itself helps to create respect and trust as team members explore their different perspectives. The team can then identify in which areas it is easily aligned, and areas where different members will contribute differently. Recent research suggests that teams should develop tight alignment around task-related issues, such as the definition of the task and objectives, while encouraging and respecting diverse perspectives around contributions to the task and ways of getting it done and social needs within the group.

Once the differences are mapped, then team members must *bridge* these differences using effective communication techniques. Especially important is decentering, or speaking and listening from the others' point of view. For example, an American, through mapping, may understand that her teammates from East Asia prefer to express conflict indirectly. However, she may not be able to bridge that difference by decentering: she may say, "I know you find it difficult to be direct in conflict, but it's OK to do it with me, I won't be offended." If the American were truly decentering, she would find ways to ask questions and check for agreement that allowed the East Asians to express conflict indirectly. Referring to a decision about direction, for example, she might ask a teammate, "How do you think people in your office would react to this decision?" This question would allow a teammate to express his own disagreement indirectly as a hypothetical third person's opinion and not his own. Equally important in bridging is refraining from blame. Problems and miscommunication in diverse teams are inevitable, and it is a natural reaction to blame others for the problem, or to attribute low motivation or other negative characteristics to them. In effective multicultural teams, team members do not blame each other when such problems arise, but engage in creative dialogue to try to understand which types of differences contributed to the misunderstanding. In this way, effective teams turn problems into opportunities for learning about each other.

It is particularly important for diverse teams to experience pieces of the task quickly, to develop respect and reliability and create a foundation for trust. For example, the more quickly team members are assigned different aspects of information gathering then come together to share initial results, the more "data" team members have about each other to build roles, processes, and, eventually, trust.

Diverse global teams experience great challenges overcoming the barriers raised by diversity. But remember that team members are often motivated by the differences; there is no doubt that being a member of a global, diverse team is interesting and an excellent learning experience. Effective leaders of global teams can leverage this motivation and, addressing the principles outlined here, can help such teams achieve their potential.

## Dispersed distribution

In addition to diverse composition, global teams are typically characterized by dispersed distribution: their members are usually based in different locations, often spanning many time zones and climates, and many members travel frequently. Communication and coordination, therefore, present major challenges for global teams. On the other hand, as a result of their dispersion and travel, members have access to a wide variety of resources and networks, and therefore can provide a broader variety of inputs to the team and links with its stakeholders.

Dispersed teams, which rely on information and communications technology to conduct much of their work together, are often referred to as "virtual teams." Although research in this field is relatively new, it has been extensive, and we can provide relatively clear advice on how to manage the virtual aspect of global teams. Early research compared virtual teams with face-to-face teams and, in laboratory situations, generally found that face-to-face teams outperform virtual ones. This research identified barriers raised by communications technology and how to overcome them. Later research has accepted that virtual teams are inevitable. Because companies create virtual teams whenever there is a need to bring together people who are geographically distributed, the tasks are often different from those assigned to face-to-face teams, and comparing their performance is neither possible nor relevant. This latter stream of research has examined the dynamics of such virtual teams and identified the key factors contributing to their performance (for further discussions and references, see also Maznevski *et al.* 2006).

### *Impact of virtual communication*

Communication via technology is much less rich than face-to-face communication, even if visual technology, such as videoconferencing or webcams, is used. Subtle nonverbal communication, such as body language and tone of voice, is greatly constrained by technology. Virtual teams therefore find it more difficult to communicate effectively, especially complex and context-sensitive information regarding the task, and emotional information regarding team processes. And even though most managers conduct a high proportion of their teamwork virtually, most report that they do not like or prefer this mode of communication. It is a "necessary evil."

While most managers are uncomfortable with virtual communication, research has shown there are only two aspects of team performance which are so difficult to achieve virtually that they should be done face-to-face if at all possible: building relationships of trust and commitment, and sharing deep-level tacit knowledge. Everyone has heard stories of relationships, including marriages, being built over the internet; however, this kind of relationship building is still the exception, not the norm. Reliability and predictability can be developed virtually through the kind of task experiences identified earlier, and in fact it is even more important for virtual teams to develop this quickly than for diverse teams to do so. But the deep trust that allows a team member to be vulnerable to others is extremely difficult to build without personal contact. Therefore, if a global team's task requires members to have this level of trust and commitment to each other – and most do – then the team must meet face-to-face.

Second, tacit knowledge is extremely difficult to share over technology. Tacit knowledge is the type of knowledge that is contextually embedded and cannot be articulated explicitly. Explicit knowledge can be written down in manuals, spreadsheets, patent applications, and so on, and can be transferred relatively easily from one person to another in such forms. Explicit knowledge is copyable and inexpensive; in fact, it can be found free of charge all through the internet. Tacit knowledge takes explicit knowledge and puts it in context, in use. Tacit knowledge comes from experience, and incorporates wisdom and judgment. It is not copyable, and it tends to be expensive. For example, a chemical engineer just graduated from university has high levels of explicit knowledge: he knows all the latest techniques and applications for combining elements; but he has less knowledge of the complex contexts of different applications. A chemical engineer who has been working on field applications for fifteen years may have less explicit knowledge than the young graduate (that is, she may not know all the latest techniques), but she has more tacit knowledge about how different compounds react to the multitude of variables in different manufacturing contexts. Tacit knowledge is best transferred during face-to-face interactions, which allow for questions, dialogue, and the richness of nonverbal communication. Therefore, if a global team's task requires high levels of tacit knowledge transfer and development – and most do – then the team must meet face-to-face.

## Create a heartbeat

The question is not, then, "should we meet face-to-face?" but "when should we meet face-to-face, and what should we do with that time?" Most teams believe they should get together at the team's launch, then whenever there is a crisis, conflict, or a major decision point: "This team is important, and so whenever we really need to see each other, when things aren't going well, we make the effort to jump on a plane and see each other." In fact, high-performing teams do something quite different. They schedule regular meetings and stick to the schedule, for example meeting once every three to four months for two days each time. They create a team heartbeat with a regular rhythm. During their face-to-face meetings they do *not* present sales reports or simple updates; instead, they engage in discussions and actions to build shared tacit knowledge and strong relationships. They might visit customers or suppliers together, work on an innovation process, or share cases about best practices or reviews of failures. These activities pump the equivalent of oxygen through the team. Research has shown that teams that have a strong heartbeat can manage all other tasks virtually in between their face-to-face meetings, and that this is both less expensive and more effective than getting together "whenever we need to" (Maznevski and Chudoba 2000).

## Discipline and focus

When teams are working via technology, the most important message is to maintain discipline and focus. Face-to-face teams can use the immediacy of personal contact to create a sense of urgency and momentum; virtual teams must create it deliberately themselves. Identifying roles, developing a project plan, monitoring progress – all the processes discussed earlier in this chapter – must be accomplished with great deliberation in virtual teams. Interestingly, teams that develop good discipline and focus find that working via technology can actually facilitate team performance, rather than hinder it. When meeting times are limited, people tend to prepare more effectively and stay focused throughout the meeting. When nonverbal cues are limited, people focus on the spoken or written word and remain much more task focused. Because of this, virtual teams often have lower levels of personal conflict than face-to-face teams. The use of structured communication tools such as conference calls, emails, and web meetings tends to decrease the dominance of extroverts and native language speakers, giving each member more of a chance to participate in a way he or she feels comfortable with. This "performance bonus" can only be achieved, though, when the team has built relationships, shared tacit knowledge, and developed discipline and focus.

## Which technology?

Virtual teams often search for the "one best technology" that will solve all the members' challenges. So far, though, that technology has not yet emerged. Some recent advances such as voice and video over broadband internet hold promise, as they add richness to normally sparse electronic communication. However, global teams usually face different infrastructures in different countries, company firewalls, people traveling, and other complications that make it difficult for them to rely on these advances. Effective virtual teams use a range of technologies, matching different technologies to different aspects of the team's task. They might use email for asynchronous communication, the telephone for one-to-one discussions, web meetings for joint discussions (some members using the phone and others using the internet for the voice aspect), and a shared workspace for keeping documents. They might also combine or sequence technologies in specific ways; for example, a good technique for communicating effectively across cultures is first to exchange email background about a topic, then to discuss it on the phone to develop a dialogue with questions and answers in real time, then to follow up via email to ensure that the main points were shared. In choosing technologies, the important thing is to select ones that all team members can use (and to provide training if necessary), and that will be supported as needed.

Like diverse composition, distributed configuration raises enormous barriers and opportunities for global teams. But also in parallel with diversity, team members are often motivated by this extra challenge, especially at the beginning of a team's life. Working with people in different locations adds variety and new perspectives, and many people find it inspiring to connect with people in other places. Effective global team leaders can take advantage of this momentum to get the team working well together and, using the findings discovered by research about dispersed teams, can turn the challenges into opportunities for high performance.

## Global teams and organizational performance

So far we have considered the effectiveness of global teams themselves; but it is also important to examine their impact on the overall performance of organizations. To this end, we will discuss two specific topics here: top management teams and connected teams.

## Top management teams: are they really teams?

The top manager and his or her direct reports are usually referred to as the top management team (TMT). The overall corporation has a global TMT, and each business unit also has a TMT which may be global or local, depending on the company's structure. The TMT's mandate is to decide on the overall direction and strategy of the company (or business unit, within the company strategy), and to take responsibility for implementing it. Team members usually act independently from each other in terms of implementation – if the TMT members are heads of geographic units, then they implement within their regions; if they are heads of product group units, then they implement for their own product areas; and so on. In fact, if the company's reward structure focuses mainly on business unit performance, then the TMT members may actually compete with each other for resources needed to implement the strategy in their own units. For this reason, there is often debate as to whether the TMT is *really* a team (e.g., Katzenbach 1997).

A lot of research on TMTs has focused on the relationship between team composition and company performance (e.g., Elron 1997), using publicly available data. This research has shown that functional diversity is usually associated with slightly higher performance, but that other sources of diversity do not affect company performance. However, this research stream cannot sort out whether a source of diversity is suppressed or used as an opportunity within the team. A few studies have indicated that effective communication and conflict resolution are associated with high-performing TMTs (that is, those whose organizations perform well), but the impact is hard to determine.

Anecdotal evidence, experience, and some more in-depth research studies suggest that a company or business unit whose TMT behaves like an effective team tends to perform better in the long term than one whose TMT behaves like a group of independent (or even competing) individuals. When TMT members follow the basic conditions and adhere to the high-performance characteristics described earlier, and when they use diversity and dispersion as opportunities, they are more likely to develop strategies that take into account the organization as a whole and that are more adapted to the current environment. In such TMTs, team members are better at helping each other to implement, for example by sharing ideas, people, and other resources. For example, one study found that when those who have the most influence in the TMT also have the most international expertise, a global TMT's company is more likely to perform well. In the short term a company can perform well when its TMT members act independently or compete; however, when the environment changes and the company must drive changes or react, then the company is better off with a "real" team as its TMT.

## Connected teams create global organizations

Today's multinational organizations typically share some negative characteristics, including impersonality and heavy complexity. Multinationals are large and distributed, and it is often difficult for their members – especially those outside of headquarters – to relate to other parts of the company. Moreover, the use of virtual workers is becoming much more common, such as salespeople with independent territories who see another member of their own company only a couple of times a month or even less. The complexity also makes these organizations heavy and unwieldy, and managers have difficulty getting information where it is needed, when it is needed. Many senior managers today are trying to learn how to motivate people and share information in this difficult situation, to maintain commitment and collaboration so that the opportunities of globalization will not be lost under the burdens. Effective global teams have some important "side effects" related to creating global organizations. "Connected teams" refers to global teams that pay attention to and nurture these higher-order benefits.

First, members of effective global teams tend to feel more committed to the organization as a whole than do people who are not members of such teams. When people have personal *and* performance-related connections with others in different parts of the organization, those other parts of the organization seem less distant and more real. Team members make the organization more tangible for each other. This may seem trivial, but for a leader trying to enhance and coordinate performance in a multinational organization, this commitment to the company and the individuals within it goes a very long way.

Second, most managers today are members of two or more global teams. As we discussed at the beginning of this chapter, global teams often cross the hierarchy and join people from different parts of the organization. Because of this, the multiple global teams that each manager is part of tend to cross *different* parts of the company. Each manager (team member), therefore, is a potential conveyor of knowledge across boundaries, and global teams can be conduits for knowledge sharing and organizational learning. This perspective is summarized in Figure 6.2. As with all other potential benefits of global teams, this knowledge sharing does not happen automatically. In fact, members of global teams tend to focus on the task at hand – which is difficult enough – and not pay attention to passing on knowledge about other aspects of company performance. But as global teams start to master their own task, their conversations often turn to "what else is happening at your end?" Effective global leaders and teams encourage this learning, and in fact sophisticated multinational companies see its advantages and facilitate it deliberately.

It is easy to argue that team performance is key to organizational performance: work is done by teams – teams make decisions and implement them – and if teams perform well, then so will the organization. In this section we have illustrated two ways in which effective global teams contribute to the performance of the organization beyond their own task mandates: the special case of top management teams, and connected teams.

## Leading global teams

We began this chapter by arguing that effective global leaders must be good both at being global team members and at leading global teams. Throughout this chapter we have identified the characteristics of effective global teams, and global leaders can use the ideas in the chapter by way of a checklist:

● Have the basic conditions been met?
● Does the team have high-performance characteristics?
● Is the team capturing the opportunities inherent in its diversity and distribution?
● If the team is a top management team, is it acting like a high-performing team to ensure the whole organization benefits?
● Are the members leveraging the team as a connected team?

But every global team is different, and therein lies the importance of leadership. Beyond the basic conditions, there are no hard and fast rules about global teams. All global teams should develop trust and respect, but the path for doing that in each team is different. All global teams should be innovative, but the focus of their innovation, the end user, is

Most managers are on two or more distributed teams, but tend to see these as separate teams or matixed teams. This is typically how connected teams are shown, emphasizing the distinct nature of the different teams:

|  | USA & Canada | Latin America | Europe | Asia | Middle East & Africa |
|---|---|---|---|---|---|
| Marketing | A | F |  |  | S |
| Production | B |  | J | N |  |
| Logistics | C | G | K |  | T |
| R&D | D |  | L | P |  |
| Finance | E | H | M | Q | U |
| Call centres |  |  |  | R | V |

For example, person A is on the "USA & Canada" team, and also on the "Marketing" team.

Here are the same teams shown as a network. Shapes with the same shading are in the same geographical team, and those of the same shape are in the same functional team. This network emphasizes the interconnections between team members, and highlights the opportunities for learning and distribution of knowledge.

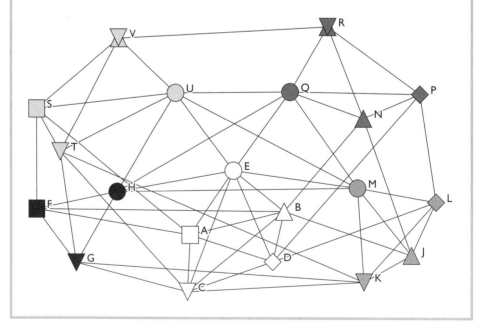

*Figure 6.2* Connected teams

different. All global teams must manage external stakeholder relationships, but all have different sets of stakeholders. And so on.

Recent research (e.g., Maznevski *et al*. 2006) has even begun to suggest that in global teams the traditional leadership role tends to be distributed across more people than in traditional teams. In traditional teams the "leader" tends to be the hierarchical head of the team, the meeting chairperson, the discussion facilitator, the decision maker, the discipline enforcer, the direction setter, and often takes other roles as well. It seems that global teams may be too complex and dynamic for one person to take on all of these roles. Experienced leaders of global teams find themselves either assigning some of these roles to others or facilitating the emergence of multiple leadership roles within the team. Although this research is still not conclusive, it resonates well with experienced leaders and probably represents an emerging trend. This would be yet another complexity for leaders of global teams, but, as with diversity and distribution, could create an opportunity for higher performance if well managed.

This infinite variety of teams and the ambiguity of leadership roles prevents the checklist from being applied like a recipe. It is more like a field guide to which characteristics to pay attention to, and which leadership tools might be most effective in different situations. The application is up to the leader, who must match the tools with the situation, including the combination of members, task, and external stakeholders. This implies that leaders of global teams must constantly observe and check the condition of the team, monitoring also its context and situation. Global teams are inherently unstable, and this monitoring can help the astute leader benefit from the instabilities (they are chances to take advantage of flexibility!) rather than be limited by them. The leader must provide some consistency of direction, but guide the team dynamically according to its needs and opportunities.

Like global leadership in general, leading global teams is a craft that combines the science of conditions and opportunities in teams – the checklist – with the art of applying the right processes at the right time. Leaders who are open to and careful about learning will develop the skills needed for this craft.

# Global leadership knowledge creation and transfer

**ALLAN BIRD AND GARY R. ODDOU**

After five years performing at a high level, an expatriate manager was transferred back from his assignment in Bonn, Germany, to his firm's New York headquarters. He had grown significantly and had acquired an extraordinary amount of knowledge. He had developed an extensive understanding of German banking regulations and practices. He had developed a far-flung network of contacts – people who could open doors, provide counsel or solve problems. Moreover, as a result of this assignment he had a deeper understanding of what the company was trying to accomplish with its global strategy, and he saw ways to implement this strategy more effectively and efficiently in Europe.

To his surprise, upon his return to New York he was put on a six-month temporary assignment assisting in the training of new employees in the United States. His superiors appeared to have little idea of how to capitalize on his German experiences within the context of existing training programs, nor could he identify ways to apply his hard-won insights within his new assignment. By the time he received a longer-term assignment working with African subsidiaries, a large portion of the learning acquired on his prior assignment had eroded. For instance, his German network of friends, so critical to the firm knowledge base there, had already begun to dissipate. Key contacts had moved or were no longer in a position to help him. As a result of the apparent poor management of his transition, personal negative feelings developed toward his company, and his motivation to help and apply his learning had also eroded.

The purpose of this chapter is to consider the role of knowledge creation and transfer in global leadership. Many models of global leadership competency (e.g., Bird and Osland 2004; Black *et al.* 1999b; Brake 1997; Kets de Vries with Florent-Treacy 1999) emphasize the important role that knowledge plays in effective leadership. Surprisingly, this aspect of global leadership has not been well researched. This chapter addresses the issue of knowledge creation and development, and also explores the transfer of knowledge. The transfer of knowledge is considered in terms of both the individual – the application of previously acquired knowledge to new situations – and the organization – the interest and receptivity of the organization to capture the knowledge the repatriate might have.

## Careers, development, and knowledge creation

In this section we shall explore the relationship between knowledge creation and the development of a knowledge capability necessary for effective global leadership. We begin by reviewing Nonaka's theory of knowledge creation and then link it to global leadership development.

In 1994, Bird proposed that a knowledge perspective be used to better capture the significance of career experience and development in career research. He argued that the traditional definition of career as "the evolving sequence of a person's work experiences over time" (Arthur *et al.* 1989: 8) ignored the essential substance of a career. He reasoned that type, duration, length, and sequence of work experiences were but outward markers of a career, and that a more meaningful understanding of careers could be constructed by focusing on the knowledge that was accumulated or discarded over time. The arc of a career could be understood in terms of the inflows and outflows and transformations of individual and organizational knowledge that derive from sequences of work experiences.

Subsequently, Bird (2001) applied the "careers as repositories of knowledge" perspective to international assignments as a way of understanding the role they might play in developing global leaders. From this perspective, international work experiences constitute the primary mechanism by which knowledge creation relevant to global leadership takes place (ibid.).

It is impossible to conceptualize careers as repositories of knowledge apart from a view of organizations as knowledge creators (Argote and Ingram 2000; Inkpen and Dinur 1998). The experience of individuals forms the substance from which knowledge is created (Nonaka 1991a). When a firm competes on the basis of cost, quality, or product differentiation, it is competing on the ability to distinguish its products or services from those of its competitors. The ability to differentiate is embedded in an invisible asset: its knowledge base (Prahalad and Hamel 1994). That knowledge base is derived, in turn, from the experience of the individuals affiliated with that firm (Nurasimha 2000). Ultimately, all advantages are informational in nature. Maintaining competitiveness and sustaining an ongoing ability to differentiate requires firms to develop their human resources in ways that enhance the supply of information and knowledge available to the firm. Firms that revitalize themselves through knowledge creation and transfer set themselves apart from competitors (Argote and Ingram 2000).

Perhaps the most important way in which organizations create knowledge is by shaping employee work experiences and then eliciting experience-based learning in ways that allow it to be shared throughout the organization and lead to the accomplishment of organizational objectives. Framed in this way, a key activity of line managers and human resource development policies that support them is to give direction to the knowledge-generating activities of employees by creating meaning – that is, by making sense of experiential data (Louis 1980b; Weick 1996).

## Explicit knowledge and tacit knowledge

There are two ways in which organizations and individuals transmit knowledge. When knowledge is transmitted to others through formal, systematic language – when it is articulable – it can be called "explicit" (Polanyi 1966). Explicit knowledge is impersonal and independent of context. For example, a mathematical equation conveys knowledge by means of an impersonal (it is not rooted in any person or situation), formal (there are rules governing the structure of equations), systematic language (mathematical symbols).

Tacit knowledge describes information that is embedded in people's experiences and which is difficult to communicate to others. By definition, tacit knowledge is personal: it is gained only through first-hand experiences and also is rooted in action and commitment (Nonaka 1991a). It is accessible to its possessor primarily in the form of intuition, speculation, and feeling. When Polanyi (1966: 4) states, "We know more than we can tell," he is describing the sum of an individual's understanding that cannot be articulated to others. A large share of the tacit knowledge that individuals possess remains beyond their ability to make it explicit (Winograd and Flores 1986).

Tacit knowledge has two variants that are relevant to learning knowledge critical for global leadership. First, one type of tacit knowledge is reflected in deeply held beliefs, paradigms, schemata, or mental models (Nonaka 1990). This knowledge helps us make sense of the world and influences our perceptions of what are appropriate values, attitudes and behaviors. A second type is technical, and consists of skills, techniques, and know-how that are context-specific. Both types are important to global leadership and to the development of global leaders.

## Types of knowledge creation

Various types of interaction between these two basic knowledge types – tacit and explicit – give rise to four types of knowledge creation (Nonaka 1991a), as shown in Figure 7.1. Sequenced together, the four create a cycle of knowledge creation.

### Tacit-to-tacit

Knowledge creation involving the transmittal of tacit knowledge between individuals represents one type. Studying under a master craftsman, apprentices may learn not only through spoken words or instructions but through observation and imitation as well. These processes of socialization lead to knowledge creation through the expansion of their knowledge – that is, newcomers imbue or modify what is learned via socialization by filtering it through their own understanding. Notwithstanding this process, however, little new knowledge is created through socialization. Moreover, the socialization form of

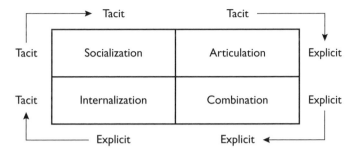

*Figure 7.1* Typology of the knowledge-creation process

Source: Bird A., "Careers as repositories of knowledge: A new perspective on boundaryless careers," *Journal of Organizational Behavior*, 15, 1994, 325–344 (page 329). John Wiley and Sons Limited. Reproduced with permission.

knowledge creation is time-consuming and difficult to manage, and more so when large numbers of people are involved.

## Explicit-to-explicit

Knowledge that is explicit can be easily transmitted. The explicitness often makes the *combination* of different knowledge transparent and easy. For example, collecting information about the financial performance of various overseas business units (explicit knowledge) brings about the creation of new knowledge: how the firm as a whole is performing in overseas markets (explicit knowledge). Combination of explicit knowledge creates new knowledge through synthesis. Unlike socialization, the new knowledge created often tends to be minimal in its scope.

The two most profound knowledge creation types involve the transition from tacit to explicit or explicit to tacit. This is also the locus where individuals' work experiences hold the potential to make their largest contribution to the organization.

## Tacit-to-explicit

Articulation is the conversion of tacit knowledge to explicit knowledge. It is significant for organizations because when knowledge that was previously inaccessible is made explicit, it can be shared. In a furniture company, for example, when a master cabinetmaker is able to articulate the thinking and techniques behind his particular style of woodworking, that information can be widely disseminated within the organization. Designers can incorporate the new knowledge into future products. Additionally, the information might even be shared with other cabinetmakers, thereby enabling them to make pieces of comparable workmanship.

## *Explicit-to-tacit*

The acquisition and subsequent application of explicit knowledge to an individual's own unique situation results in an expansion of the tacit knowledge base. In addition to *internalization* of explicit knowledge, this knowledge creation may lead to a reframing of knowledge that constitutes knowledge creation as well. It is also important to note that transference of knowledge from explicit to tacit can lead to self-renewal of the employee and a deepening commitment.

There are similarities between tacit-to-tacit and explicit-to-tacit knowledge creation types. The primary difference between "socialization" and "internalization" lies in the informational source. In socialization (tacit-to-tacit) a master or role model is the primary information source contributing to new knowledge creation. New knowledge is initially being created through replication, with the receiver's knowledge base contributing little to the newly created knowledge. In the case of explicit-to-tacit knowledge creation the receiver's knowledge base contributes most of the information. By helping the receiver to see things in a different light or think in a different way (both being forms of new knowledge), explicit knowledge stimulates learning.

## International assignments as spirals of knowledge creation

Through iteratively cycling through the four knowledge creation modes it is possible to trace the knowledge arc of a career path. Different experiences spark shifts from one mode to another. Nonaka (1991b) provides an example of how this sequencing of knowledge creation modes plays out. In doing so, he outlines the nature of experience in each mode as well as the modal shifts in describing the experience of one team member on a product development team at Matsushita Electric Company charged with improving the design and performance of a home bread-making machine. Though a prototype had been developed, it produced unacceptable bread. The crust was hard and the inside was doughy. One team member, Ikuko Tanaka, suggested they study the technique of Osaka International Hotel's baker, who had a reputation for making the best bread in Osaka. She arranged to work as an apprentice with the baker. One day she noticed that the baker had a distinctive technique of stretching the dough when kneading it. She returned to the product development team and shared her insights. Acting on this new understanding, they made several modifications to the bread-maker's design. Matsushita engineered the "twist dough" method into its design and came out with a new machine that set a sales record for kitchen appliances.

Nonaka (1991b: 99) continues:

1   First, [Ikuko Tanaka] learns the tacit secrets of the Osaka International Hotel baker (socialization).
2   Next, she translates these secrets into explicit knowledge that she can communicate to her team members and others at Matsushita (articulation).

3    The team then standardizes this knowledge, putting it together into a manual or workbook and embodying it in a product (combination).

4    Finally, through the experience of creating a new product, Tanaka and her team members enrich their own tacit knowledge base (internalization). In particular, they come to understand in an extremely intuitive way that products like home bread-making machines can provide genuine quality. That is, the machine must make bread that is as good as that of a professional baker.

It is interesting that Nonaka (1994) uses a project team experience to illustrate the sequence of knowledge creation modes. This has implications for understanding knowledge creation as part of a global leadership development process, particularly as enacted through international assignments. When individuals join a project or work team they may experience a form of *socialization*. Dialogue within the team, in turn, leads to *articulation*. As when ideas and concepts generated by the team are incorporated into existing knowledge bases or joined with existing data, there is a modal shift to *combination*. Experimentation with various new combinations of knowledge may lead to "learning by doing" that becomes *internalization*. In a similar vein, managers who venture out on international assignments often undergo a profound socialization as they work to adjust to their new surroundings and the requirements of their new work. As they acquire some facility or proficiency in the assignment, they will likely share their experiences and observations with others, leading to *articulation* of their newly acquired tacit knowledge. Combining this knowledge with explicit knowledge about their work context, organization, competitive environment, and so forth involves a process of *combination*. As they fully incorporate all of this learning while still expatriates, or upon repatriation, they will have internalized this understanding, resulting in more knowledge creation.

As individuals repeat this sequence of work experiences, their store of knowledge grows. Development, then, can be understood as the path of an individual's work experiences through the various knowledge creation modes. The sequences of modes can be visualized as an outwardly expanding spiral.

## Four types of knowing

Though the knowledge creation cycle provides a description of the developmental trajectory that work experiences may take, it does not delineate the content of that development. Knowing that work experiences involve moving through a sequence of knowledge creation modes does not tell us anything about the types of knowledge embedded in that development. A way of categorizing types of knowledge that is particularly useful for understanding knowledge acquisition and transfer related to developing global leaders can be found in Kidd and Teramoto's (1995) four-class taxonomy of "knowings." Each of the four is discussed below.

*Know who* refers to a person's social capital. It is the actual and potential resources embedded within, available through, and derived from the network of relationships an individual is able to access. Examples of *know who* would include such knowledge as having a contact in the Chinese government willing to make introductions on one's behalf to local, state-owned enterprises, or being acquainted with key individuals in the Ireland Development Agency. Knowing who involves an acquaintance with others *and also* the ability to tap into resources through those relationships.

*Know how* covers knowledge related to a person's set of skills and knowledge about how to accomplish tasks or how to do work. For example, methods for structuring payment protocols to take into account the effects of hyperinflation in Argentina represent one type of know how. Another would be methods for giving or saving *face* in Chinese business relationships.

*Know what* addresses the nature and extent of a person's understanding about specific projects, products, services, or organizational arrangements. Knowledge of the firm's supply-chain management procedures and the various suppliers and transportation services in Malaysia or an understanding of the structure of the South African subsidiary's information system constitute types of *know what*.

*Know why* relates to the nature and extent of a person's identification with the firm's culture, intention and strategy – for instance, knowing why the firm chose to set up a manufacturing operation in Honduras rather than Kenya. Knowing why gives meaning and purpose to organizational and individual action.

Through time, the volume and value of each type of knowing may increase or decrease. Additionally, specific types of knowledge may be acquired, lost, and recovered. Figure 7.2 presents a graphic depiction of an idealized career developing over time.

## Types of knowing in international assignment and global leader development

The "careers as repositories of knowledge" perspective offers significant value for the study of global leader careers, particularly from a developmental standpoint. Two recurring themes in research on global leadership development have been the use of international assignments – with their extensive range of new experiences as a mechanism for growth – and the role of knowledge acquisition.

Personal experience is the essential element in knowledge creation and the basis for all tacit knowledge. Each phase of knowledge creation draws on the current or past experience of individuals. Nevertheless, the value of experiences is variable. Frequent experiences such as driving to and from work, for example, provide little that is useful for new knowledge creation. The experiences most likely to lead to significant knowledge creation possess three characteristics: variety, quality, and affective intensity (Nonaka 1994). All three are present in the experiences associated with international assignments and leading in a global context.

Variety refers to the range of experiences acquired over a given period of time. International assignments, unlike most other work experiences, provide extraordinary opportunities for variety. Living and working in another country present a wide range of

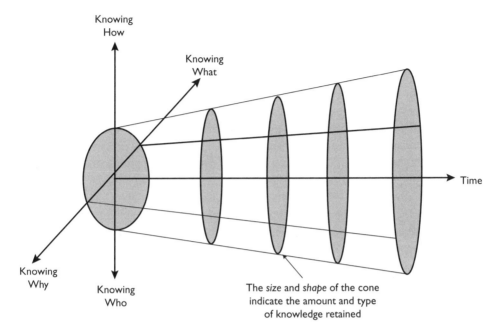

Time

Knowing
How

Knowing
What

Knowing
Why

Knowing
Who

The *size* and *shape* of the cone
indicate the amount and type
of knowledge retained

*Figure 7.2* Four types of knowing over time

Source: Stephens, G. K., Bird, A., and Mendenhall, M. E. (2002). "International careers as repositories of
knowledge: A new look at expatriation." D. C. Feldman (ed.) *Work Careers: A Developmental Perspective.*
San Francisco: Jossey-Bass, pp. 294–320 (p. 303). Reprinted with permission by John Wiley and Sons
Limited.

new experiences. Often managers encounter a mixture of customs, norms, beliefs, and
attitudes across a wide range of situations and circumstances. The physical environment
itself is likely to be quite different, with differing climate, terrain, and weather.
Additionally, there will be new foods and beverages to sample and adjust to. Possibly
there will be a new language to learn. Most importantly, there will be a new position with
new colleagues, new reporting relationships, and new responsibilities and demands.

The quality of experiences is likely to be richer and deeper than in previous,
noninternational assignments. Moreover, managers are likely to pay greater attention to
and reflect longer on these experiences because their expectations about anticipated
outcomes are more likely to be undermet or overmet in overseas assignments (Black *et
al.* 1991). Additionally, mistakes and failures are likely to be more frequent (Mendenhall
2001b), leading managers to reevaluate core assumptions about themselves, about others,
and about their work context. Managers may also find they experience unexpected
successes (ibid.).

The heightened quality of experience, with its attendant amplified attention and deeper
reflection, in turn increases the probability that individuals will experience greater

knowledge creation. In other words, international assignments spur knowledge creation, particularly around self-knowledge, because they evoke stronger affective reactions than other types of assignments (Mendenhall 2001b). The knowledge creation may be further enhanced because of the heightened emotional impact that international assignment experiences often carry.

International assignments can be characterized as infrequent events that provide managers with significant opportunities and material for tacit knowledge creation. No doubt this explains why Osland (1995) characterizes international assignments as transformative experiences for many managers. For many, the experiences of an international assignment have no comparable counterpart in prior work they have done. It is this poignancy of experience – the extent of variety, the depth of quality, and the intense emotionality – that may also help explain why research on global leadership development has emphasized the importance of international assignments, but has had difficulty in understanding how best to study the knowledge acquired through those experiences.

## Application to global leadership development

International assignments associated with global leadership development possess unique properties when viewed through the lens of knowledge creation. This section considers those distinctive properties and explores their implications.

## Syntactic and semantic issues

Work experiences have both a syntactic and a semantic aspect, to borrow two terms from linguistics. Syntax refers to the structure of a sentence; semantics to its meaning. Human resource managers must consider both the structure of work experiences and their meaning if international assignments are to lead to significant knowledge creation beneficial to global leadership development and the overall competitiveness of the firm. Syntactic dimensions of work experience include such things as the duration of the assignment, the sequencing of assignments, and the structure of assignments. There are several important issues to consider here.

The duration of international assignments may often be established arbitrarily. Short-term assignments of nine months or less are usually based on the completion of a particular task or project, while long-term assignments often follow a standard length of two to three years. In setting the length of the assignment, there is frequently little regard for the impact on knowledge acquisition or dissemination (Black *et al.* 1999a). Clearly, not all international assignments are alike in terms of the variety, quality, and intensity of experience they provide, which means that the knowledge creation process may vary in length as well. For example, similar cultures, similar legal regulations, and a common language may make it possible for a US manager to quickly learn how to get a new subsidiary fully operational in New Zealand. That same manager might take considerably longer to accomplish the same feat in China. The difference is not solely one of culture, language, and/or legal regulations, but also involves the acquisition of the right sorts of experiences that will allow useful new knowledge to be created. In a related vein, whether a particular culture is characterized by high- or low-context communication preferences may influence, in turn, whether the most effective knowledge creation methods will be tacit or explicit (Dulek and Fielden 1991). Chinese culture is characterized by a communication style in which much of the message is embedded in the situation rather than in explicit written documents or verbal exchanges (Hall 1966). US managers in China may need to acquire a substantial range of local experiences before they are able to accurately make sense of what is going on around them. In China the most effective knowledge-creation type early in the assignment may be the tacit-to-tacit exchange – socialization – whereby a newly arriving manager works closely with a local Chinese manager or experienced expatriate. That same manager when assigned to Australia may be able to create knowledge through combination (explicit-to-explicit), as the US manager and local counterparts share their understanding of plant setup and management.

Sequence is another issue that human resource managers should consider when using international assignments in developing global business leaders. Gunz (1989) suggests that although many large organizations carry out career planning to identify logical sequencing of positions and promotions for managerial personnel, the knowledge creation process does not factor into that planning. An international assignment may be appropriate as the next step on a career path headed to the top of the organization, but inappropriate for moving a manager through the next phase of the knowledge creation cycle or providing a manager with the right type of experiences. For example, after eighteen months in a domestic department where he focused on mortgaged-based securities, one manager at a US investment bank was transferred to Tokyo, where his new position was to oversee a Japanese securities trading operation. There was little, if any, room within the new assignment for internalization of knowledge acquired in the previous position.

Disruption in the knowledge creation process may also occur upon repatriation (Gupta and Govindarajan 1991; Black *et al.* 1999a; Stroh 1995), particularly if personnel in the receiving unit are not open to the experiences of the repatriate. Adler (2002) calls this the "xenophobic response," wherein colleagues' and supervisors' fear and rejection of the foreign knowledge that repatriates contribute subsequently constrain the transfer of knowledge. Many firms find it difficult to access, with any depth of understanding, what a manager has learned or to position the manager so that foreign experiences can be effectively used in broader knowledge-creation activities. The case of the American manager returning from Germany that opened this chapter provides an obvious instance of disruption of the knowledge-creation process and also of a firm's inability to tap into or transfer knowledge.

It is ironic that, although firms send managers on international assignment to get experience that will lead to knowledge acquisition in a wide variety of ways, many firms seem incapable of appreciating how successful they have been, often underestimating the growth in knowledge that managers have experienced. Repatriates report that work takes on broader significance. Moreover, they have a changed perspective of their role within the firm and within the world, as well as a changed understanding of where the firm fits in the world.

## Employee transformation

There are three aspects of international assignment experiences that help to explain the significant transformations managers may undergo. The commingling of work and nonwork experiences, common to both short and long-term assignments, often lead to learning and insight about oneself, one's family, global business, and the world in general. In turn, these insights inevitably extend to a changed view of the work setting, the meaning of work, and the nature of the organization. Short-term assignments that do not include the relocation of the family, but which include extended absences or the development of local social support systems, may also lead to a new perspective on work, the company, and larger "purpose of life" issues. Oddou (2002) gives a fairly comprehensive list of the transformations expatriates usually experience.

A second aspect of international assignments that influences transformation is the compression into a short span of time of myriad novel, intense, significantly different experiences. Compression of so many powerful experiences may lead to a proliferation of new mental maps, an explosive increase in the repertoire of schemata and scripts for dealing with a multitude of commonplace and not-so-commonplace events. Typical of this phenomenon in a more superficial way is the matter of the proper way to greet people in a business setting. Prior to an international assignment in Japan, a typical US manager would probably employ a handshake as the most common form of greeting and introduction. After working in Japan for several months or years, that same manager would return home with an expanded set of greetings and introductions that would now include bows of various depths and rigidity as well as handshakes of varying strength and duration.

Other transformations can relate to very deep-seated values or attitudes. For example, an expatriate in Vietnam was having a conversation with a Vietnamese colleague one day. The Vietnamese colleague asked him how he, the expatriate, could support the US president with respect to the war in Iraq. When asked to clarify, the Vietnamese colleague said that the expatriate's president was responsible for killing civilians, just like Saddam Hussein. Neither one was better than the other, the Vietnamese colleague stated. This perspective was a completely new one for the expatriate. He had always defined whether something was good or bad on the basis of the results or the intent. The Vietnamese colleague, however, represented a cultural viewpoint that intent counted for nothing if the results were not also good. Although this example was not readily applicable to the expatriate's job in a tangible way, the ability to understand a very different perspective enabled him to better accept that there are other views of events that he had never questioned. Such increased mental flexibility is a valuable characteristic to acquire for any businessperson, but is particularly important for global leaders (Black *et al.* 1999b).

*Table 7.1* Repatriate resource capabilities and application potential

| Resource type | New resource capabilities | Application value |
|---|---|---|
| Cognitive | • New global knowledge (of foreign operations, interdependencies, etc.)<br>• New broader and different perspectives or worldview<br>• Increased ability to conceptualize diverse information<br>• Increased cognitive complexity | • Understanding of the foreign culture<br>• Understanding of the foreign operation<br>• Clearer and more accurate worldview<br>• Personal understanding of the interdependencies of global business operations |
| Relational | • New sources of information (e.g., people contacts)<br>• New quality or depth of relationships | • Names of individuals in the foreign operation (internal to the firm and those external – politicians, community leaders, other firms' personnel) that can be sources for gathering information more efficiently and accurately<br>• Favor-granting relationships with individuals in the foreign operation (internal to the firm and those external – politicians, community leaders, other firms' personnel) that can be helpful in exploiting opportunities and defending against threats |
| Attitudinal | • Increased self-efficacy | • More initiating behavior<br>• Greater self-reliance when necessary<br>• Increased sense of "can-do-it" |
| Behavioral | Managerial skills:<br>• More effective communication skills<br>• More effective motivation skills<br>• More effective planning skills<br>• More effective organizing skills | • Greater ability to consider diversity in planning tasks<br>• Greater understanding of different communication styles<br>• Better understanding of and ability to manage or work with people with different motivations |

Because many, if not most, firms do not view repatriate knowledge as a valuable resource or competitive advantage, such gains can be of little consequence to the firm. In fact, repatriates report that firms seldom take a strategic perspective when positioning them upon return (Downes and Thomas 1999; Forster 1999; Harzing 2001), reducing the chances that their hard-earned knowledge will be applicable to their new situation. A case study of a Spanish bank revealed that the bank showed little interest in what repatriates learned abroad; repatriates felt their knowledge was "undervalued or not wanted at all" (Bonache and Brewster 2001: 159). Upon reentry, repatriates typically do not get to use much of the knowledge acquired on foreign assignments (Harvey 1989; Osland 1995; Stroh and Caligiuri 1997). However, a recent study of Japanese repatriates found that those who were able to transfer the global competencies they learned abroad reported higher levels of commitment (Furuya et al. 2005). Repatriates are often dissatisfied with their reentry, and their turnover rate is much higher than that of their domestic counterparts (Black and Gregersen 1999; Price Waterhouse 1997; Stroh et al. 1998). If they resign, firms lose repatriate knowledge assets, most likely to a competitor.

These losses are of the types discussed earlier. *Knowing who* losses may occur as some friendships, acquaintances, and relationship networks wane. *Knowing what* losses may take place as a manager's knowledge of some products and services or specific aspects of some organizational arrangements are forgotten, become outdated, or are no longer relevant. As a manager's identification with the firm shifts or changes, understanding of what is relevant or strategic may be lost. Finally, the move to a new position and new responsibility may result in less practice and application of well-developed skills so that knowledge of certain techniques or the ability to use some skills may wither. In short, international assignments are a time of knowledge growth and development, but also loss and decay.

The failure on the part of firms to value and actively draw out repatriate knowledge greatly limits its successful transfer. Repatriates in Berthoin Antal's (2001) study identified the three major barriers. First, a lack of interest and the absence of processes or structures to communicate knowledge hindered the dissemination of repatriate knowledge. Second, the lack of a global mindset in the parent firm, coupled with a lack of real dedication to being multinational, constituted another set of barriers. However, failure to assign repatriates to jobs that utilized their international expertise was perhaps the most significant obstacle. Thus, she recommends adding another stage to the expatriation–repatriation process – knowledge sharing – that would occur after reentry and involve an active knowledge management process (ibid.).

In the following section we will explore those variables that it is important to address in order to facilitate the transfer of repatriate knowledge. Although researchers have suggested HR tools that could facilitate repatriate knowledge transfer (Lazarova and Tarique 2005; Tsang 1999), we actually know very little about the conditions under which repatriate knowledge might be captured by the firm.

Scholars have complained that our knowledge of how organizations manage their personnel lacks good conceptual underpinning (Kochan et al. 1992; Welch 1994), which is certainly true for repatriate knowledge transfer.

# A communication perspective on the repatriate knowledge transfer process

Transferring information is a type of communication process – whether explicit or tacit. In the explicit communication of knowledge, the repatriate can write the information down and pass it along to others, for example. With tacit knowledge, although the repatriate might not write information down, he or she acts in such a way that the information can be observed, and therefore communicated and captured. It is useful, then, to use as a basic framework the early work that Shannon and Weaver (1949) did on the components of a basic communication model. This approach has precedence in light of researchers who have used a communication model to study knowledge or information flows in other contexts (Bryant and Nguyen 2002; Gupta and Govindarajan 2000). Further, Minbaeva's (2005) literature review noted that the knowledge transfer process in MNCs is affected by the characteristics of the knowledge (the message), the knowledge sources and transferors (the sender), the recipients (the receiver), and their relationship (the context). The nature of the knowledge (explicit or tacit) to be transferred is, of course, an important part of the transfer process. This has previously been addressed in earlier sections of this chapter. The following discussion will focus on the rest of the communication model. The research work by Oddou, Osland and Blakeney (Oddou and Osland 2003; Osland *et al.* 2005; Blakeney *et al.* 2006a, b; Oddou *et al.* in press) provides the principal basis for this discussion.

## Repatriate characteristics

First, there is an assumption that the repatriate is already motivated to transfer the learning acquired from the international experience. Such motivation can be related to personal career interests, i.e., self-centered (Lazarova and Tarique 2005). For example, a repatriate who is focusing on a promotion or other organizational reward is more likely to want to look for opportunities to improve the organization. Another important motivation where similar behaviors are manifested is personal commitment to the firm, i.e., other-centered (Meyer and Allen 1997). Certainly, however, the *degree of motivation* is also a variable that must be considered.

### Ability to transfer knowledge

The other major repatriate "characteristic" is the repatriate's ability to transfer knowledge. Variables that have traditionally been viewed as relating to the ability to influence include one's perceived competence or expertise (Cross and Prusak 2003; French and Raven 1959). The greater the perceived expertise of the individual, the more potential influence he or she can have. The social networks of which one is a member (Boisot 1998) is also a factor. Au and Fukuda (2002) found that individuals who held boundary-spanning roles (i.e., were members of social networks) had more organizational power than those who did not. Certainly, the repatriate who is in a project management position and interacting regularly with six or seven people from different areas has the potential to exert more influence than a repatriate who returns as an outside salesperson working primarily with external clients. In addition, the actual position one has and how it might be related to the acquired knowledge the repatriate has obtained is important. For example, Berthoin Antal (2001) found that when reentry jobs have international dimensions and are similar to the foreign assignment, the repatriates' knowledge is more relevant to their work and to their coworkers.

## Firm characteristics

### People

Firms are composed of people and systems. Therefore, it is important to address both aspects when considering knowledge transfer. The people who are most in contact with the repatriate are those who are more likely to allow or encourage or otherwise accept and apply the knowledge of the repatriate. Some of the more important aspects about these individuals that relate to knowledge transfer include (1) the relevance of the repatriate's knowledge that the repatriate's colleagues perceive for their work milieus (Zander and Kogut 1995), (2) colleagues' openness to learning new information in general (Berthoin Antal 2001), and (3) how collaborative the work culture is and the nature of the leadership style of the repatriate's manager (Politis 2001).

### Systems

Organizations have systems that include policies and procedures, as well as informal routines created by their organizational culture. These "routines" affect the organization's ability to absorb information (Zahra and George 2002). More than likely, such routines are a reflection of the attitudes of the members of the organization. Gold *et al.* (2001) found that organizations that reflected the importance of continuous improvement, experimentation, and openness to new ideas were related to learning organizations. Organizational routines need to be created around these activities.

## Shared context

When the repatriate returns to the company and is given a particular work setting, the repatriate and colleagues in that work setting share a context. How the individual and the organization share that context is meaningful for the transfer of knowledge (Wood 1997). Kodama (2005b) refers to this as shared space and argues that it is necessary in order to create a context for knowledge creation. Although not a physical space, it is a space in which ideas can be exchanged, discussed, and possibly applied. Such a space is created from trust. Trust between two parties is critical in knowledge transfer (Andrews and Delahaye 2000; Argote *et al.* 2003), and creates a consistent atmosphere of openness in a knowledge market (Cross and Prusak 2003).

## Implications for knowledge transfer

Based on our understanding of what variables affect knowledge transfer, a number of things can be done to enhance this process:

1 Firms can attempt to create more strategic planning around the careers of their international assignees. In fact, this might start in the selection of the assignee, ensuring that the knowledge to be gained in the foreign assignment is strategic to the employee's growth and the firm's needs. This will create continuity in the knowledge-creation process.

2 Firms can institute, as a few do, debriefing sessions where the repatriate gives a debriefing to the firm upon return, explaining what was learned and experienced, what networks were developed that might be of use, etc.

3 Firms can also create knowledge-sharing sessions around themes. Such sessions can be carried out during the lunch hour, and company sponsored. Themes can be country focused or issue focused. Doing these kinds of things creates routines in the organization that facilitate knowledge transfer and absorption.

4 Firms can train the managers of repatriates about the issues surrounding reacculturation and culture shock so as to facilitate the repatriate's return and resocialization process into a new work culture. Doing so will likely increase the repatriate's personal commitment to the firm and also allow opportunities to discuss experiences and learning.

5 Firms could incorporate the inclusion of a "back-home project" in which the expatriate, as a transition back to the home country and organization, is given a relevant project to work on before actually returning from the foreign assignment. This might allow more opportunities to transfer learning as well as better prepare the expatriate for network development and socialization.

## Conclusion

In conclusion, today's world of global business requires that companies must "innovate by learning from the world" (Doz *et al.* 2001: 1). Today's economy is often referred to as a knowledge economy, knowledge that firms must recognize, capture, and manage in order to create a sustainable competitive advantage (Inkpen 1998). Exposure to new ideas and business practices as well as foreign cultures and markets via international assignments contributes to the creation of knowledge that can be used to build and sustain competitive advantage (Tallman and Fladmoe-Lindquist 2002) and transform individuals in ways that make them more valuable employees of the organization (Oddou and Mendenhall 1991; Osland 1995).

The motivation and ability of the repatriate to transfer the knowledge acquired in the international assignment combined with the ability and interest of the firm to learn and apply new information are keys to the transfer process. Without such transfer, the ability to build and sustain a competitive advantage is less realizable. Firms can do a number of things to increase the likelihood of knowledge transfer, including selecting the appropriate person to take the foreign work experience, training their managers to understand the personal challenges these individuals experience upon return, and creating organizational routines that will create a knowledge-sharing environment.

# Leading global change

JOYCE S. OSLAND

> There is no more delicate matter to take in hand, nor more dangerous to conduct, nor more doubtful in its success, than to be a leader in the introduction of changes. For he who innovates will have for enemies all those who are well off under the old order of things, and only lukewarm supporters in those who might be better off under the new.
>
> (Machiavelli, *The Prince*, trans. N. H. Thomson)

> We have to be willing to cannibalize what we're doing today in order to ensure our leadership in the future. It's counter to human nature, but you have to kill your business while it is still working.
>
> (Lew Platt, former CEO of Hewlett-Packard)

Leadership professor Jim Clawson believes that being a leader boils down to one's point of view, rather than one's title or status (2006: 4). In his opinion, the leadership point of view has three elements: "(1) seeing what needs to be done; (2) understanding all the underlying forces at play in a situation; and (3) having the courage to initiate action to make things better" (ibid.: 6). This chapter is all about making organizations better and making a difference. One can readily argue that it is more difficult to see what needs to be done on a global level and understand all the underlying forces in a more complex setting. It is undoubtedly more problematic to successfully change the mindset and behavior of followers and partners who come from diverse cultural and organizational backgrounds. Global leaders face the arduous task of steering the change efforts and aligning extremely large and far-flung multinational corporations. While leading and managing change is always challenging, no matter where it takes place, we make the assumption that it is more difficult in a global setting. That said, global leaders are in a position to have a broad impact with their ideas and to foster the agility, innovation, and rapid learning capacity crucial to business survival and success.

In this chapter we shall talk about the universal aspects of managing change as well as the factors that seem particularly important in global change efforts. Since innovation and change go hand in hand, we will describe how global leaders can promote and lead innovation. To understand the context in which global change occurs, we shall begin by summarizing the cultural differences that influence change and innovation.

## The role of culture in change

Change interventions that work in one country do not always succeed elsewhere (Faucheux *et al.* 1982; Weick and Quinn 1999). To avoid failure, several cultural factors should be taken into consideration in global change efforts. Culture affects not only the predisposition to change but how change itself is viewed and implemented.

Cultures vary in their beliefs about how change occurs (Bartlett and Ghoshal 2000). When most European and Japanese companies want to make a change, they follow this process: (1) focus on changing the attitudes and mentalities of their key people; (2) modify the flow of communication and decision-making processes; and (3) consolidate the changes by realigning the structure to mirror the changes that have already occurred. US companies, however, take a different approach, based on different assumptions about change. They begin by modifying the organizational structures with the hope that a new structure will cause changes in interpersonal relationships and processes, leading eventually to changes in individual attitudes and mentalities. Bartlett and Ghoshal (2000) note, however, that these different national biases seem to be disappearing as global companies learn different approaches from one another.

There is not extensive research on cultural differences and global change. We can, however, infer from the research on culture the likely impact of certain cultural beliefs and values. Table 8.1 summarizes the cultural value dimensions that seem to influence predisposition to change.

Cultures vary in their level of comfort with change and whether they see change as basically positive or negative. Cultures that have a preference for order and are high in uncertainty avoidance should be more likely to avoid change and the risks that it entails. Cultures that strongly avoid uncertainty are less comfortable with ambiguity and risk (Hofstede 1980b). For this reason, it is helpful to clearly delineate the change process for them so they know what to expect at each stage. Members of cultures characterized by flexibility and low uncertainty avoidance, should be more open to change. Because of its history, change is highly valued in the United States.

> In the Old World respect came from a valuable heritage, and any change from that norm had to be justified. In America, however, the *status quo* was no more than the temporary product of past changes, and it was the resistance to change that demanded an explanation. A failure to change with the times was more than just a private misfortune; it was a socially and organizationally subversive condition. This attitude still persists in America, particularly in the corporate world.
>
> (Bridges 1995: 20)

It may explain, in part, why some U.S. firms go on to launch repeated change projects without first ensuring that previous projects are completely implemented.

Kluckhohn and Strodtbeck (1961) categorized cultures according to their perspective on time as either past-, present-, or future-oriented. Future-oriented cultures are seen as

*Table 8.1* Cultural dimensions related to change

| More disposed to change | Less disposed to change |
| --- | --- |
| • Low uncertainty avoidance | • High uncertainty avoidance |
| • Flexibility | • Order |
| • Mastery | • Harmony |
| • Future oriented | • Past oriented |
| • Internal locus of control | • External locus of control |
| • Human nature as mutable | • Human nature as immutable |

*Factors that influence implementation*

1 Human nature as trustworthy vs. untrustworthy
2 Low or high power distance
3 Importance of hierarchy
4 Communication styles
5 National history

being more open to both change and innovation because their focus lies on the need to adapt to what is coming next. We usually expect more resistance to change in cultures that value the past and tradition. Historical precedent receives more attention than innovations. In past-oriented cultures, managers are expected to be less proactive about making changes, and change processes may take more time (Osland 2004).

The same is true of cultures that believe people are at the mercy of uncontrollable forces rather than masters of their own destiny. Cultures whose members are characterized by external focus of control (also called outer-oriented) believe that other forces, such as fate or luck, control one's destiny (Rotter 1966; Hampden-Turner and Trompenaars 2000). Accordingly, we would expect them to be less likely to initiate change or to be highly proactive in their strategy and planning efforts. Employees may not be held personally accountable for accomplishing changes since this is not viewed as completely within their own control. In contrast, cultures whose members believe that people control their own destiny, having an internal locus of control (also called inner-oriented), tend to take matters into their own hands and are more likely to see themselves as change agents.

A culture's relationship with its environment can impact the target of change. Do those living in a particular culture believe in mastering the environment or living in harmony with it (Kluckhohn and Strodtbeck 1961)? Cultures with a preference toward mastery are generally more dynamic, competitive, and likely to use technology to change the environment and accomplish their goals. They are more likely to dam rivers to obtain hydroelectric power than to refrain out of concerns about upsetting the delicate balance of nature by altering the river. The latter is more characteristic of cultures that value harmony with nature. Rather than changing the environment, they believe in understanding and working with it.

Another change target-related cultural difference is rooted in beliefs about human nature. Cultures see humans as either mutable (capable of change) or immutable (incapable of change) (Kluckhohn and Strodtbeck 1961). In cultures where human nature is viewed as immutable or unchangeable, there may be less confidence that change projects involving new behaviors and mindsets are feasible. People within such cultures are more likely to subscribe to the belief that "You can't teach an old (or even young) dog new tricks." By contrast, members of cultures who believe that human nature is mutable will likely put more faith in training and behavioral change.

A related view of human nature can affect the change implementation process. Kluckhohn and Strodtbeck (1961) differentiated between cultures that saw humans as basically good, mixed, or evil. We believe it is more helpful to characterize this dimension as trustworthy versus untrustworthy and associate it with the length of time needed to build trust in different cultures. In cultures where human nature is viewed as basically good, or trustworthy, trust in general comes more quickly. In cultures that believe human nature is basically evil, or untrustworthy, it takes longer to build trust. Since trust in leaders and change agents is essential in change projects, it seems logical that trusting cultures may be quicker to go along with change projects and assume that the leader has the best interests of the organization in mind. In cultures that see humans as untrustworthy, we hypothesize that it will take longer to build trust and commitment to the change, unless the leader already enjoys the followers' trust.

Power is another cultural factor that can influence the change process. High power distance cultures accept that power is distributed unequally, whereas low power distance cultures believe in equality and a more even distribution of power (Hofstede 1980b). Power distance values can determine who is invited to the table to provide input and plan the change and who will lead the change. Will egalitarian values hold sway or will only those at the very top of the organization be involved in planning and leading change? Schwartz (1994) noted that in hierarchical cultures, the social fabric is maintained by a hierarchical structure of ascribed roles. Any change that disturbs this hierarchy by changing the roles or the distribution of power could be viewed as threatening and a source of resistance to change.

Participation and equality and power sharing are among the core values of organization development (OD) consulting, which leads organizations through planned change. These values are congruent with low power distance but not high power distance. In low power distance cultures, participation is generally the best way to allow employees to feel some sense of ownership of the change process and thereby reduce resistance to change. They can then see themselves as architects of the change rather than as victims. Employees from cultures characterized by high power distance, however, are more likely to expect leaders to make decisions without their input and are less satisfied when empowerment programs are put in place. Research found less satisfaction resulting from empowerment in high power distance Asian cultures than in low power distance Canada (Eylon and Au 1999) and again in high power distance India compared with the United States, Poland, and Mexico (Robert et al. 2000).

Communication differences should also be considered in change projects. Style differences can prevent people from accurately perceiving, analyzing, and decoding intercultural communication. People in collectivist cultures are more likely to encounter situations in which there is a preference for high-context, indirect, and self-effacing (modest) communication and silence (Ting-Toomey 1999). They show greater concern for saving face and not standing out from the group (e.g., the Japanese saying, "The nail that sticks up is hammered down"). In contrast, people in individualistic cultures are more likely to encounter situations characterized by a preference for low-context, direct, and self-enhancing communication and talkativeness (ibid.). These communication styles are defined in Table 8.2. One can readily imagine change-related situations in which

*Table 8.2* Communication style differences

| | |
|---|---|
| Low versus high context | Pertains to the extent to which language is used to communicate the message. **Low context**: relies on explicit verbal messages to convey intention or meaning. The onus lies on the speaker to send a clear, easily decoded message. (Examples: Germany, Switzerland, United States) **High context**: relies mostly on information contained in the physical context or internalized in the person. The onus lies on the listener to "read" meaning into the message. (Examples: Asia, Latin America) |
| Direct versus indirect | Pertains to the extent to which language and tone of voice reveal or hide the speaker's intent. **Direct**: speakers specify their intentions in forthright statements. (Examples: Western cultures) **Indirect**: speakers hide their meaning in nuances in their verbal statements. (Examples: Eastern and Middle Eastern cultures, most of Latin America) |
| Self-effacing versus self-enhancing | Pertains to how one refers to one's effort or performance. **Self-effacing**: emphasizes the importance of humbling oneself via verbal restraints, hesitations, modest talk, and the use of self-deprecation. (Examples: Asian cultures) **Self-enhancing**: emphasizes the importance of boasting about or drawing attention to one's accomplishments and abilities. (Examples: Arab, African-American) |
| Silence | Pertains to the meaning of silence. **Silence conveys a message**. It can mean respect for someone of a higher status, careful consideration of the speaker's words, displeasure of a child's behavior, harmony, etc. (Examples: China, Japan, Korea) **Silence has no meaning**. Therefore, it is usually filled with words (Examples: Latin America, United States) |

Source: Based on research by Ting-Toomey, S. (1999) *Communicating Across Cultures*. New York: Guilford Press.

global leaders would want to communicate their vision and receive input and feedback without running the risk in misunderstandings due to cultural communication problems.

Global leaders should also consider national history in change efforts. Countries that have sovereignty issues, for instance, can be particularly sensitive to changes imposed by a foreign headquarters. Hungary's political structure and state-owned companies exert a strong influence on views of change and its implementation, and one can expect special considerations in managing change in transition economies (Fehér and Szigeti 2001).

We have a few caveats about culture. There are still other cultural values, unique to a specific culture, that could influence change efforts. The value dimensions in Table 8.1 can provide us with the "first best guess" (Adler and Gundersen 2007) about the preferences, and behavioral predispositions of another culture with regard to change, but they require more research and will never predict cultural behavior with total accuracy. For one thing, they describe modal preferences and there are many individual differences within cultures. Second, cultures are much more complex than these value dimensions convey; other factors can trump these values in specific contexts (Osland and Bird 2000). These cultural value dimensions should, however, be on a global leader's radar screen whenever organizational change is under discussion.

Is culture an insurmountable obstacle to change? No. It is possible to work around and leverage cultural beliefs and values. For example, you can empower employees to implement change in a high power distance culture when the change is tied to other values in the culture. Total Quality Management (TQM) was successfully implemented in Morocco because authority figures were used as role models and TQM was linked to Islamic values and norms (Gelfand *et al.* 2007). Without a deep knowledge of the culture, it would not have been possible to leverage them. In a Central American TQM project the general manager absented himself from key problem-solving meetings so that senior managers would more openly share their opinions; if he were present, they would have deferred to him unquestioningly. He was wise enough to realize that this modification was necessary in a culture with high power distance (Osland 1996). While expert leaders understand and respect cultural constraints, they also know when and how to get around them. Percy Barnevik described this expertise in an interview:

> Global mangers have exceptionally open minds. They respect how different countries do things, and they have the imagination to appreciate why they do them that way. But they are also incisive, they push the limits of the culture. Global managers don't passively accept it when someone says, "You can't do that in Italy or Spain because of the unions," or "You can't do that in Japan because of the Ministry of Finance." They sort through the debris of cultural excuses and find opportunities to innovate.
>
> (Champy and Nohria 1996a: 67)

To do so, global leaders may have to adapt their own change-related behavior to match the cultural scripts used in different locations, find ways to leverage cultural differences, and contextualize the change in ways that are appropriate for different cultures. We will discuss contextualization later in the chapter.

## Introduction to change management

Change management, which is based on knowledge of behavior science, is a concerted, planned effort to increase organizational effectiveness and health. It involves an intentional and structured transition to a desired end state. Organizational change is usually categorized in terms of magnitude as either incremental or transformative. Incremental change (also known as first-order change) is linear, continuous, and targeted at fixing or modifying problems or procedures. Transformative change (also called second-order change or gamma change) modifies the fundamental structure, systems, orientation, and strategies of the organization (Burke and Litwin 1992). Transformative change is radical, generally multidimensional and multilevel, and involves discontinuous shifts in mental or organizational frameworks. To borrow Wilbur's (1983) analogy, whereas incremental change is analogous to rearranging the furniture in a room to make it more comfortable or functional, transformative change questions whether this is even the room or floor where we should be. Given the complexities of global organizations, Champy and Nohria (1996a) contend that incrementalism is a luxury that businesses can no longer afford; to avoid falling behind, they recommend radical change and moving ahead quickly.

## Change process models

The process of change is often viewed in terms of unfreezing, moving, and refreezing (Lewin 1947). *Unfreezing* entails overcoming inertia and developing a new mindset. This stage is accompanied by stress, tension, and, once people's defense mechanisms have been breached, a strongly felt need for change. In the *moving* stage, the change begins, which involves relinquishing old ways of behavior and testing out new behaviors, values, and attitudes that usually have been proposed by a respected source. As one would expect, this stage is characterized by confusion. *Refreezing* occurs when the new behavior is reinforced, internalized, and institutionalized or, to the contrary, rejected and abandoned. Whatever the outcome, this stage represents a sense of returned equilibrium.

In a study of multinational organizations, the change process was described as follows: *incubation* (questioning the status quo), *variety generation* (middle-up experimentation) leading to *power shifts* (change in the leadership structure), and then the process of *refocusing* (Doz and Prahalad 1987). In another study, Ghoshal and Bartlett (1996) observed the following sequential and overlapping process – *simplification, integration, and regeneration* – in successful large-scale strategic transformations at General Electric (GE), ABB, Lufthansa, Motorola, and AT&T. Simplification involves a more laser-like change focus that clarified the strategy, such as GE's "being number one or two in the industry." In the integration phase, shared values and realigned cross-unit relationships bring people together. Welch's focus on interunit collaboration and the sharing of best practices in GE is a good example of integration. In regeneration, the last phase, efforts are made to build an organization that is capable of renewing itself. This was the purpose of Welch's "boundarylessness" push at GE (Ghoshal and Bartlett 1996).

Kotter and Cohen (2002) provide a more detailed breakdown of the sequential stages in the change process used in successful change efforts:

1 *Increase urgency.* Unfreeze occurs by demonstrating the need for change with undeniable evidence, something that people can see, touch, and feel that touches their emotions.
2 *Build the guiding team.* A group powerful enough to guide the change is created and teambuilding is used to build a trusting, effective team.
3 *Get the vision right.* The guiding creates a succinct, inspiring, moving, and appropriate vision for the future.
4 *Communicate for buy-in.* The change is communicated in ways that are simple and heartfelt and that take into consideration the feelings of those who will be affected.
5 *Empower action.* Obstacles are removed from their path so that more people feel able to contribute their efforts to the change and are rewarded for doing so.
6 *Create short-term wins.* Easy, visible, and early successes build momentum, lessening the likelihood of resistance and increasing the support of powerful players.
7 *Don't let up.* People make wave after wave of change, tackling ever more difficult challenges until the vision is realized.
8 *Make change stick.* Change is institutionalized by the organizational culture, storytelling, promoting change heroes, socializing new recruits, and ensuring continuity.

One of the most important contributions of this model is Kotter and Cohen's (2002) finding that leaders have to include the emotional aspects of change to be successful. For example, building a rational business case for change is not enough. The feelings that block change require incontrovertible evidence that touches people's emotions and helps them feel the need for urgency.

Not everyone views change as an orderly progression, in part because they view the reality of change as more haphazard and dependent on luck and circumstance. Some describe change as a "strategic layering" process, in which firms continuously build capabilities in response to environmental demands (Evans and Doz 1989). Another school of thought views change as a spiral process. Management teams focus on a change initiative until it looks as if they might be going too far in that direction. Then, to avoid the pathologies that could result from the initial change effort, they switch their focus to something else (Evans et al. 2002). The top management team of a firm in the midst of decentralizing, for example, may switch its attention to integration mechanisms when decentralization begins to cause too many coordination problems. When the integration mechanisms begin to look too cumbersome, they will spiral on to another focus.

Unlike change in a single location or operations in a single country, global change involves a broader range of action. This means that global leaders have to anticipate changes to a greater degree. The process of looking ahead to predict future needs and adjustments is called anticipatory sequencing (Evans and Doz 1989). The challenge of building the future into the present is daunting, as noted in the epitaph for a change agent, "How are you supposed to change the tires on a car when it's going at 60 miles per hour?"

Table 8.3 summarizes basic lessons about successful domestic and international organizational change.

*Table 8.3* Common lessons about change

*Leadership*

- There has to be a vision for the change so that people have a purpose to believe in.
- Top management support for planned change, or at least benign neglect, is crucial.
- In addition to top management support, there needs to be a "critical mass" – the smallest number of people or groups who must be committed to a change for it to occur.
- Thoughtful management of resistance to change is the responsibility of change leaders.
- The more discretion managers have, the more changes they will make.
- Leaders of change have to be self-aware.
- Leaders have to be role models for the change.

*Communication*

- The end result of the change must be clearly communicated so people are willing to leave behind what they know for something new.
- It is almost impossible to "overcommunicate" a change – people need to hear about it several times in a variety of mediums before the message is accurately received.

*Trust*

- Lasting change won't happen unless there is a sufficient level of trust within the organization.

*Context*

- Change almost always requires reexamining and rethinking the assumptions people hold about the environment, the way the organization functions, and their working relationships with other people. There is often a mourning period before people can let go of the way things used to be.
- Change requires new assumptions, attitudes, behaviors, and skills, which must eventually be institutionalized so the change can endure.
- Constant change is a source of stress for employees, so organizations have to balance both change and continuity.

*Tactics*

- Since tactics that work in one part of the organization cannot always be transferred successfully to another area, standardized change efforts may not be possible.
- Multiple interventions are necessary; one is seldom sufficient.

*Table 8.3 Continued*

- People have to possess the skills required by the change, which may necessitate training.
- Evaluation and incentive systems have to support the change and reward the desired behaviors.
- Changing one element in a system will not work unless we bring all the other elements into alignment to support the change.

*Implementation process*

- Change is a process rather than an event or a managerial edict.
- A good idea is not enough – the change process has to be skillfully managed for implementation to be effective.
- The change process occurs in multiple steps that cannot be bypassed.
- While there are linear steps in planned change, implementation is seldom linear.
- Changes require a fertile context – an organizational culture with values and norms that complement the change and a climate of renewal and growth.
- Changes need time to take root.
- Change is hard to sustain; some innovations succeed initially, but conditions eventually revert to their previous state.
- Change requires perseverance.
- There are costs associated with any change, and we can expect a predictable slump in performance before a successful change starts to show results.

*Resistance*

- Resistance is a natural response to change.
- Three common types of resistance are blind, ideological, or political resistance.
- Changes often upset the political system in organizations and come into conflict with the vested interests of people who prefer the status quo.
- Allowing people to participate in some aspect of the change process and educating them about the change are positive ways to reduce resistance.

Sources: Armenakis, A. and Bedeian, A. G. (1999) "Organizational Change: A Review of Theory and Research in the 1990s". *Journal of Management* 25(3): 293–315; Burke, W. W. (2002) "The Organizational Change Leader." In *The Many Facets of Leadership*, Goldsmith, M., Govindarajan, V., Kaye, B., and Vicere, A. (eds.) Upper Saddle Creek, NJ: Financial Times Prentice Hall: 83–97; Cummings, T. C. and Worley, C. G. (2004) *Organization Development and Change*. Cincinnati, OH: Southwestern; Jick, T. and Peiperl, M. (2003) *Managing Change: Cases and Concepts*. Boston: Irwin; and Lawson, E. and Price, C. (2003) "The Psychology of Change Management." *The McKinsey Quarterly*, Special Edition: The Value in Organization: 31–34.

# Global change

Research conducted by Prosci with more than 1,000 organizations from fifty-nine countries shows that people must achieve five building blocks in order for change to be realized successfully. These building blocks, known as the ADKAR model, consist of the following factors (Hiatt 2006):

- *awareness* – of why the change is needed;
- *desire* – to support and participate in the change;
- *knowledge* – of how to change;
- *ability* – to implement new skills and behaviors;
- *reinforcement* – to sustain the change.

There is very little empirical research on global change efforts. Therefore, the research findings in this chapter are supplemented with information from interviews and case studies of global leaders who are successful change agents. These sources indicate that the factors shown in Table 8.4 play an especially important role in global change or have special meaning in a global context (Osland 2004). Many of these are universal change lessons that are equally important in domestic settings.

Some of these factors are present in the following story of change efforts by Paolo Scaroni. Scaroni successfully turned around two firms, Pilkington (a UK glassmaker) and Enel (an Italian electric utility), before taking the CEO position at ENI, an Italian oil and gas company (Ghislanzoni 2006). When asked for his advice on leading change, his answer was to keep things simple and avoid complexity. At Pilkington he built a

*Table 8.4* Key factors in global change

- Leaders as catalysts
- Vision that is clear, motivating and linked to performance goals
- Change message that is easily grasped and repeated
- Building a community and generating trust
- Clear expectations and operationalization of the vision at all organizational levels
- Alignment of organizational design components to complement changes
- Use of teams to drive the change
- Accountability for results at all levels and for units and individuals
- Measurement and evaluation during the process
- High standards of performance
- Results-driven approach
- Reinforcement systems
- Persistence
- Creating a context for change by modifying the organizational culture and establishing vehicles for learning and participation
- Cultural contextualization of the change

community and integrated and centralized finance and purchasing. Scaroni dubbed this "Building One Pilkington" and repeated this message over and over. In another turnaround at Enel he refocused around core competencies to avoid distraction and decrease the problems to a manageable number.

ENI was in good shape when Scaroni took over, but he believes that organizations can always be improved. His challenge was to foster growth and make changes in an organization that did not need to be turned around. The specific change he wanted to make was completing the integration process that would definitively signal ENI's transformation from a holding company.

Scaroni creates a sense of urgency by setting stretch goals that were reinforced by mechanisms like bonuses and the compensation system. When the business environment is intensely competitive, this creates an inherent sense of urgency. In less competitive environments,

> the only thing you can do to create the appropriate sense of urgency is to benchmark yourself against others so you can see what others have been doing and where you should be doing better. Stretch targets are always a good way to get people to improve quickly.
> (Ghislanzoni 2006: 61–62)

Scaroni was asked whether he had employed a different leadership style at Eni than he had at Pilkington or Enel. He answered:

> Not really. I normally try to find three or four strategic concepts that sum up the direction in which the company should be moving, build up an organization that believes in these concepts and repeat, repeat, repeat them throughout the organization. I am convinced that communication is a very powerful tool for running very large organizations such as this one. It works fine if people know exactly where they are going, but in order to know this, they need to be able to grasp some easy concepts. If it takes more than one minute to explain a strategy, something is wrong. In my view, it has to be that simple. Successful things are simple; I have never seen successful things that are very complicated. You provide simple guidelines and then repeat them throughout the organization.
> (ibid.: 59)

Scaroni's strategic goals involve changing both the mindset and the behavior of thousands of employees. While this is the essence of global change, it is never an easy task. The next section describes in greater depth the factors that play a critical role in global change.

## Leaders as catalysts

Kotter (1990c) once stated that leadership, unlike management, is about coping with change. Leaders are catalysts, as we see in BP CEO John Browne's description of how leaders can institutionalize breakthrough thinking:

The top management team must stimulate the organization, not control it. Its role is to provide strategic directives, to encourage learning, and to make sure there are mechanisms for transferring the lessons. The role of leaders at all levels is to demonstrate to people that they are capable of achieving more than they think they can achieve and that they should never be satisfied with where they are now. To change behavior and unleash new ways of thinking, a leader sometimes has to say, "Stop, you're not allowed to do it the old way," and issue a challenge.

(Prokesch 2000: 302–303)

Champy and Nohria (1996b) claim that a leader must possess these personal traits to manage change:

- driven by a higher ambition;
- able to maintain a deep sense of humility;
- committed to a constant search for the truth;
- able to tolerate ambiguity, uncertainty and paradox;
- personally responsible for the consequences of their actions;
- highly disciplined in their everyday lives;
- always authentic.

Most of these characteristics, such as humility, authenticity, inquisitiveness, and cognitive complexity, were identified in Chapter 2's global leadership competency lists. Global leaders have to live with ambiguity and paradox when making changes, because the need to take quick action may preclude the luxury of extensive diagnoses. The results of major changes are seldom completely predictable. Discontinuous thinking and a global mindset help leaders come up with the right change goals and tactics at the right time. Good change agents know that they must first understand and then change people's mental maps in order to implement a change. This involves mindful communication and the ability to engender trust, which rest on authenticity. Finally, the articulation of a vision and the ability to communicate this vision are key competencies for global leaders, as will be seen in the following sections.

## Creating the right vision

The capability that was most valued in a large study of global managers from eight countries was *the ability to articulate a tangible vision, values, and strategy* (Yeung and Ready 1995). The other five capabilities they identified all contribute to successfully managing global change: *being a catalyst for strategic change, being results-oriented, empowering others to do their best, being a catalyst for cultural change*, and *exhibiting a strong customer orientation*. Being close to the customer helps identify the right vision and promote a culture that is open to change. Larry Bossidy, former CEO of Honeywell and Allied Signal, said:

I think that the closer you come to the customers, the more you appreciate the need to change. And the more inwardly focused you are, the less you understand that need. As we get more and more customer focused, we don't have to preach about the need to change. People know it.

(Tichy and Charan 1995: 247–248)

Without a clear vision for global change, employees will not leave "the known" for "the unknown" and change their behavior. Stories from successful global CEOs reveal (1) a clear vision for change that made sense to followers, (2) that they communicated over and over again, (3) accompanied by a blueprint for achieving the vision.

Selecting the right change target depends on the environmental scanning and creative abilities of the global leader and others in the organization. In some firms the top management team or employee groups help with this function, even though leaders are ultimately responsible for ensuring that it takes place and is accurate. Senior management at Nokia assigns five to fifteen themes of critical interest to the firm to cross-functional strategic planning teams involving as many as 400 employees every six months (Gratton and Ghoshal 2005). The teams interview experts inside and outside Nokia and summarize their findings in reports called strategy road maps. As with strategic planning, consensus is building that determining the vision for change should be a participative effort rather than the sole responsibility of one leader.

> Conditions associated with the global economy's new competitive landscape – shorter product life cycles, ever-accelerating rates and type of change, the explosion of data and the need to convert it to useable information – prevent single individuals from having all the insight necessary to chart a firm's direction. . . . Insightful top managers recognize that it is impossible for them to have all of the answers, are willing to learn along with others, and understand that the uncertainty created by the global economy affects people at the top as well as those lower down in the organization.
>
> (Ireland and Hitt 2005: 65)

Change targets should be results driven (e.g., increase market share) rather than activity based (e.g., train 1,000 employees in emotional intelligence). The change should be closely linked to business issues and performance so that employees can readily see its relevance. Changes are more likely to succeed if they are in line with the organization's history and core values (except when those values are part of the problem and modifying the organizational culture is the change goal). Understanding the organization's culture also clarifies what should *not* be changed because it serves as the organizational glue or strongly relates to key success factors. Alan Lafley, Procter and Gamble CEO, stated that the company's purpose and values were not going to change, but strategy and execution would be improved, "[s]o I was very clear about what was safe and what wasn't" (Gupta and Wendler 2005: 4).

One of the ways a single person can begin to influence a large organization is to envision a feasible and powerful future and paint a picture of that vision for others. Larry Bossidy is a proponent of the "burning platform" theory of change in which the leader is the catalyst. When an oil rig catches fire and the foreman orders the worker to jump into the ocean, they don't automatically obey. Fear of the ocean or sharks and so forth will hold them back until they see the flames actually burning the platform.

> The leader's job is to help everyone see that the platform is burning, whether the flames are apparent or not. The process of change begins when people decide to take the flames seriously and manage by fact, and that means a brutal understanding of reality. You need to find out what the reality is so that you know what needs changing. I traveled all over the company with the same message and the same charts, over and over. Here's what I think is good about us. Here's what I'm worried about. Here's what we have to do about it. And if we don't fix the cash problem, none of us is going to be around. You can keep it simple: we're spending more than we're taking in. If you do that at home, there will be a day of reckoning.
>
> (Tichy and Charan 1995: 247–248)

Bossidy increased the perceived need for change by highlighting what Peter Senge calls the "creative tension" that results from perceiving the gap between the ideal situation (the organization's vision) and an honest appraisal of its current reality. By focusing attention on problems or opportunities and taking their change story to many groups of employees at all levels in the organization, global leaders can "turn up the heat" and create a sense of urgency.

As organization development (OD) consultant Richard Beckhard stated,

> For change to be possible and for commitment to occur, there has to be enough dissatisfaction with the current state of affairs to mobilize energy toward change. There also has to be some fairly clear conception of what the state of affairs would be if and when the change was successful. Of course, a desired state needs to be consistent with the values and priorities of the client system. There also needs to be some client awareness of practical first steps or starting points toward the desired state.
>
> (1991: 664)

## Communicating the vision

Bossidy's statement quoted earlier, "I traveled all over the company with the same message and the same charts, over and over" (Tichy and Charan 1995: 248), is typical of global leaders. To personally convince employees about the need to embrace the change, the message has to be consistent and repeated. Without consistency, the message is distorted as it is passed up and down hierarchies and across cultural borders, much like the children's game of "Telephone." Without repetition and the commitment demonstrated by leaders, employees "sit out" change efforts, assuming that this is just another in a long line of management fads that will pass when a new CEO is named or when the current top management team's attention is drawn to a more pressing issue. Sharing evidence and making a case for change that touches people's emotions to increase the level of dissatisfaction with the status quo, reiterating the perceived need for change and painting a vivid picture of the desired end state, are essential parts of the unfreezing process.

The change message is communicated more effectively when it contains a simple metaphor or slogan that travels well across cultures. Even though Procter and Gamble hires the smartest students from the best schools, Alan Lafley says the need to communicate at a "Sesame Street level of simplicity" was one of his most significant lessons after becoming CEO (Gupta and Wendler 2005).

> So if I'd stopped at, "We're going to refocus on the company's core businesses," that wouldn't have been good enough. The core businesses are one, two, three, four. Fabric care, baby care, feminine care, and hair care. And then you get questions: "Well, I'm in home care. Is that a core business?" No. "What does it have to do to become a core business?" [become the industry global leader, have the best structural economics in the industry, and show a consistent growth rate and strong cash flow ROI]. So then business leaders understand what it takes to become a core business.
>
> (Gupta and Wendler 2005: 3)

The simplicity and repetition are needed in part because of Procter and Gamble's diversity and size: 100,000 people from over 100 cultures. But Lafley is also trying to "unclutter employee thinking" so they can stop, think, and internalize the strategy and go on to make their own decisions (ibid.: 3).

The following example of a bank transformation includes lessons about communicating the vision. Hired to improve a large European retail bank with 30,000 employees, the new CEO began by setting performance targets (Lawson and Price 2003). This was not sufficient for the change he had in mind. Unless the employees changed both the way they worked and their mindset, they would not be able to offer better customer service at a lower cost. The bank's culture had to be transformed from a bureaucracy to a "federation of entrepreneurs" who quickly solved customer problems.

The first step was to develop a convincing story to provide employees with a purpose to believe in. The CEO drafted his story and improved it with feedback from his executive directors. In turn, each of them created a version of the story for their area and delegated the responsibility for one aspect of the story to a team member, who developed a performance scorecard for each deliverable.

The story was then retold by the employees' immediate boss all the way down the hierarchy, giving emphasis to the relevant points for each different audience. In other words, how could each unit and employee provide better service with fewer costs? This process, called dialogue-based planning, was a series of sense-making efforts that involved several iterations, feedback on the stories, and both upward and downward communication flows. For example, employees reported that out-of-order document imagers frequently prevented them from making customer copies efficiently. These were replaced in each branch, and that information was added to the story as an example of a change that helped both employees and customers. For the CEO, the secret to having employees believe and accept the story was to have it describe "how life could be better for all of the bank's stakeholders, not just investors and analysts" (Lawson and Price 2003: 37).

The tactics that come to mind for communicating a change may be limited to persuasive speeches, newsletters, and memos. However, change agents also influence and communicate change by:

- encouraging the participation of those who will be impacted by the change in the process;
- supporting human resource management practices (hiring criteria, performance appraisal systems, compensation, employee development programs);
- giving importance to symbolic activities (rites and ceremonies, celebrations);
- instituting diffusion practices (best-practice programs and transition teams);
- managing internal and external information; and
- instituting formal activities that demonstrate support for change initiatives (modified organizational structures and new job descriptions) (Armenakis *et al.* 1999b).

Corrado Passera, CEO of Banca Intesa, recommends using the press to communicate change successes in turnarounds of large organization:

> Change will only be effective if people are really convinced that they are working for a successful business. Internal results undoubtedly matter, but even they won't count for much if everyone keeps reading in the newspapers that the business is still a poor performer. . . . People will not believe you unless you can change the organization's image in the media.
>
> (Ghislanzoni and Shearn 2005: 77)

## Building a community

Charles Handy, noted British management thinker, predicts that companies in the future will not be property owned by shareholders but communities to which people belong. Rather than workers, employees will be citizens with rights and a share of the profits that they create (Handy 2001). While they may not go as far as Handy predicts, successful global leaders do indeed create communities. This theme is heard repeatedly in global leader interviews, witness Scaroni's slogan "Building One Pilkington" (Ghislanzoni 2006).

> The leaders of large, multicultural, and geographically distant organizations have to bring the members of their heterogeneous groups together before they can act in concert. A sense of community may be the "glue" in global organizations that builds enough consistency to risk major changes and survive the unanticipated consequences inherent in change efforts.
>
> (Osland 2004: 134)

Building work communities in organizations led to innovation, action, and change in a study of global leaders (Wellsfry 1993).

Community is born out of shared values, shared language, trust, and a sense of belonging and identification. The trust that accompanies community building lays the groundwork for successful change. Employees seldom exert themselves for leaders they do not trust, which underscores the need for integrity and credibility. Trust is also an issue for the teams charged with carrying out change projects. The author co-facilitated a series of organizational change seminars in various countries that were attended by change teams from different firms. As facilitators, we readily observed that some teams were highly competitive and dysfunctional, while others operated like effective teams with a high level of trust. When we checked back informally on the teams' progress, we were not surprised to find that the changes directed by the dysfunctional teams were less successful. Their preoccupation with personal agendas and feuds translated into less energy to devote to their change project and less attention to the external forces that threatened their projects. Transformational change can be a difficult, even treacherous, journey and is best undertaken with trustworthy companions in community.

The vision itself can contribute to building a community. When Sir Colin Marshall announced his vision that British Airways would be "the world's favorite airline," BA was actually ranked close to the bottom of the barrel. Instead of laughing at this goal, his employees were motivated by it. Many people prefer working for successful rather than poorly performing organizations for the sake of their self-esteem and the opportunity to make positive contributions. Therefore, change targets, even audacious ones like this, unleash employee motivation and can bring them together if the blueprint for change is clear and the process is carefully managed. Marshall wanted to signal a change in BA's culture from a sole focus on technology and airline safety to a customer focus. One of the interventions that helped it successfully make this transition was a two-day "Managing People First" session that focused on relationship building. About 150 people from various departments and locations were invited, which built community. Marshall demonstrated his commitment and perseverance by attending every one of these sessions.

> I spent two to three hours with each group. I talked with people about our goals, our thoughts for the future. I got people's input about what we needed to do to improve our services and operations. The whole thing proved to be a very useful and productive dialogue. We found it so valuable, in fact, that in cases when I was away, we offered people the opportunity to come back and have a follow-up session with me. So I really did talk to all 110 groups in that five-year period.
>
> (Burke 2002: 93)

When a sense of community is lacking in an organization, employees are less likely to make the effort or the necessary sacrifices to realize a vision. Even when people recognize the need for change, self-interest or inertia can prevail if there is no perception that this harms the community. Therefore, many successful changes incorporate community building, as shown in the following example of a "grassroots" change in which a global leader tried to bypass the bureaucracy and change the mindset and behavior of the frontline employees and work directly with them (Pascale 1999).

Steve Miller, group managing director of Royal Dutch/Shell Group of Companies, set up a "retailing boot camp" for six- to eight-person teams at a time from six different operating companies throughout the world. After receiving training to identify and take advantage of market opportunities, the teams went home to apply their new skills. Sixty days later they returned to present their analyses and plans to the other teams and provide feedback to one another. They had another sixty days to perfect their business plans, which they then presented in a fishbowl session with Miller and his direct reports; the other teams observed, so they could learn vicariously from each team's interchanges with senior management. In exchange for promised results, Miller and his staff approved their plans and made financial commitments to support them. The teams returned to the field to implement their plans and returned two months for a follow-up session in which they analyzed and learned from what succeeded or failed. Thus, this was a plan to empower, challenge, provide resources, and hold frontline people accountable (Pascale 1998).

One result was US$300 million worth of audited results to Shell's bottom line. Another outcome was that the corporate culture became more participative and innovative. The third consequence was community building for the grassroots teams, senior management, and, by extension, their individual networks. Shell had never before taken mid-level employees and exposed them to employees from different countries or to senior management. As Miller stated,

> The whole process creates complete transparency between the people at the coal face (Shell's term for its front-line activities in the worldwide oil products business) and me and my top management team. At the end, these folks go back home and say, "I just cut a deal with the managing director and his team to do these things." It creates a personal connection, and it changes how we talk with each other and how we work with each other. After that, I can call up those folks anywhere in the world and talk in a very direct way because of this personal connectedness. It has completely changed the dynamics of our operations.
>
> (Pascale 1998: 110)

## Operationalizing the change

Percy Barnevik, former ABB CEO, and his team spent 200 days a year communicating their vision and message and helping units figure out what the vision meant in terms of their own work (Ghoshal and Bartlett 1996). This is called operationalizing the vision. Not only does it set clear expectations for each employee and unit but it also helps align the organization and symbolizes the leader's commitment to change. A vision without a blueprint for change simply frustrates employees.

## Organizational alignment

Sometimes the change goal or target is to better align the organization. Many of Scaroni's integration efforts at ENI are directed at internal alignment. Even when the change target has an external focus (e.g., market share, new strategic direction), however, organization design components have to be aligned. For example, a new strategy usually requires concurrent, complementary changes in policies, employee skills, staffing, systems, cultural norms, and structure (Pascale and Athos 1981). Organizations are interdependent systems; changing only one component can result in the systemic resistance that occurs when other components of the organization block the change. For instance, if employees do not possess the skills to use a new IT tool and these skills are not evaluated in the performance management system, implementation will fail. The compensation mechanisms that reinforce new ways of thinking and behaving demanded by a change should simultaneously reward personal results, group results, short-term results, and long-term results (Ghislanzoni and Shearn 2005). Ensuring the "fit" among components is a key aspect of institutionalizing change. In a study of 500 of the largest European firms, there were significant performance benefits only in the firms that changed structures, processes, and boundaries simultaneously. The firms that changed only structures and boundaries but failed to make their processes complementary not only failed to improve their performance but were *worse* off after the change (Whittington *et al.* 1998)!

Given the rapidly changing environment, global leaders have to expect to carry out ongoing alignment. Organizational evolution usually consists of periods of incremental change punctuated by discontinuous or revolutionary change. Thus, global leaders and managers face the paradoxical demands of "increasing the alignment or fit among strategy, structure, culture, and processes, while simultaneously preparing for the inevitable revolutions required by discontinuous environmental change" (Tushman and O'Reilly 1996: 11). In addition to paying attention to the future, this entails a willingness to tear apart what has just been painstakingly cobbled together. As we saw in the Lew Platt quotation at the beginning of the chapter, "We have to be willing to cannibalize what we're doing today in order to ensure our leadership in the future" (Evans *et al.* 2002: 423). While alignment is a necessity for institutionalizing change, it can also be a barrier to future change if leaders are not willing to cannibalize it. In this sense, alignment can be viewed as a double-edged sword.

### *Measurement*

Following the truism that "people do only what is measured," successful global change projects have a clear, understandable focus that can be measured. Changes should be monitored with a reasonable number (three to five) of carefully thought out metrics. The use of metrics like the Balanced Scorecard allows multinational enterprises (MNEs) to target critical success factors and hold employees accountable for achieving them.

Recommended general metrics measure the most important performance and health indicators, such as:

- financial performance;
- operations (quality and consistency of key value-creation processes);
- organizational issues (depth of talent, ability to motivate and retain employees);
- state of product market and position (quality of customer relationships);
- the nature or relationships with external parties, such as suppliers, regulators, and nongovernmental organizations.

(Dobbs *et al.* 2005: 67)

Leaders should remember to include several types of measures: performance measures, evaluation of the change itself, and systemic measures of the long-term health of the organization. The concern for organizational health implies a longer time horizon that lays the groundwork for the future (Dobbs *et al.* 2005). Review processes that are carefully monitored also allow global leaders to keep tabs on the progress of change in far-flung MNCs.

Taking a long-term view of change is important, since some changes that are successful in the short run may eventually revert back to the status quo; other changes look like failures in the short term, only to prove successful years later. Thus, *when* a change is measured makes a notable difference.

## Change tactics and contextualization

Accounts of global change produce seven general guidelines:

- Begin with the basics of planned change.
- Know your company well enough to understand which interventions and tactics will be most effective.
- Understand when solutions and interventions have to be universal (global or corporate-wide) or particularistic (local).
- Contextualize training and tactics when made necessary by cultural differences.
- Modify mindsets through training that is culturally appropriate.
- Establish specific, measurable goals.
- Provide rewards and incentives for change.

Goss *et al.* (1996), consultants who specialize in helping firms make the changes they will need for the future, have this specific advice for staying out ahead:

1 *Assemble a critical mass of key stakeholders.*
2 *Conduct an organizational audit* to identify assumptions, influential functional units, key systems that drive the business, core competencies or skills, shared values, and idiosyncrasies.
3 *Create urgency and discuss the undiscussable* so employees are motivated to question basic assumptions.

4 *Harness contention* to jumpstart the creative process.
5 *Engineer organizational breakdowns*, such as setting impossible deadlines, so that organizational problems become visible.

Such general tactics are very constructive, but they have to be adapted to fit the conditions and history of the specific organization. ABB's philosophy on making global change, shown below, represents the lessons learned from its own experience with cross-border mergers. Other companies have learned different lessons or operate in different conditions.

1 Immediately reorganize operations into profit centers with well-defined budgets, strict performance targets, and clear lines of authority and accountability.
2 Identify a core group of change agents from local management, give small teams responsibility for championing high-priority programs, and closely monitor results.
3 Transfer ABB expertise from around the world to support the change process without interfering with it or running it directly.
4 Keep standards high and demand quick results (Barnevik 1996: 81).

One of the challenges of global change is that not all solutions and interventions are effective throughout a firm's global operations. The vision cannot be operationalized the same way, given local differences that are influenced by culture, history, and local business practices. No matter how well designed corporate-wide solutions and interventions are, they may require some type of contextualization – modification to fit the local context. This is one of the major lessons about global change. Those who know the local people and culture best need the autonomy and discretion to tailor the change effort so it is appropriate. In the bank transformation each boss developed his or her own story to communicate and operationalize the vision.

Training is a common change tactic because changes require a different mindset, new skills, or new ways of working. Broad-scale training programs signal a deep commitment to the change by the company and send a strong symbolic message to employees.

However, training programs in global firms have to be contextualized to ensure their relevance and acceptability to different cultures. For this reason, training designs should include room for learning to go in more than one direction. Global change and training are more than the transmission of knowledge from an expert source to a non-expert receiver. Instead, global change is a matter of knowledge creation among different communities; it involves mutual learning (Tenkasi and Mohrman 1999).

> Global firms benefit most when training sessions produce general lessons, recommendations for the rest of the company, and knowledge about necessary local adaptations.
>
> (Osland 2004: 145)

## Creating a context for change

Organizational scholars have long accepted Ashby's (1956) concept of requisite variety, which states that organizations have to be as complex as their environments. This is one of the arguments for developing a global mindset in the workforce. The complexity of employee views in a global firm should equal the complexity of the global environment. Heterogeneous, complex perspectives help firms to perceive opportunities, problems, and solutions that a homogeneous mindset cannot see. In addition, the innovation and creativity so central to many successful change efforts is stifled when employees cannot contribute their diverse views.

The social architecture aspect of a global leader's role involves building an organizational culture with these characteristics that set the stage for change (Osland 2004):

- *entrepreneurship* – to foster initiatives and a concern for performance;
- *diversity* – to attract and retain employees of all types so different views can be heard;
- *learning and innovation* – to promote renewal and growth and ward off stagnation and obsolescence;
- *participation* – so that diverse views can be heard and employees can express their ideas and feel a sense of ownership;
- *trust* – so that employees believe in the wisdom and fairness of their leaders and colleagues;
- *collaboration* – so that employees are willing to contribute their efforts to the change effort.

Honda is an example of a firm that successfully created a context for change through its organizational culture and *waigaya* sessions.

> Contrary to what many Westerners might think about the importance of consensus in Japanese culture, institutionalized conflict is an integral part of Japanese management. At Honda, any employee, however junior, can call for a waigaya session. The rules are that people lay their cards on the table and speak directly about problems. Nothing is out of bounds, from supervisory deficiencies on the factory floor to perceived lack of support for a design team. Waigaya legitimizes tension so that learning can take place.
>
> (Goss *et al.* 1996: 136–137)

Organizational cultures that value learning are more open to change and innovation. If companies are actively learning, the need for change becomes obvious. As BP CEO John Browne stated, "Learning is at the heart of a company's ability to adapt to a rapidly changing environment. It is the key to being able both to identify opportunities that others might not see and to exploit those opportunities rapidly and fully" (Dess and Picken 2000: 31). Taking the time to learn what will be successful before leaping to a global implementation plan is another way to benefit from a learning orientation. Another practice of learning organizations is action learning, which brings together diverse global teams to study specific issues and make recommendations (Dotlich and Noel 1998). The Nokia teams that produce strategy road maps are an example of action learning.

## Innovation

Global change and learning organizations are closely tied to innovation. We have mentioned previously the challenge global leaders face in building organizations that simultaneously manage the present and create the future. In large part, innovation is the solution. Innovation, which is defined as the implementation of new ideas at the individual, group, or organizational level, is closely linked to organizational survival in the global economy. At a 2006 leadership forum, IBM CEO Samuel J. Palmisano commented, "The way you will thrive in this environment is by innovating – innovating in technologies, innovating in strategies, innovating in business models." In IBM's latest survey of CEOs and government leaders, innovation, particularly with respect to new business models, was a major topic of interest and an area that requires personal leadership.

> With product innovation, if you stand up on your soapbox and you cheer a little bit, that will certainly help. But the reason I think that the CEOs have to lead this is because, fundamentally, the biggest breakthroughs are a result of changing the business model and the processes and the culture. . . . Go back even 10 years ago. Was it natural for IBM to go collaborate around the future of innovation or the future of our technologies? . . . Was it natural for IBM to join into the open-source community to talk about standards around lots of technologies? These weren't natural things to occur. . . . If the CEO doesn't give people permission to go change behavior and to collaborate, then it's not going to happen. Everybody is looking for the signal. They want to know whether things are really changing fundamentally.
>
> (Hamm 2006)

In addition to signaling that innovations have to be taken seriously, leaders create the architecture needed to foster innovation, follow up on innovations, and repeatedly communicate their importance and publicize successes and failures (Loewe and Dominiquini 2005). While leaders play a crucial role in innovation, they are never the sole reason why some companies are more innovative than others.

Boston Consulting, at the behest of *BusinessWeek*, carried out a survey that asked executives to name the most innovative companies in the world outside their own industry (*BusinessWeek Online* 2006). The 1,070 respondents included 46 percent from North America, 30 percent from Europe, and the remaining 16 percent from Asia and the Pacific region. The results showed some regional differences in their answers. However, the top twenty-five companies were, in order, Apple, Google, 3M, Toyota, Microsoft, GE, Procter and Gamble, Nokia, Starbucks, IBM, Virgin, Samsung, Sony, Dell, IDEO, BMW, Intel, eBay, IKEA, Wal-Mart, Amazon, Target, Honda, Research In Motion, and Southwest. Many of these firms were chosen because they are good at design, although that was not their only definition of innovation. Five common themes make up the lessons from these firms: (1) opening the doors of R&D labs to work with customers, suppliers, and expert networks; (2) leadership from the top to drive and protect innovation; (3) using a variety of innovation metrics; (4) redesigning the organization to foster coordination and collaboration; and (5) customer insight, based on a close connection with customers and techniques that get at how customers think.

Innovation paid off financially for the world's twenty-five most innovative companies, based on a comparison between their median statistics and those of the median Standard and Poor's Global 1,200 company. The median profit margin growth of the innovative companies was 3.4 percent over the past decade compared to 0.4 percent, and their median annual stock return over the same time period was 3.2 points higher (14.3 percent versus 11.1 percent) than the comparison group median (*BusinessWeek Online* 2006).

Despite the proven worth of innovation, research shows that, according to employee evaluation, most companies are not good at innovation (Loewe and Dominiquini 2006). Only 85 percent of new ideas ever get to market, and 50–70 percent of those that do are failures (Booz Allen and Hamilton 1982; Cooper 2001; Tucker 2002). "While operating around the world may help companies generate ideas for innovations, the complexity of the global network is likely to render the evaluation and optimal exploitation of innovation ever more difficult" (Koudal and Coleman 2005: 22). To increase global markets and reduce costs, organization functions, including R&D, are geographically dispersed to an unprecedented degree. Thus, it is no wonder that the ability to coordinate innovation across complex global operations was identified as the key success factor in a recent study of 650 firms (ibid.). Additionally, those firms that invested heavily in innovation infrastructure showed profits up to 70 percent higher than those that did not. They put their money into (1) product development capabilities; (2) supply chain process infrastructure such as flexible manufacturing, design quality and the use of common platforms; (3) sophisticated information systems used to synchronize and support innovations across the value chain; and (4) closer collaboration with customers and suppliers (ibid.). Mondi, a European paper and packaging firm, is an example of investing in technology to support innovation. The firm has a web-based "Innovation Zone" where employees contribute ideas that others build upon and improve (ibid.).

Best Buy took an innovative approach to learning about customer insight. Innovation teams generated hundreds of new ideas by observing the behavior of consumers in their normal habitat. Instead of focusing solely on their typical customer – young male "techies" – employees went to observe the American Girl Store in Chicago to understand what draws girls and their mothers to this destination retail store. They also went to Amish country and to poor barrios in Mexico City to comprehend the frustrations of less technologically proficient people (Loewe and Dominiquini 2006: 26).

Innovation cannot be limited to employees who work in R&D or product development. It is expected of all employees, as shown in Whirlpool's logo, "Innovation from everyone everywhere." Truly innovative firms make a concerted effort to hire creative personalities. Lotus Development was an extremely successful start-up founded in 1982 to market Lotus 1-2-3. When the firm hit 1,000 employees, it started hiring primarily outside MBAs from Fortune 500 companies who transplanted the management techniques appropriate for routine work in big firms. Subsequently, Lotus had difficulty developing and marketing new products. Mitchell Kapor, chairman of the board and former CEO, and Freada Klein, head of organizational development and training, put to the test one of their own hypotheses for the diminished creativity. They tested it by carrying out an experiment. They took the résumés of the first forty people hired at Lotus, changed the names on the résumés, and put them into the current applicant pool. None of these "applicants" even made it to the interview stage because their backgrounds had too many "wacko and risky things." Instead of linear business careers, they had had eclectic experiences such as community organization, transcendental meditation teaching, and clinical psychology. To Kapor and Klein, this was evidence that Lotus was systematically weeding out applicants like the creative people who were responsible for the firm's only hit product (Sutton 2001: 8).

Getting creative people through the door and hiring them is only the first step. Research has identified a long list of organizational conditions, shown in Table 8.5, that either enhance or repress individual creativity in organizations. They can be categorized as

*Table 8.5* Contextual effects on creativity

| *Creativity enhancers* | *Creativity killers* |
| --- | --- |
| Focus on intrinsic motivation | Excessive focus on extrinsic motivation |
| Creativity goals | Limits set by superiors |
| Developmental feedback | Critical evaluation |
| Supportive supervision | Close, controlling supervision |
| Healthy competition | Competition in a win–lose situation |
| Participative decision making | Control of decision making |
| Hiring creative individuals | Control of information |
| Enriched, complex jobs | Time pressure |
| Provision of necessary resources, particularly time | Political problems |
| Clear organizational goals | Emphasis on the status quo |
| Instructions to employees to be creative | |
| Recognition and rewards for creativity | |
| Encouraging of risk taking | |
| No punishment for failure | |
| Autonomy | |
| Productivity | |
| Workforce diversity | |
| Opportunities for internal and external interaction | |
| Diverse teams skilled at working together | |
| Supportive climate | |
| Organizational culture that promotes innovation | |
| Flexible, flat structures | |
| Close interaction and relationships with customers | |

Source: Osland, J. S., Kolb, D., Rubin, I., and Turner, M. (2007) *Organizational Behavior: An Experiential Approach.* Upper Saddle River, NJ: Prentice Hall: 325.

designing complex jobs, unleashing and rewarding creativity, adopting a managerial style that fosters creativity, and creating an organizational culture and developing a structure that promote collaboration, interaction, and trust. It has to be easy for employees to present their ideas and get a hearing for them without fighting bureaucratic requirements. John Chambers, Cisco CEO, has birthday breakfasts with employees that give him an opportunity to get feedback and hear ideas (Shalley and Gilson 2004). The organizational culture has to reward risk and refrain from punishing people for errors. Associated Enterprises celebrated mistakes by bestowing an award, the "screw-up of the week," accompanied by an ugly statue that traveled around the office. Thomas Edison once said, "I make more mistakes than anyone else I know, and sooner or later, I patent most of them." Google, definitely an example of a culture that rewards creativity, allows employees to spend 20 percent of their work week developing their own ideas.

The SAS Institute in North Carolina, the world's largest privately held software company, is a good example of a company that manages creativity and innovation well (Florida and Goodnight 2005). SAS has 10,000 employees and 40,000 customer sites worldwide. The company sells its services in an innovative fashion via subscriptions. Since 98 percent of the subscriptions are renewed, its income is relatively steady and predictable. So is its workforce. Its turnover rate is only 3–5 percent in an industry that averages 20 percent, saving it around US$85 million annually in recruitment and replacement costs. The company's revenues have grown annually for twenty-nine years. CEO Jim Goodnight credits SAS's success and creativity to three guiding principles (ibid.):

1.  *Help employees do their best work by keeping them intellectually engaged and by removing distractions.* According to an *Information Week* survey, information technology workers are motivated more by challenging jobs than by salary and financial incentives. SAS keeps its employees stimulated via training, employee white papers on new technologies, a constant stream of new products, and internal R&D expos where technical staff educate nontechnical staff about new products.

SAS asks workers each year what nonwork tasks distract them from their work. Their answers guided the establishment of in-house medical facilities for workers and their families, a day care center and a cafeteria where kids can eat lunch with their parents, workout facilities, and a Work–Life Department that helps workers' children make the right college choice and finds home health care for workers' elderly parents. Dry cleaning, massage, haircut, and auto-detailing services are also available on site at a discount. SAS believes these programs, plus flexible work hours that allow employees to meet their family needs, pay off in higher employee retention and productivity.

The company keeps bureaucratic requirements to a minimum and understands that creativity requires downtime. An SAS proverb is: "After eight hours, you're probably just adding bugs [errors]." SAS believes that creative capital is built by long-term relationships among developers, support staff, salespeople, and customers. Therefore, it focuses on careful selection and retention. Its hiring decisions, which can take months to make, are designed to ensure that prospective employees fit the culture. All employees receive the same benefits package, and no jobs are outsourced. "SAS recognizes that 95 percent of its assets drive out the front gate every evening. Leaders consider it their job to bring them back the next morning" (Florida and Goodnight 2005: 127). Goodnight claims that they "hire hard, manage open, and fire hard." Employees are not terminated when they make errors but for failing to meet performance standards after receiving a second chance with a corrective action plan.

2.  *Make managers responsible for sparking creativity and eliminate arbitrary distinctions between "suits" (managers) and "creatives" (employees doing creative work).* All SAS managers do hands-on work in addition to their managerial responsibilities. Even the CEO still writes code to send a symbolic message that everyone in the firm is a creative, despite their job assignment, on the same team working toward the same goal. The manager's role is to stimulate creativity by asking good questions, convening groups to exchange ideas, removing obstacles, and getting employees what they need to accomplish their work.

3.  *Engage customers as creative partners to enable the company to deliver superior products.* Because SAS is privately held, it tracks customer satisfaction and opinions, rather than stock prices, which then guide the 26 percent of its budget devoted to R&D. SAS surveys customers annually on desired new features, and stores customer complaints and suggestions in a database. This information is fed into product design and updates. At user conferences SAS aims for creative interchanges.

> SAS may be the only company that prints the names of its software developers in product manuals. Customers can – and do – call them up. And because employee loyalty is so high, the developers actually answer the phone: they haven't moved down the road to start-up number seven.
>
> (Florida and Goodnight 2005: 131)

SAS aims to build mutual loyalty in customers by releasing products only when they are bug-free.

SAS takes an integrative approach by aligning all the puzzle pieces that culminate in innovation: hiring and retaining creative employees, creating a culture designed especially for creatives, fostering a managerial style that catalyzes and enables creativity, partnering with customers, building long-term relationships, and investing heavily and consistently in innovation infrastructure.

## Conclusion

The research on global change leadership is more anecdotal than empirical and therefore warrants further study. The role of global leaders in innovation has received less attention than that of domestic leaders, although much more is known about innovation from a strategic and product development point of view. Our message in this chapter is that global leaders are especially skilled at catalyzing and managing global change and designing innovative organizations. They practice many of the universal lessons about change management but perhaps place greater emphasis on some actions or utilize somewhat different change levers. Although we have not repeated the lessons of Chapter 6, "Leading global teams," global leaders rely heavily on teams to carry out their vision. From accounts of successful global change agents, they also rely on inspiring visions that have to be carefully crafted to cross cultural and organizational boundaries without losing meaning. Perhaps the most surprising finding is how much time and travel global leaders devote to communicating the vision and working with employees at various levels to operationalize the vision and clarify what that means for themselves and their work unit. This signifies a great deal of persistence and commitment. Furthermore, their efforts in this regard also generate trust and build the community that lays the groundwork for change.

The organizational architecture identified as a competency of global leaders in Chapter 2 in very evident in both global change and innovation. Global leaders align the various organizational components to support changes and then take the puzzle apart and realign them yet again to fit future needs. They build organizational cultures that support change and innovation and create a context for change so that it is not an uphill battle and so that the need for change becomes self-evident to many employees. The size and complexity of global organizations make architectural design and modification a challenging task. Thorough alignment also requires persistence.

Global leaders take cultural differences and local history and conditions into consideration when planning and implementing change. Rather than allow cultural difference to be an obstacle, they leverage cultural values that support the desired change. Implementation plans, and training in particular, are contextualized so they are appropriate for the local context.

To be effective change agents, global leaders require knowledge related to future trends and knowledge about change management and innovation, the impact of culture, and a deep understanding of the organization. Change agents and leaders also need self-knowledge in the form of self-awareness. A leader's vision comes from reflection on the tasks they find most engaging and what they see as their purpose in life. There is a truism that it is impossible to change an organization without changing oneself in the process. This is captured best by an African proverb:

> When I was a young man, I thought I would change the world.
>
> When I was middle-aged, I thought I would change my village.
>
> Now that I am an old man, I think I will change myself.

# Global leadership development

## 9

### GARY R. ODDOU AND MARK E. MENDENHALL

In the early to mid-1990s, Alcatel, a French telecommunications giant, went on a merger and buying spree such that in a very short amount of time it had 200 operations in France itself and over 700 in the rest of the world, representing a huge increase in the number of its operations. These mergers with, and acquisitions of, foreign operations created significant management challenges for Alcatel. The telecommunications giant was struggling with the immediate issues of determining what to standardize and what to localize. It needed to build a common corporate culture yet allow decentralization as appropriate. It needed to understand how to manage foreign units that wanted greater independence yet also encourage cross-unit collaboration in order to leverage experience economies among its vast domestic and foreign operations. To manage such an operation, Alcatel needed a new management mentality, one that would reflect a keener understanding of countries – their cultures, politics, economics; of the individual operations it had acquired – their history, their organizational cultures, their distinctive competencies; and of management and organizational principles – balancing the needs of local independence and system interdependence.

The biggest single long-term challenge Alcatel had to deal with over the next decade, therefore, was how to identify, select, and develop its managers to make sure they had the potential to manage this complex organization in an increasingly dynamic and competitive world. Though perhaps on a larger scale than many, Alcatel's experience with its mergers and acquisitions was not unusual.

A decade ago, Gregersen et al. (1997) researched Fortune 500 companies, of which 85 percent said they did not have adequate numbers of capable global leaders. Further, of those few "global leaders" they did have, only about 30 percent of them were rated as having the necessary competencies to really be effective. Very significantly, the human resource directors of these firms in their survey rated "having effective global leaders" as the number one priority of their firms. Mendenhall et al. (2003) found that similar conditions extant in large global firms across industries.

In this chapter we will focus on the development of global leaders, including general leadership methods that apply to global leadership development (GLD), conceptual issues that underlie effective GLD, and two examples of very different GLD practices and how they each can positively affect global leadership development.

## General leadership development methods

Firms' general approaches to developing global leaders have usually involved altering existing traditional leadership development approaches to try to incorporate a global perspective in their managerial cadres. From a review of the literature and of current company *traditional* leadership development programs benchmarked against best practices, the following appear to be the most common components (Day and Halpin, 2001):

- 360-degree feedback;
- executive coaching;
- job assignments;
- mentoring;
- networking;
- reflection;
- action learning;
- outdoor experiences.

For many firms, all of these are still part of their approach to developing leaders who operate in multiple markets and/or simply across country boundaries in one capacity or another. If modified appropriately, such methods can become an important part of global leadership development. Adapting what used to be general leadership methods requires a change of mindset, though. For example, mentoring is more effective if a less experienced manager is being guided by someone with significant learning accrued from global business experience rather than by someone who has risen through the organization when global markets were not really necessary for adequate profit or by someone who does not otherwise reflect a global mindset.

Executive coaching will be more effective if the coach has had international work experience and can relate the issues the manager might be struggling with to the context of global business and the competencies needed to be effective. Action learning projects need to involve members of the firm from different countries, such as with global teams tasked to analyze global operations of the firm or some other relevant issue. Reflection needs, in part, to be based on survey instruments that are specifically designed to indicate the manager's intercultural competencies or the manager's cultural profile as it compares and contrasts to other cultures with which he or she works. Job assignments need to include international ones, where the manager is exposed to cultural and business differences and also has the opportunity to develop global networks of people. Outdoor, experiential exercises are best done with international team members.

One of the primary challenges will be whether firms can appropriately modify their general leadership development programs to address the peculiar requirements of global leadership development. Before we broach the actual methods used to develop global leaders, several points are worth mentioning. First, as was noted earlier in the book, current global leadership models that have been proposed tend to focus on competencies that would benefit any manager in any situation, whether domestic or cross-cultural. Earlier arguments in previous chapters have explained that there is not so much a difference in kind as a difference in the degree of importance and the degree of reach of some of the competencies. For example, being able to communicate clearly across cultures is both the same and different in a multicultural and domestic context.

On the one hand, the underlying principles related to using a medium that is consistent with the relationships and issues involved in the communication, as well as the appropriate language, are principles that are true of any communication situation irrespective of the culture(s) involved. However, which language to use, what gestures to use, understanding the meaning of silence during the communication, and knowing specifically how the relationships among the communicators might affect the communication are culturally contextual and require additional understanding and knowledge when in a cross-cultural communication. In summary, although the principles of effective leadership in domestic and in global contexts overlap a great deal, it is the multicultural context that makes all the difference in terms of how those principles are applied.

In addition to understanding the complexity inherent in global leadership situations and how that can affect leadership development, it is also important to see the commonalities across the different global leadership models that have been proposed. Most or all of the models extol the importance of the individual's personal competencies (e.g., tolerance of ambiguity, integrity, maturity, etc.), and all of them emphasize the importance of being able to develop and manage relationships effectively. Additonally, the importance of business experience and acumen is underscored by each of them, representing a tripartite dimensionality that global leadership program design must address.

The previous discussion has addressed primarily content issues relative to GLD. Relative to the *process* of global leadership development, Black and Gregersen (2000) have said, "The primary objective of global leadership training is stretching someone's mind past narrow domestic borders and creating a mental map of the entire world." Even the smallest of businesses need to be aware of the global business arena. A restaurant that gets its shrimp from South America needs to understand the issues related to sourcing from foreign countries and have alternative plans in case tariffs close off its source of shrimp, or changing global climate patterns alter the sea temperature in that part of the world and lessen the availability of shrimp, thereby increasing the cost, or requiring another source to be sought. Clark Foam, a very small firm, was the clear majority supplier of surfboard blanks to surfboard manufacturers worldwide. In 2006 it closed its doors almost overnight. Manufacturers were caught totally unprepared. Had they understood the dynamics of today's volatile marketplace, they would have already been sourcing from foreign suppliers as well. Indeed, almost all of the new suppliers came from foreign countries. Without an understanding of global sourcing, even small firms or seemingly insignificant industries will not be able to operate most efficiently or profitably. In the following sections we will examine the following aspects of GLD: (1) the basic types of learning contexts and approaches, (2) the conceptual process and outcomes of effective training that leads to transformation, and (3) the different strategies that firms have to help "globalize" their managers.

## The learning context of GLD methods

Learning the kind of competencies needed for global leaders requires classroom-type education as well as experiential education. Research shows that approximately 20 percent of our education comes through formal classroom training, 30 percent through information exchanges with others, and 50 percent from personal work experience (Dodge 1993). The classroom is best for disseminating information efficiently that represents research and experience that might otherwise only be acquired after a lifetime of actual business experience. Classrooms can gather in-company personnel from all around the world and help company managers forge networks efficiently as well, which can then contribute to that 30 percent of information exchange. Current issues affecting the firm can be delivered by leading-edge individuals. Classrooms, however, have their limitations. A key disadvantage of the classroom-type experience is that it typically is more of an intellectual experience, and therefore not always memorable. Experiential education is both intellectual and emotional. It activates both the intellectual and the emotional memories. Experiential education involves giving managers exposure to actual business operations in geographically dispersed, functionally different operations of the firm. They confront cultural differences that actually impact their real performance; it is a case study in "living color."

Through such experiences a network can be developed that is much deeper than, though perhaps not as inclusive as, the network available in company seminars, for example. Such experiences also test the mettle and capabilities of the manager in real-life business experiences. Because experiential education involves intellectual and emotional memory, the lessons learned are not easily forgotten. In summary, both classroom (e.g., seminars) and experiential education are important and complementary, and have a part in the development of global leaders.

## Conceptual process and outcome of effective GLD programs

As has been discussed, most firms have a fairly common set of learning approaches they use to train their personnel. The underlying process that creates the learning, however, is rarely made explicit. Nonetheless, there is a process at the conceptual level that is critical to training and learning. For GLD programs to be effective, they must address this process and recognize the value it brings. Black and Gregersen's proposed model for GLD (2000) embodies the essential elements of this learning process: *Contrast, Confrontation and Replacement* (Black and Gregersen use the term *"Remapping"*).

For us to learn, we must acquire new information or see the same thing from a different perspective. As individuals with certain cultural maps about how the world works and how business operates, we need to experience contrasts to those views and confront our beliefs. Without such contrasts that lead to confronting our traditional way of seeing or doing, there is no change. Joyce Osland (1995, 2000) described this process as "Letting go" and "Taking on" (see Table 2.2 in Chapter 2). Although her focus is on the experience that international assignees go through as they confront differences and have to deal with them, it is the same process for anyone undergoing change. Consider the following example of a German purchasing agent.

## Case scenario: contrast, confrontation, and replacement

A purchasing agent in Germany who now has to deal with the *contrasting* inconsistencies in communication with a supplier in Malaysia because of local power outages and differences in notions of urgency is forced to *confront* his mental map of how business is done in other parts of the world. To be effective in dealing with the agent's Malaysian counterpart, the agent must *replace* his previous notion (i.e., mental map) that business can be conducted with the same methods and communications, resulting in the same efficiency, everywhere in the world. However, a changed mental map can occur at different levels – at a superficial level or a deep level. A superficial-level change might be something along the lines of the agent's realization that Malaysia has a poor electricity infrastructure, negatively affecting the timeliness of communications, and second that the Malaysian vendor is not very motivated. Such a remapping is superficial because it localizes the difference in operating methods to a particular person and to a physical infrastructure issue rather than a deeper underlying cultural issue that often is the more important variable affecting the efficiency of operations.

A deeper-level replacement of the purchasing agent's mental map would relate to an improved understanding of not only the physical infrastructure but the cultural "infrastructure" as well. Managers in developed countries place great value on urgency because of the value placed on customer service in the highly competitive world they operate in. This value puts pressure on the manager to get the rest of the world to conform to that assumption about competition – that the customer is king. This is a belief that fits well with the concept that planning is critical and the ability to satisfy the customer is a competitive edge. For a deeper-level understanding to occur, the purchasing agent might have to ask others about the interaction or do some research, or be observant over time to see patterns that develop across individuals and contexts in dealing with Malaysia. Understanding that Malaysia is a high-context culture, where relationships are critical and in-groups and out-groups differentiate the level of responsiveness between two people, would represent a much deeper level of remapping.

This deeper level of remapping represents a fundamental level of learning that can then be applied to multiple contexts as the purchasing agent goes about planning business with other foreign businesspeople in other, similar cultures. More fundamental lessons at this level of learning include the realization that knowledge of cultures is important when planning an operation, that when there is a critical interdependency that involves foreign operations and great distances it is important to allow for more time and for greater possibilities for things to go wrong, and that it is critical to develop a good relationship with the agent's counterpart in the foreign country (in this case, Malaysia) in order to be better informed and have better access to information that might be helpful.

It is important to help managers understand that a superficial addition to their existing mental maps (e.g., Malaysia requires more time) is not as efficient or effective as actually replacing the mental map with a more sophisticated one. Kurt Lewin (1947) referred to this process of confronting our mental maps and replacing them with new ones as "unfreezing," changing and "refreezing" within a context of dynamic stability. That dynamic stability applied to global leadership development and the change process to become a global leader is at the heart of the "contrast, confrontation and replacement" process.

The German purchasing agent experienced a contrast to his usual way of doing business and had to confront the situation (unfreezing). In this case he could either try to force the Malaysian salesman to change the situation in Malaysia (unlikely) or change his own perspective on how to work with the Malaysian company more effectively (changing). When we experience a contrast in customs, beliefs, etc. that does not allow us to conduct business the way we are used to, we have forces that continue to push us toward doing business the old way and we have forces that are pushing us to do business in a new way (i.e., resulting in a dynamic stability). The German continues to feel pressure from his own company to obtain the necessary supplies in a timely matter. That pressure does not disappear, and motivates the German to continue to act in his normal way. However, there are also pressures that are pushing the German to realize that he cannot always expect to realize the same time economies in Malaysia as he normally could in his own country. Those pressures, by contrast, motivate the German to act in a different way from his customary behavior.

These competing pressures force a reconstruction of the previous "map." The conclusion or learning arises from creating a better understanding of all the variables at play and an effective way to work within that new context (changing). Finally, as our new way or new "map of the world" is reinforced through additional similar experiences across individuals, countries, and business operations, it becomes a new, usable "legend" that helps us be more effective in managing our businesses (refreezing). And the process must continue in order that our "legend" becomes increasingly refined and accurate, because, as noted in Chapter 1, the global context will continually change over time.

In terms of global leadership development it may be useful to merge concepts from both content and process theories reviewed earlier in the book (Chapter 3) in designing global leadership development curricula. The process theories focus on global leadership as a transformational process – of letting go and taking on new mental constructs and models.

## Enablers of transformation

To accomplish the kind of transformations we are speaking of does not occur automatically just because one experiences a contrasting experience that creates a confrontation. In other words, the German purchasing agent does not automatically move from one type of approach to time and relationships (the German's) to another (the Malaysian's). In fact, it is possible – or even likely – that the German will simply make a quick judgment about the Malaysian culture being inefficient. Such stereotypes are common and certainly do not allow for the development of a new understanding. In Lewin's terms, there is no "unfreezing" and therefore no "changing" that occurs.

In order for there to be a transformation, the individual needs to have certain competencies that enable this process. For example, if the German purchasing agent is able to tolerate ambiguity, the agent is less likely to draw quick – and, most likely, inappropriate – conclusions about the Malaysian vendor. This allows the agent time to inquire about the challenges the vendor might be facing or the specific cultural context in which the vendor lives. Such an inquiry demonstrates another enabling competency: curiosity or openness. To actually discover the relevant information to better understand the Malaysian's culture, the German might have to initiate conversations with the vendor himself, or with people familiar with Malaysian culture. This, in turn, demonstrates another enabling competency: interpersonal initiation. If the agent takes a strong interest in the vendor himself, rather than in the issue as a general cultural concept, he further demonstrates another competency that can lead to an effective transformation: relationship development. Wanting to develop and effectively manage their vendor–purchasing agent relationship is more likely to lead to a cooperative, long-term collaboration.

Thus, having the enabling competencies is absolutely necessary for appropriate transformations to occur in managers seeking to become effective global leaders. The enabling competencies help ensure appropriate transformations, and transformations lead to better global managers and leaders. A complete global leadership development program needs to include a diagnosis of the leader's enabling competencies as well as experiences that can more easily lead to meaningful transformations. (For a discussion of various assessments of enabling competencies, see Chapter 4.)

## Strategies for globalizing personnel

Regardless of the enabling competencies an individual might have, for this change or developmental process to occur, firms need to strategize to put their personnel into situations where this transformation process of contrast – confrontation – replacement can happen. Some years ago, Oddou *et al.* (2000a) queried multinational Japanese, US and European firms about their methods for developing their personnel to become more globally qualified. Their research showed that there were five main training elements that were part of the process of globalizing personnel:

- international business travel;
- international business seminars with in-company personnel;
- international business seminars with noncompany personnel;
- international project teams/task forces;
- international assignments (both expatriation and inpatriation).

This research was directed specifically to understand what methods multinational corporations (MNCs) in different parts of the world are using and were anticipating using in the future to develop greater global perspectives in their employees. Although a comparative view of global leadership development is not the focus in this chapter, the findings, both surprising and expected, are of interest, as they probably reflect cultural differences about GLD that are important to recognize. The surprising findings related to the Japanese multinationals. Although they reported an expected increase in international business travel, as did the others, they also reported a clear increase in expatriation, while the European and US MNCs reported either some increase or maintenance of their present trend. More surprising, however, was the anticipated *decrease* in multinational task forces and inpatriate assignments by the Japanese MNCs. It appears that the Japanese MNCs were expecting to maintain a strong Japanese perspective and to implement staffing and training methods that were consistent with a more monocultural perspective. Both the US and the European MNCs reported anticipating a much greater emphasis on international task forces and also on inpatriation, reflecting more open cultural stances.

Turning attention back to the specific training methods themselves, in the following sections two of the aforementioned methods of globalizing personnel will be discussed. The purpose of this is to show how these two methods enable the process of transformation even though they are in many ways on opposite ends of the spectrum: international business travel and international assignments. International business travel tends to be very short term (a few days to a couple of weeks) and can be very superficial in a cross-cultural learning sense because there is far less need to learn the local language, learn the local customs, or understand more than superficially the foreign counterparts and their organizational culture. The employee is often personally taken care of from arrival to departure without having to venture into the foreign culture and problem-solve on her or his own. Rarely does the international business traveler need to learn the transportation system or where to shop for this or that. Quite often, the international business traveler is little more than a tourist in a business context.

Many firms, and many businesspersons themselves, create these kinds of cultural bubbles and isolate themselves from having to come in contact with the local culture. They are picked up at the airport by a chauffeur who waits for them at the exit with their name on a white piece of paper. They follow the chauffeur into and out of buildings and parking spaces to the car that awaits them. The chauffeur takes care of the luggage, opens the door to the car for the businessperson to step in, and speeds away, negotiating the signs and distances on the way to the hotel or the company the businessperson is visiting. If it is to a hotel, the hotel employees usher the business traveler to the reception desk and from there to the room itself, possibly without the traveler ever having to figure out anything on her or his own. A similar process occurs at the company site when the traveler arrives there. And so it goes for many business travelers. There is no need to use their analytical abilities to figure things out, no need to ask, or try to ask, in the foreign language about directions or transportation, no need to translate signs directing them to certain places, no need to navigate traffic into the city, and so on. In other words, the traveler may not be confronted with and therefore have to deal with any direct contrasts between his or her own culture and that of the foreign land. Without confrontation there is no real meaningful contrast, no unfreezing or change, and certainly no replacing of one's mental maps of how things are done, what is right and wrong, what works and what does not work.

## Leveraging travel for global leadership development

For traveling to be part of global leadership development, it has to be designed strategically to that end. The company or traveler has to build in time to the travel for mistakes and discoveries to be made. The businessperson has to be willing to take risks and able to manage negative emotions or tensions that are created in trying to find his or her own way. The businessperson has to observe carefully the actions and words of others and the effects they have. He or she has to figure out ways to try to build trust quickly by being open, accepting, and appropriately appreciative. Damiran (1993) speaks of this kind of traveler as a contrast to the tourist as follows:

> A traveler and a tourist can visit the same city, but experience it very differently. A tourist's goals are typically to see all the sights, learn their names, make and collect stunning pictures, eat the foods, and observe the rituals of the city. A traveler, on the other hand, seeks to understand the city, to know and live briefly among the people, to understand the languages, both verbal and nonverbal, and to participate in the rituals of the city. At the end of equally long visits, the tourist is likely to have seen more monuments, but the traveler is more likely to know how to use the public transportation.

J. Bonner Ritchie (Oddou et al. 2000b) recounted an experience he had as a traveler that broadened his global mindset. While walking through the Muslim Quarter in the Old City of Jerusalem, he stopped to look at a brass vase. He asked the shopkeeper the price. Upon hearing the price, even though he wasn't seriously in the mood for buying, Bonner said, "Too much." The shopkeeper asked how much he would offer. He said he wasn't sure as he began walking down the street. The shopkeeper followed and threw out a lower figure: "60 shekels." Bonner, willing to play the game, responded, "25 shekels." The merchant in turn said, "40 shekels." They went through another round and settled at 35 shekels.

The important part of his experience was not the transaction, though without the transaction no development would have occurred. After settling on a price, because the shopkeeper had noticed that Bonner seemed uncomfortable with the bidding negotiation, he asked Bonner why that was so. The merchant reminded Bonner that in the United States, Americans do not buy homes or cars on a fixed price basis, so why should negotiation be omitted from other transactions? He suggested it was not only more enjoyable to prolong the interaction but fairer to do so. Surprised, Bonner asked him why it was fairer. The merchant responded that this way, the seller and buyer can arrive at a price that is mutually acceptable and that such a price is going to reflect the buyer's ability to buy and need to buy – it will likely be a higher price for someone who has more money and a greater need and a lower price for someone who is poorer or with less of a need. And so, the merchant reasoned, a lower price was not a better deal but a fairer deal.

Bonner had entered the negotiation with a sense of discomfort because doing business this way for this type of product was not his normal way. Though not a lot was at risk in this situation, Bonner had to confront the effectiveness of his usual way of buying such products with the local way of doing so and figure out what was equitable. Bonner's assumption that a fixed price meant a fair price is a cultural belief he had been accustomed to in the United States. The fairness was in a reasonable profit margin the merchant determined and the clarity of the price so the buyer can make an "informed" decision. It gives all the responsibility to the buyer, in a sense, to determine fairness. Bonner did not want to be taken advantage of by paying a higher price than he should, particularly because he was a foreigner and suspected the merchant might try to gouge him to obtain a higher profit margin than should be expected. Bonner was assuming this way of doing business gave the merchant all the responsibility and power to determine what was fair. From this traveler transaction, Bonner learned that "fairness" was a clear factor embedded in negotiations in such contexts, that equity or fairness was best reached in a more flexible, fluid context where the needs and motivation of the two parties could be understood in a conversation. This cultural *contrast* resulted in Bonner's *confronting* his understanding of "fairness" and "responsibility" in reaching equitable transactions. He gained a better appreciation for cultures that are more flexible and allow individual circumstances to influence transactions to reach a greater sense of equity.

This change in Bonner's mental map (*replacement* or *remapping*) would never have occurred had Bonner not ventured beyond his hotel room and hotel restaurant or if he had allowed himself always to be "protected" by a host employee who could have intervened. Bonner never would have had to learn another perspective.

## International assignments

On the other side of the spectrum from international travel is an international assignment. International assignments are the longest type of exposure to foreign business and culture (one to three years, usually) and require a tremendous amount of interaction and integration into all aspects of the culture. The international assignee lives the culture every single day.

Still, as will be discussed in the following section, an international business traveler who is curious and motivated to learn can have an adventure that goes well beyond the experience of a tourist. International assignments require the greatest degree of integration with the culture. It is the necessity of integration that causes the greatest degree of culture shock. By definition, culture shock is the absence of familiar "markers," which causes a disorientation and inability to perform according to habitual expectations. In the *general* culture an expatriate must normally deal with differences in language, rules of the road, shopping, on down to such mundane but essential things as differences in car insurance and the payment of utility bills and more. Within the *work environment* the assignee might also deal with language differences but he or she more certainly deals with work culture differences in performance appraisal systems, meeting behavior, and so forth. The assignee might or might not have family members with him or her. Family members each are dealing with another subset of the culture and will bring additional and supplementary contrasts to the cultural experience.

When one of the authors of this chapter was in France with his family, they moved into the home they were to be in for six months while on an assignment there. The washing machine had just broken down. The previous family gave them the number of a repairman to call. The author called, and the repairman said he would be out within a couple of days. The repairman never came. He called again after a few more days and the repairman said he'd be out right away, but that it was taking a while because the washing machine was German and he had to order the part from Germany (he had never even come out to the house to see what was wrong, to know what part might have to be ordered!). Either way, he never came. The author's wife began to complain and was getting upset with him from having to do so much washing by hand (because they didn't know if there were any public washing machines even available). He called the repairman again and told him (in good French) that the repairman was unprofessional. With that, the repairman got upset and both of us hung up our phones, mutually dissatisfied.

One day, about two weeks later, while eating at the home of the parents of the people whose house they lived in, the mother asked how everything was and the author told her that except for the problem with the washing machine, things were great. She asked what was wrong and they explained what had happened. She immediately said not to worry, that the repairman had been a previous employee of theirs for many years in their import–export firm, and that she would call him. He came out the next day with a replacement washer.

There was a lesson to be learned there. But the lesson would not have been learned had the author not had to personally *confront* the *contrast* in the "repair process" in France and the United States. In the United States he was used to a repair person making an appointment and usually coming approximately when the appointment was made. When that did not happen in France, he had to confront the difference but without any explanation for why the repairman had behaved this way. When he saw how quickly his previous employer got him to come, he began to realize that this was a country where relationships could mean everything. The author had no relationship with the repairman and so there was apparently no obligation; he could take as long as he wanted and it was acceptable. The mother of the people whose house they lived in had had a long relationship with him. That previous relationship apparently was enough to motivate the repairman to do something even though he was no longer in the parents' employ.

The author now had to modify his understanding of how things can get done (*replacement*). In the United States the relationship between repairman and the customer is a neutral one. However, because customer service is a competitive advantage for business survival in the United States, a deep relationship is not needed. The required relationship is established simply by being a customer; business is business. This notion was in stark contrast to his experience in France, where the relationship is established over years of familiarity, and not by virtue of being classified as a customer over a phone conversation. And so the author realized that to get things done in France, he had to establish and maintain relationships. He had to replace his mental model of supplier–customer relationships to fit a broader definition. This was just one of the many "maps" that was altered during his time in France as an expatriate.

## Strategies for globalizing personnel and general leadership development

You might recall the common elements of *general leadership development* programs cited earlier: 360-degree feedback, executive coaching, job assignments, mentoring, networking, reflection, action learning, and outdoor experiences. How do these elements support or enable the potentially strategic globalizing training methods? First, you might recall that all of the strategies firms were using in Oddou *et al.*'s research (2000a) among Japanese, European and US MNCs are job assignments of one type or another. Job assignments provide the experiential context which generates the cultural contrasts that lead to one's confronting the "normal" way with a "different" way (unfreezing).

The more *experiential* (or action/"outdoor" learning) or more holistic (emotional, behavioral and intellectual) the experience or contrast characterizing the experience, the greater the impact. In addition, the greater the number of *sources* of feedback that tells the manager his or her behavior or decision was or was not appropriate (360-degree feedback), again the more impact the contrast will have. These contrasts cause us to reflect and possibly seek out perspectives from mentors or coaches to help us understand the contrast and how to manage it. All this can more easily lead to the unfreezing and changing of our mental maps. Of course, in the process of working with foreign counterparts in these job assignments, the manager is also building global networks, another important common component of general leadership models. Figure 9.1 illustrates these relationships.

Most global leadership development programs take an eclectic approach to the challenge of developing global leaders, with an emphasis on classroom and information exchange types of approaches. As was discussed earlier, Dodge (1993) found that 20 percent of managerial learning is best suited for classroom-type scenarios, and 30 percent involves exchanging information with others, and learning from them. More in-depth learning occurs from actual, personal work experience – if it is facilitated in a productive way. A major multinational's global leadership development program, as described on its website, is a good case in point.

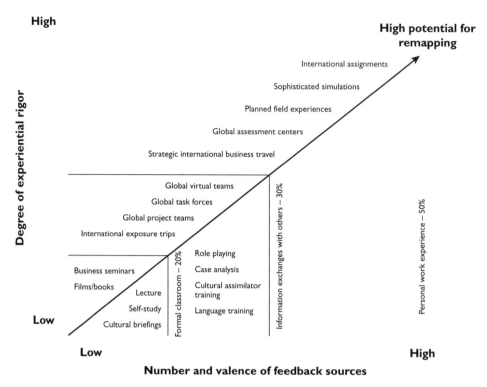

*Figure 9.1* Relationship of experiential rigor and number of feedback sources on mental remapping potential in global leadership development programs

## Colgate's global leadership development program

To be eligible for Colgate's program, the participant must have an MBA and have specific performance potential indicators. Thus, the program already assumes a higher level of development through classroom instruction as well as on-the-job demonstrated performance. Colgate's approach emphasizes continuous learning, leadership and global training programs. It encompasses an individual development planning (IDP) system that encourages the participants to plan their own development by identifying their strengths, skills, and career aspirations. It also contains several of the elements of general leadership programs as well as international exposure, one of the principal methods to globalize personnel cited earlier.

The MBA leadership development program consists of the following major elements, and we will append the nature of the approach (**C** = classroom, **IE** = information exchange with others, and **E** = experiential) to the elements below.

● cross-functional training – including sales, marketing, finance, product supply chain, and a technical department assignment.   **E**

- international assignment exposure.   **E**
- classroom training on specific functional and managerial skills.   **C**
- program led by senior managers and mentors.   **C and IE**

Finally, the individual is continually assessed through a competency-based performance management system.

As can be seen, this program includes a heavy work experience component, regular feedback through performance appraisal, a broad perspective on the organization through the cross-functional assignments, exposure to foreign people and work practices, personal development through classroom-type instruction, and insights and relationship development through senior managers.

Contrast the above comprehensive but more traditional approach to the Seiten Wechsel ("perspective change") program that was run by the Union Bank of Switzerland in the late 1990s (Mendenhall and Stahl 2000: 258). Colgate's program, certainly results in important personal transformations as a result of the different experiences, which inherently include contrasts. Seiten Wechsel includes a component that specifically is directed toward ensuring personal transformation. Part of the ongoing management development efforts of this firm was intended to broaden and expand the perspectives of its managers so they could better understand people who were different from them. UBS managers were assigned to work for one week, full time, with not-for-profit agencies that dealt with various social problems; for example, some managers were assigned to work with terminally ill HIV patients while others were required to care for the homeless at government-sponsored shelters. In other cases, managers were assigned to work with juvenile delinquents or with immigrants from war-ravaged countries who were seeking asylum. Though often painful and challenging, this experience provided the managers with powerful contrasts and challenged them to expand their perspectives and worldviews. The results indicated that this intensive global simulation experience helped the UBS managers to significantly "reduce subjective barriers and prejudices, learn more about themselves, broaden their horizons, and increase their interpersonal skills – all of which are competencies associated with global leadership" (ibid.: 258). Interestingly, 60 percent of the managers who participated in the Seiten Wechsel program continued to support the institution that they served in after the program finished (ibid.).

The Seiten Wechsel program is an excellent example of a global leadership development technique that can be classified in the "personal work experience" dimension of managerial learning. Managers were placed in situations where they had to extend the reach of their existing competencies to handle, cope, and be productive in milieus that were alien to them. Thus, it is possible to develop global leadership competencies without actually sending people overseas. Also, such in-depth simulations can be used to increase the number of managers who are trained to develop global competencies, as this type of global leadership competency training does not require managers to be sent overseas on either long- or short-term assignments, which of course can be quite expensive and budget-prohibitive.

## Conclusion

As the world becomes increasingly interdependent, complex, uncertain, and dynamic, the challenge to understand and operate within that world will become ever more difficult. Firms typically have responded to this environment by creating strategic allies in foreign countries in order to operate more easily in global markets. However, creating strategic foreign allies also increases the need to interact effectively on an operational basis with foreign counterparts in the strategic alliance. This requires managers who can understand and work with people who are different from them and who must work in a cultural milieu that is also different. Simultaneously, forging alliances with foreign firms can decrease the need to develop a keen understanding of that foreign culture itself, because the strategic ally is better positioned to do so. This might only postpone or inhibit the probable necessity of mutual understanding.

Another response to the kind of environment reflected in our current global marketplace is organizational redesign. Alcatel, for example, was struggling with some design issues to try to address a very complex global operation: overall centralization versus decentralization of authority and communications within the corporation; common culture versus decentralized work cultures in a context of allowing some foreign operations more autonomy, given their cultural needs and the business they were in. Some of these challenges can in part be taken care of by redesigning reporting relationships, creating new organizational structures for problem solving across cultures, and so on.

In both these common ways to respond to an ever more challenging global marketplace, the more the managers (and all employees, for that matter) have a global mindset, the more effective the strategies will be, as well as the operations and the specific working relationships of employees representing a diverse set of values and mindsets. Global leadership training is essential. As Black *et al.*'s research (1999b) pointed out, firms have a great deal of progress to make to respond to the need for the quality and quantity of global leaders we need. As more entrants come into the marketplace, we will need increasing numbers of these individuals. The more the training creates contrasts by confronting managers with different ways of being and doing, the more the manager will likely change and evolve to have a better mental map of the world and thereby achieve greater effectiveness and efficiency.

# Bibliography

Adler, N. J. (1994) "Competitive frontiers: Women managing across borders." In N. J. Adler and D. N. Izreali (eds.) *Competitive frontiers: Women managers in a global economy*. Cambridge, MA: Blackwell: 22–40.

Adler, N. J. (1997) "Global leadership: Women leaders." *Management International Review*, 37(1): 171–196.

Adler, N. J. (1998) "Did you hear? Global leadership in charity's world." *Journal of Management Inquiry*, 7(2): 135–143.

Adler, N. J. (2001) "Global leadership: Women leaders." In M. Mendenhall, T. Kühlmann, and G. Stahl (eds.) *Developing global business leaders: Policies, processes and innovations*. Westport, CT: Quorum Books: 73–97.

Adler, N. J. (2002) *International dimensions of organizational behavior*, 4th edn., Cincinnati, OH: South-Western/Thomson Learning.

Adler, N. and Bartholomew, S. (1992) "Managing globally competent people." *Academy of Management Executive*, 6(23): 52–64.

Adler, N. J. and Gundersen, A. (2007) *International Dimensions of Organizational Behavior*. Cincinnati, OH: South-Western Publishing.

Adler, P. (1975) "The transitional experience: An alternative view of culture shock." *Journal of Humanistic Psychology*, 15: 13–23.

Alldredge, M. and Nilan, K. (2000) "3M's leadership competency model: An internally developed solution." *Human Resource Management*, 39(2/3): 133–146.

Ancona, D. G. and Caldwell, D. F. (1992) "Bridging the boundary: External activity and performance in organizational teams." *Administrative Science Quarterly*, 37: 634–661.

Andrews, K. M. and Delahaye, B. I. (2000) "Influences on knowledge processes in organizational learning: The psychosocial filter." *Journal of Management Studies*, 37(7): 797–810.

Argote, L. and Ingram, P. (2000) "Knowledge transfer: A basis for competitive advantage in firms." *Organizational Behavior and Human Decision Processes*, 82: 150–169.

Argote, L., McEvily, B., and Reagans, R. (2003) "Managing knowledge in organizations: An integrative framework and review of emerging themes." *Management Science*, 49, 571–582.

Argyris, C. (1979) "How normal science methodology makes leadership research less additive and less applicable.: In J. G. Hunt and L. L. Larson (eds.) *Crosscurrents in leadership*. Carbondale, IL: Southern Illinois University Press: 47–63.

Armenakis, A. and Bedeian, A. G. (1999) "Organizational change: A review of theory and research in the 1990s." *Journal of Management*, 25(3): 293–315.

Armenakis, A., Harris, S. G. and Feild, H. S. (1999a) "Paradigms in organizational change: Change agent and change target perspectives." In R. Golembiewski (ed.) *Handbook of organizational behavior*. New York: Marcel Dekker.

Armenakis, A. A., Harris, S. G., and Feild, H. S. (1999b) "Making change permanent: A model for institutionalizing change." In W. Pasmore and R. Woodman (eds.) *Research in organization change and development*, vol. 12. Greenwich, CT: JAI Press: 97–128.

Arthur, M. B., Hall, D. T., and Lawrence, B. S. (1989) *Handbook of Career Theory.* New York: Cambridge University Press.

Arthur, W. Jr. and Bennett, W. Jr. (1997) "A comparative test of alternative models of international assignee job performance." In Z. Aycan (ed.) *New approaches to employee management*, vol. 4, *Expatriate management: Theory and research.* Greenwich, CT: JAI Press: 141–172.

Ashby, W. R. (1956) *An introduction to cybernetics.* New York: Wiley.

Au, K. Y. and Fukuda, J. (2002) "Boundary spanning behaviors of expatriates." *Journal of World Business*, 37(4): 285–296.

Barnevik, P. (1996) in an interview in J. Champy and N. Norhria (eds.) *Fast forward: The best ideas on managing business change.* Cambridge, MA: Harvard University Press.

Barrick, M. R. and Mount, M. K. (1991) "The Big Five personality dimensions and job performance: A meta-analysis." *Personnel Psychology*, 44: 1–26

Bartlett, C. A. and Ghoshal, S. (1994) "What is a global manager?" In *Global strategies: Insights from the world's leading thinkers.* Boston, MA: Harvard Business School Press: 77–91.

Bartlett, C. A. and Ghoshal, S. (1989) *Managing across borders: The transnational solution.* Boston, MA: Harvard Business School Press.

Bartlett, C. A. and Ghoshal, S. (2000) *Transnational Management.* Boston, MA: Irwin McGraw-Hill.

Bartlett, C. A., Doz, Y., and Hedlund, G. (1990) *Managing the global firm.* New York: Routledge.

Bartunek, J. M., Gordon, J. R. and Weathersby, R. P. (1983) "Developing 'Complicated' Understanding in Administrators." *Academy of Management Review*, 8(2): 273–284.

Bass, B. M. (1990) *Bass and Stogdill's handbook of leadership: Theory, research and managerial applications*, 3rd edn. New York: Free Press.

Bateson, G. (1980) *Mind and nature: A necessary unity.* New York: Bantam Books.

Bateson, M. C. (1994) *Peripheral Visions: Learning along the way.* New York: HarperCollins.

Beckhard, R. (1991) "Strategies for large system change." In D. A. Kolb, I. M. Rubin, and J. S. Osland (eds.) *The Organizational Behavior Reader.* Upper Saddle River, NJ: Prentice Hall: 662–674.

Beechler, S. and Javidan, M. (2007) "Leading with a global mindset." In M. Javidan, R. Steers, and M. Hitt (eds.) *Advances in International Management*: Special Issue on Global Mindset, 19: 131–169.

Bennett, M. J. (1993) "Towards ethnorelativism: A developmental model of intercultural sensitivity." In R. M. Paige (ed.) *Education for the intercultural experience*, 2nd edn. Yarmouth, ME: Intercultural Press: 21–71.

Bennis, W. G. (1959) "Leadership theory and administrative behavior: The problem of authority." *Administrative Science Quarterly*, 4: 259–260.

Bennis, W. (1989) *On becoming a leader.* Reading, MA: Addison-Wesley.

Bennis, W. (1997) "Cultivating creative genius." *Industry Week*, 246(15): 84–89.

Bennis, W. and Thomas, R. J. (2002) *Geeks and geezers: How era, values, and defining moments shape leaders.* Cambridge, MA: Harvard Business School Press.

Berry, J. W. (1983) "Acculturation: A comparative analysis of alternative forms." In R. J. Samuda and S. L. Woods (eds.) *Perspectives in immigrant and minority education.* New York: University Press of America: 65–78.

Berthoin Antal, A. (2001) "Expatriates' contributions to organizational learning." *Journal of General Management*, 26(4): 62–84.

Bettenhausen, K. L. (1991). "Five years of groups research: What we have learned and what needs to be addressed?" *Journal of Management*, 17: 345–381.

Bikson, T. K., Treverton, G. F., Moini, J., and Lindstrom, G. (2003) *New challenges for international leadership: Lessons from organizations with global missions.* Santa Monica, CA: Rand.

Bingham, C. B., Felin, T., and Black, J. S. (2000) "An interview with John Pepper: What it takes to be a global leader." *Human Resource Management*, 39(2/3): 287–292.

Bird, A. (1994) "Careers as repositories of knowledge: A new perspective on boundaryless careers", *Journal of Organizational Behavior*, 15(4): 325–344.

Bird, A. (2001) "International assignments and careers as repositories of knowledge", in M. Mendenhall, T. Kühlmann, and G. K. Stahl (eds.) *Developing global business leaders: Policies, processes and innovations*. Westport, CT: Quorum.

Bird, A. and Osland, J. (2004) "Global competencies: An introduction." In H. Lane, M. Maznevski, M. Mendenhall and J. McNett (eds.) *Handbook of global management*. Oxford: Blackwell: 57–80.

Black, J. S. (2006) "The mindset of global leaders: Inquisitiveness and duality." In W. H. Mobley and E. Weldon (eds.) *Advances in Global Leadership*, 4: 181–200.

Black, J. S. (1988) "Work-role transition: A study of American expatriate managers in Japan." *Journal of International Business Studies*, 19(2): 274–291.

Black, J. S. and Gregersen, H. B. (1990) "Expectations, satisfaction and intention to leave of American expatriate managers in Japan." *International Journal of Intercultural Relations*, 14: 485–506.

Black, J. S. and Gregersen, H. B. (1999) "The right way to manage expatriates", *Harvard Business Review*, 77(2): 52–54, 56, 58, 60–62.

Black, J. S. and Gregersen, H. (2000) "High impact training: Forging leaders for the global frontier." *Human Resource Management*, 39(2/3): 173–184.

Black, J. S., Mendenhall, M., and Oddou, G. (1991) "Toward a comprehensive model of international adjustment: An integration of multiple theoretical perspectives." *Academy of Management Review*, 16(2): 291–317.

Black, J. S., Gregersen, H., Mendenhall, M., and Stroh, L. (1999a) *Globalizing people through international assignments*. New York: Addison-Wesley Longman.

Black, J. S., Morrison, A., and Gregersen, H. (1999b) *Global explorers: The next generation of leaders*. New York: Routledge.

Blakeney, R., Oddou, G., and Osland, J. (2006a) "The effects of repatriate characteristics on knowledge transfer." Paper presented at the Academy of Management meetings, Atlanta, GA.

Blakeney, R., Oddou, G., and Osland, J. S. (2006b) "Repatriate assets: factors impacting knowledge transfer." In M. J. Morley, N. Heraty, and D. G. Collings (eds.) *International HRM and International Assignments*. New York: Palgrave Macmillan: 181–199.

Boisot, M. H. (1998) *Knowledge assets: Securing competitive advantage in the information economy*. Oxford: Oxford University Press.

Bonache, J. and Brewster, C. (2001) "Knowledge transfer and the management of expatriation." *Thunderbird International Business Review*, 43(1): 145–168.

Booz Allen Hamilton (1982) *New Products Management for the 1980s*. New York: Booz Allen Hamilton.

Boyacigiller, N. A. and Adler, N. J. (1997) "Insiders and outsiders: Bridging the worlds of organizational behavior and international management." In B. Toyne and D. Nigh (eds.) *International business: An emerging vision*. Columbia, SC: University of South Carolina Press: 396–416.

Boyatzis, R. E. (1982) *The competent manager: A model for effective performance*. New York: John Wiley.

Brake, T. (1997) *The global leader: Critical factors for creating the world class organization*. Chicago: Irwin Professional Publishing.

Bridges, W. (1995) "Managing organizational change." In W. W. Burke (ed.) *Managing Organizational Change*. New York: American Management Association: 20.

Brislin, R. W. (1981) *Cross-cultural encounters: Face-to-face interaction.* New York: Pergamon.

Bryant, S. and Nguyen, T. (2002) "Knowledge acquisition and sharing in international strategic alliances: The role of trust." Paper presented at the annual meeting of the Academy of Management, Washington, DC.

Burke, W. W. (2002) "The organizational change leader." In M. Goldsmith, V. Govindarajan, B. Kaye, and A. Vicere (eds.) *The Many Facets of Leadership.* Upper Saddle Creek, NJ: Financial Times Prentice Hall: 83–97.

Burke, W. W. and Litwin, G. H. (1992) "A causal model of organizational performance and change." *Journal of Management,* 18: 523–545.

Busco, C., Frigo, M. L., Giovannoni, E., Riccaboni, A., and Scapens, R. W. (2006) "Integrating global organizations through performance measurement systems." *Strategic Finance,* 87(7): 30–35.

*BusinessWeek Online.* "The world's most innovative companies." http://www.businessweek.com/magazine/content/06_17/b3981401.htm (accessed January 1, 2006).

Buss, A. H. (1989) "Personality as traits." *American Psychologist,* 44(11): 1378–1388.

Caligiuri, P. M. (1995) "Individual characteristics related to effective performance in cross-cultural work settings (expatriate)." Unpublished doctoral dissertation, Pennsylvania State University, University Park.

Caligiuri, P. (2000) "The Big Five personality characteristics as predictors of expatriate's desire to terminate the assignment and supervisor-rated performance." *Personnel Psychology,* 53: 67–89.

Caligiuri, P. (2004) "Global leadership development through expatriate assignments and other international experiences." Paper presented at the Academy of Management, New Orleans, August 2004.

Caligiuri, P. and DiSanto, V. (2001) "Global competence: What is it and can it be developed through global assignments?" *Human Resource Planning,* 24(3): 27–38.

Canney Davison, S. (1994) "Creating a high performance international team." *Journal of Management Development,* 13: 81–90.

Champy, J. and Nohria, N. (1996a) *Fast forward: The best ideas on managing business change.* Cambridge, MA: Harvard University Press.

Champy, J. and Nohria, N. (1996b) "The eye of the storm: The force at the center." In J. Champy and N. Nohria (eds.) *Fast forward: The best ideas on managing business change.* Cambridge, MA: Harvard University Press: 263–264.

Charan, R., Drotter, S., and Noel, J. (2001) *The leadership pipeline.* San Francisco: Jossey-Bass.

Chen, G. M. and Starosta, W. J. (1999) "A review of the concept of intercultural awareness." *Human Communication,* 2: 27–54.

Clawson, J. G. (2006) *Level three leadership: Getting below the surface.* Upper Saddle River, NJ: Prentice-Hall.

Coleman, J. S. (1988) "Social capital in the creation of human capital." *American Journal of Sociology,* 94: S95–S120.

Colgate (2007) http://colgate.51job.com/mba_insidepage.php (accessed May 29, 2007).

Conger, J. A. and Ready, D. A. (2004) "Rethinking leadership competencies." *Executive Forum,* Spring Issue: 41–47.

Cooper, R. G. (2001) Winning at new products: Accelerating the process from idea to launch. Cambridge, MA: Basic Books.

Cornett-DeVito, M. and McGlone, E. (2000) "Multicultural communication training for law enforcement officers: A case study." *Criminal Justice Policy Review,* 11: 234–253.

Corporate Leadership Council (2000) *The new global assignment: Developing and retaining future leaders.* Executive Inquiry. Washington, DC: Corporate Leadership Council.

Costa, P. T. and McCrae, R. R. (1985) *The NEO PI Personality Inventory.* Odessa, FL: Psychological Assessment Resources.

Costa, P. T. and McCrae, R. R. (1992) "Four ways five factors are basic." *Personality and Individual Differences*, 13: 653–665.

Coutu, D. L. (2004) "Putting leaders on the couch: A conversation with Manfred F. R. Kets de Vries." *Harvard Business Review*, 82(1): 64–71.

Cross, R. and Prusak, L. (2003) "The political economy of knowledge markets in organizations." In M. Easterby-Smith and M. Lyles (eds.) *The Blackwell Handbook of Organizational Learning and Knowledge Management*, Malden, MA: Blackwell: 454–472.

Cummings, T. C. and Worley, C. G. (2004) *Organization Development and Change*. Cincinnati, OH: Southwestern.

Dalton, M. A. (1998) "Developing leaders for global roles." In C. D. McCauley, R. S. Moxley, and E. Van Velsor (eds.) *The Center for Creative Leadership Handbook of Leadership Development*. San Francisco: Jossey-Bass: 379–402.

Dalton, M., Ernst, C., Deal, J., and Leslie, J. (2002) *Success for the new global manager: What you need to know to work across distances, countries, and cultures*. San Francisco: Jossey-Bass and the Center for Creative Leadership.

Dalton, M. and Wilson, M. (2000) "The relationship of the five-factor model of personality to job performance for a group of Middle Eastern expatriate managers." *Journal of Cross-cultural Psychology*, 31(2): 250–258.

Damiran, S. K. (1993). "School and situated knowledge: Travel or tourism?" *Educational Technology*, 33(3): 27–32.

Davis, S. and Finney, S. (2006) "A factor analytic study of the Cross-Cultural Adaptability Inventory." *Educational and Psychological Measurement*, 66(2): 318–330.

Day, D. and Halpin, S. (2001) "Leadership development: A review of industry best practices." Technical report 1111, US Army Research Institute for the Behavioral and Social Sciences. Army Project no. 622785A950.

Deardorff, D. K. (2006) "Identification and assessment of intercultural competence as a student outcome of internationalization." *Journal of Studies in International Education*, 10(3): 241–266.

De Dreu, C. K. W. and Weingart, L. R. (2003) "Task versus relationship conflict, team performance and team member satisfaction: A meta-analysis." *Journal of Applied Psychology*, 88: 741–749.

De Fruyt, F., McCrae, R. R., Szirmák, Z., and Nagy, J. (2004) "The Five-Factor personality inventory as a measure of the Five-Factor Model: Belgian, American and Hungarian comparisons with the NEO-PI-R." *Assessment*, 11: 207–215.

Deller, J. (1998) "Personality scales can make a difference in expatriate selection: The case of Germans working in Korea." Paper presented at the International Congress of Applied Psychology, San Francisco, August 1998.

Den Hartog, D. N., House, R. J., Hanges, P. J., Ruiz-Quintanilla, S. A., Dorfman, P. W., and Associates (1999) "Culture specific and cross-culturally generalizable implicit leadership theories: Are attributes of charismatic/transformational leadership universally endorsed?" *Leadership Quarterly*, 10(2): 219–256.

Denison, D., Hoojiberg, R., and Quinn, R. (1995) "Paradox and performance: Toward a theory of behavioral complexity in managerial leadership." *Organization Science*, 6: 76–92.

Dess, G. G. and Picken, J. C. (2000) "Changing roles: Leadership in the 21st century." *Organizational Dynamics*, 28(3): 31.

Dinges, N. G. and Baldwin, K. D. (1996) "Intercultural competence: A research perspective." In D. Landis and R. S. Bhagat (eds.) *Handbook of intercultural training*, 2nd edn. Thousand Oaks, CA: Sage: 106–123.

DiStefano, J. J. and Maznevski, M. L. (2000) "Creating value with diverse teams in global management." *Organizational Dynamics*, 29: 45–63.

Dobbs, R., Leslie, K., and Mendonca, L. T. (2005) "Building the healthy corporation." *McKinsey Quarterly*, 3: 62–71.

Dodge, B. (1993) "Empowerment and the evolution of learning." *Education and Training*, 35(5): 3–10.

Dotlich, D. L., and Noel, J. L. (1998) *Action learning: How the world's top companies are re-creating their leaders and themselves.* San Francisco: Jossey-Bass.

Downes, M. and Thomas, A. S. (1999) "Managing overseas assignments to build organizational knowledge." *Human Resource Planning Journal*, 22(1): 33–48.

Doz, Y. and Prahalad, C. K. (1987) "A process model of strategic redirection in large complex firms: The case of multinational corporations." In A. M. Pettigrew (ed.) *The management of strategic change.* Oxford: Basil Blackwell: 63–83.

Doz, Y. L., Santos, J., and Williamson, P. (2001) *From global to metanational.* Boston, MA: Harvard Business School.

Drath, W. H. (1998) "Approaching the future of leadership development." In C. D. McCauley, R. S. Moxley, and E. Van Velsor (eds.) *Handbook of leadership development.* San Francisco/Greensboro: Jossey-Bass/Center for Creative Leadership: 403–432.

Dreyfus, H. L. and Dreyfus, S. E. (1986) *Mind over machine: The power of human intuitive expertise in the era of the computer.* New York: Free Press.

Driskat, V. U. and Wheeler, J. V. (2003) "Managing from the boundary: The effective leadership of self-managing work teams." *Academy of Management Journal*, 46: 435–457.

Dulek, R. E. and Fielden, J. S. (1991) "International communication: An executive primer." *Business Horizons*, 34(1): 20–29.

Earley, P. C. and Mosakowski, E. A. (2000) "Creating hybrid team cultures: An empirical test of transnational team functioning." *Academy of Management Journal*, 43: 26–49.

Elliot, J. (1989) *Requisite organization: The CEO's guide to creative structure and leadership.* Arlington, VA: Cason Hall.

Elron, E. (1997) "Top management teams within multinational corporations: Effects of cultural heterogeneity." *Leadership Quarterly*, 8(4): 393–412.

Emerson, V. (2001) "An interview with Carlos Ghosn, President of Nissan Motors, Ltd. and Industry Leader of the Year." *Journal of World Business*, 36: 3–10.

Evans, P. and Doz, Y. (1989) "The dualistic organization." In P. Evans, Y. Doz, and A. Laurent (eds.) *Human resource management in international firms: Change, globalization, innovation.* London: Macmillan: 219–242.

Evans, P., Pucik, V., and Barsoux, J.-L. (2002) *The global challenge: Frameworks for international human resource management.* Boston, MA: McGraw-Hill.

Eylon, D. and Au, K. Y. (1999) "Exploring empowerment cross-cultural differences among the power distance dimension." *International Journal of Intercultural Relations*, 23: 373–385.

Fantini, A. E. (2000) "A central concern: Developing intercultural competence." http://www.sit.edu/publications/docs/competence.pdf (accessed January 3, 2003).

Faucheux C., Amado G., and Laurent A. (1982) "Organizational development and change." *Annual Reviews of Psychology*, 33: 343–370.

Fehér, J. and Szigeti, M. (2001) "The application of change management methods at business organizations operating in Hungary: Challenges in the business and cultural environment and first practical experience." In D. Denison (ed.) *Managing Organizational Change in Transition Economies.* London: Lawrence Erlbaum: 344–361.

Fennes, H. and Hapgood, K. (1997) *Intercultural learning in the classroom.* London: Cassell.

Fiske, A. P. (1992) "The four elementary forms of sociality: Framework for a unified theory of social relations." *Psychological Review*, 99(4): 689–723.

Florida, R. and Goodnight, J. (2005) "Managing for creativity." *Harvard Business Review*, 83: 124–131.

Fondas, N. (1997) "Feminization unveiled: Management qualities in contemporary writings." *Academy of Management Review*, 22(1): 257–282.

Forster, N. (1999) "Another 'glass ceiling'?: The experiences of women professionals and managers on international assignments." *Gender, Work and Organization*, 6(2): 79–90.

Freeman, R. E. (2004) "The stakeholder approach revisited." *Zeitschrift für Wirtschafts- und Unternehmensethik*, 5: 228–241.

French, J. R. P. and Raven, B. (1959) "The bases of social power", in D. Cartwright (ed.) *Studies in Social Power*, Ann Arbor, MI: University of Michigan Press: 150–167.

Friedman, R. A. and Polodny, J. (1992) "Differences in boundary spanning roles: Labor negotiations and implications for role conflict." *Administrative Science Quarterly*, 37(1): 28–47.

Furuya, N. (2006) "Repatriation management effectiveness: A mechanism for developing global competencies through a comprehensive process of repatriation." Unpublished dissertation, University of Tsukuba, Japan.

Furuya, N., Stevens, M. J., Oddou, G., and Bird, A. (2005) "The effects of HR policies and repatriate self-adjustment on global competency transfer." Paper presented at the Annual Meetings of the Academy of International Business, Quebec City.

Furuya, N., Stevens, M., Oddou, G., Bird, A., and Mendenhall, M. (2006) "Predictors and outcomes of Japanese repatriation effectiveness: Managing the learning and transfer of global competencies." *2006 Best Papers Proceedings of the Association of Japanese Business Studies*, Beijing.

Furuya, N., Stevens, M., Oddou, G., Bird, A., and Mendenhall, M. (2007). "The effects of HR policies and repatriate adjustment on global competency transfer." *Asia-Pacific Journal of Human Resources*, 45: 6–23.

Gelfand, M., Erez, M., and Aycan, Z. (2007) "Cross-cultural organizational behavior." *Annual Review of Psychology*, 58: 479–514.

Ghislanzoni, G. (2006) "Leading change: An interview with the CEO of Eni." *McKinsey Quarterly*, 3: 54–63.

Ghislanzoni, G. and Shearn, J. (2005) "Leading change: An interview with the CEO of Banca Intesa." *McKinsey Quarterly*, 3: 73–81.

Ghoshal, S. and Bartlett, C. A. (1996 ) "Rebuilding behavioral context: A blueprint for corporate renewal." *Sloan Management Review*, 37(2): 23–37.

Gill, A. and Booth, S. (2003) "Identifying future global leaders." *Strategic HR Review*, 2(6): 20–25.

Gold, A. H., Malhotra, A., and Segars, A. H. (2001) "Knowledge management: An organizational capabilities perspective", *Journal of Management Information Systems*, 18(1): 185–214.

Goldsmith, M., Greenberg, C., Robertson, A., and Hu-Chan, M. (2003) *Global leadership: The next generation*. Upper Saddle River, NJ: Prentice Hall.

Goldstein, D. and Smith, D. (1999) "The analysis of the effects of experiential training on sojourners' cross-cultural adaptability." *International Journal of Intercultural Relations*, 23: 157–173.

Goss, T., Pascale, R. T., and Athos, A. (1996) "The reinvention roller coaster: Risking the present for a powerful future." In J. Champy and N. Nohria (eds.) *Fast Forward: The Best Ideas on Managing Business Change*. Cambridge, MA: Harvard University Press: 124–139.

Govindarajan, V. and Gupta, A. K. (2001) "Building an effective global business team." *Sloan Management Review*, Summer: 63–71.

Graen, G. B. and Hui, C. (1999) "Transcultural global leadership in the twenty-first century: Challenges and implications for development." In W. H. Mobley, M. J. Gessner, and V. Arnold (eds.) *Advances in Global Leadership*, 1: 9–26.

Gratton, L. and Ghoshal, S. (2005) "Beyond best practice." *MIT Sloan Management Review*, 46(3): 49–57.

Green, S., Hassan, F., Immelt, J., Marks, M., and Meiland, D. (2003) "In search of global leaders." *Harvard Business Review*, 81(8): 38–45.

Gregersen, H., Black, S., and Morrison, A. J. (1997) "Developing global leaders for competitive advantage." *Strategic Human Resource Development Review*, 1: 77–102.

Gregersen, H. B., Morrison, A. J., and Black, J. S. (1998) "Developing leaders for the global frontier." *Sloan Management Review*, 40: 21–32.

Gudykunst, W. B. (1994) *Bridging differences: Effective intergroup communication*, 2nd edn. London: Sage.

Gunz, H. (1989) "The dual meaning of managerial careers." *Journal of Management Studies*, 26: 225–250.

Gupta, A. and Govindarajan, V. (1991) "Knowledge flows and the structure of control within multinational corporations." *Academy of Management Review*, 16: 768–792.

Gupta, A. K. and Govindarajan, V. (2000) "Knowledge flows within multinational corporations." *Strategic Management Journal*, 21: 473–496.

Gupta, R. and Wendler, J. (2005) "Leading change: An interview with the CEO of P&G," *McKinsey Quarterly*, July: 1–6.

Hall, E. T. (1966) *The Hidden Dimension*. New York: Doubleday.

Hall, E. T. and Hall, M. R. (1990) *Understanding Cultural Differences*. Yarmouth, ME: Intercultural Press.

Hall, D. T., Zhu, G., and Yan, A. (2001) "Developing global leaders: To hold on to them, let them go!" In W. Mobley and M. W. McCall Jr. (eds.) *Advances in Global Leadership*, vol. 2. Stamford, CT: JAI Press.

Hamm, S. (2006) "Innovation: The view from the top." *BusinessWeek Online*. http://www.businessweek.com/magazine/content/06_14/b3978073.htm (accessed January 2, 2006).

Hammer, M. R., Bennett, M. J., and Wiseman, R. (2003) "Measuring intercultural sensitivity: The Intercultural Development Inventory." *International Journal of Intercultural Relations*, 27(4): 421–443.

Hampden-Turner, C. (1994) "The structure of entrapment: Dilemmas standing in the way of women managers and strategies to resolve these." *Deeper News*, 5(1): 1–43.

Hampden-Turner, C. and Trompenaars, F. (2000) *Building cross-cultural competence: How to create wealth from conflicting values*. Chichester, UK: John Wiley.

Handy, C. (2001) *The elephant and the flea: Looking backwards to the future*. London: Hutchinson.

Harris, J. G. (1973) "A science of the South Pacific: Analysis of the character structure of the Peace Corps volunteer." *American Psychologist*, 28: 232–247.

Harris, J. G. (1975) "Identification of cross-cultural talent: The empirical approach of the Peace Corps." *Topics in Culture Learning*, 3: 66–78.

Harrison, D. A. and Shaffer, M. A. (2005) "Mapping the criterion space for expatriate success: Task- and relationship-based performance, effort and adaptation." *International Journal of Human Resource Management*, 16(8): 1454–1474.

Harrison, D. A., Price, K. H., and Bell, M. P. (1998) "Beyond relational demography: Time and the effects of surface- and deep-level diversity on work group cohesion." *Academy of Management Journal*, 41: 96–107.

Harrison, D. A., Shaffer, M. A., and Bhaskar-Shrinivas, P. (2004), "Going places: Roads more or less traveled in research on expatriate experiences." In J. J. Martocchio (ed.) *Research in Personnel and Human Resources Management*, vol. 22. Greenwich, CT: JAI Press, 203–252.

Harvey, M. (1989) "Repatriation of corporate executives: An empirical study." *Journal of International Business Studies*, 20(1): 131–144.

Harvey, M. and Novicevic, M. M. (2004) "The development of political skill and political capital by global leaders through global assignments." *International Journal of Human Resource Management*, 15(7): 1173–1188.

Harzing, A. W. (2001) "Of bears, bumble-bees and spiders: The role of expatriates in controlling foreign subsidiaries." *Journal of World Business*, 36: 366–379.

Hedlund, G. (1986) "The hypermodern MNC: A heterarchy?" *Human Resource Management*, Spring: 9–35.

Helfat, C., Harris, D., and Wolfson, P. (2006) "The pipeline to the top: Women and men in the top executive ranks of U.S. corporations," *Academy of Management Perspectives*, 20(4): 42–64.

Hiatt, J. (2006) *ADKAR: A model for change in business, government and our community*. Loveland, CO: Prosci Research.

Hofstede, G. (1980a) "Motivation, leadership and organization: Do American theories apply?" *Organizational Dynamics*, (9)1: 42–63.

Hofstede, G. (1980b) *Culture's Consequences*. Thousand Oaks, CA: Sage.

Hofstede, G. (2001) *Culture's consequences: Comparing values, behaviors, institutions and organizations across nations*, 2nd edn. London: Sage.

Hollenbeck, G. P. (2001) "A serendipitous sojourn through the global leadership literature." In W. Mobley and M. W. McCall (eds.) *Advances in Global Leadership*, vol. 2. Stamford, CT: JAI Press.

Hoopes, D. S. (1979) "Intercultural communication concepts and the psychology of intercultural experience." In M. Pusch (ed.), *Multicultural education: A crosscultural training approach*. Yarmouth, ME: Intercultural Press: 9–38.

Hosking, D. M. and Morley, I. E. (1988) "The skills of leadership." In J. G. Hunt, B. R. Baliga, H. P. Dachler, C. A. Schriesheim, and R. Steward (eds.) *Emerging leadership vistas*. Lexington, MA: Lexington Books: 89–106.

House, R. J., Hanges, P. J., Javidan, M., Dorfman, P. W., and Gupta, V. (eds.) (2004) *Culture, leadership and organizations: The GLOBE study of 62 societies*. Thousand Oaks, CA: Sage.

Howell, W. C. and Fleishman, E. A. (eds.) (1982) *Human performance and productivity*, vol. 2, *Information processing and decision making*. Hillsdale, NJ: Lawrence Erlbaum.

Inkpen, A. (1998) "A note on the dynamics of learning alliances: Competition, cooperation and relative scope." *Strategic Management Journal*, 212: 775–779.

Inkpen, A. C. and Dinur, A. (1998) "Knowledge management processes and international joint ventures." *Organization Science*, 9: 454–468.

Ireland, R. D. and Hitt, M. A. (1999) "Achieving and maintaining strategic competitiveness in the 21st century: The role of strategic leadership." *Academy of Management Executive*, 13(1): 43–57.

Ireland, R. D. and Hitt, M. A. (2005) "Achieving and maintaining strategic competitiveness in the 21st century: The role of strategic leadership." *Academy of Management Executive*, 19(4): 63–77.

Javidan, M. and House, R. J. (2001) "Cultural acumen for the global manager: Lessons from Project Globe," *Organizational Dynamics*, 29(4): 289–305.

Javidan, M., Dorfman, P., Sully de Luque, M., and House, R. (2006) "In the eye of the beholder: Cross cultural lessons in leadership from Project GLOBE." *Academy of Management Perspectives*, February: 67–90.

Jehn, K. A. (1994) "Enhancing effectiveness: An investigation of advantages and disadvantages of value-based intragroup conflict." *International Journal of Conflict Management*, 5: 223–238.

Jehn, K. A. (1995) "A multimethod examination of the benefits and detriments of intragroup conflict." *Administrative Science Quarterly*, 40: 256–282.

Jick, T. and Peiperl, M. (2003) *Managing change: Cases and concepts*. Boston, MA: Irwin.

Jokinen, T. (2005) "Global leadership competencies: a review and discussion." *Journal of European Industrial Training*, 29(2/3): 199–216.

Kanter, R. M. (1997) *World class: Thriving locally in the global economy*. New York: Simon and Schuster.

Kashima, T. (2006) "Phenomenological research on the intercultural sensitivity of returned Peace Corps volunteers in the Athens community." Unpublished master's thesis. Ohio University.

Katzenbach, J. R. (1997) "The myth of the top management team." *Harvard Business Review*, 75(6): 83–91.

Kayworth, T. R. and Leidner, D. L. (2001/2002) "Leadership effectiveness in global virtual teams." *Journal of Management Information Systems*, 18(3): 7–40.

Kealey, D. J. (2003) *The intercultural living and working inventory: History and research.* http://www.dfait-maeci.gc.ca/cfsa-icse/cil-cai/ilwi-ici-background-en.as (accessed December 12, 2003).

Keller, R. T. (2001) "Cross-functional project groups in research and new product development: Diversity, communications, job stress and outcomes." *Academy of Management Journal*, 44: 547–555.

Kelley, C. and Meyers, J. (1992) *Cross-cultural adaptability inventory: Action planning guide.* Minneapolis, MN: Reid London House.

Kelley, C. and Meyers, J. (1995a) *The Cross-Cultural Adaptability Inventory.* Minneapolis, MN: National Computer Systems.

Kelley, C. and Meyers, J. (1995b) *The Cross-Cultural Adaptability Inventory Manual.* Minneapolis, MN: National Computer Systems.

Kelley, T., Littman, J., and Peters, T. (2001) *The art of innovation: Lessons in creativity from Ideo, America's leading design firm.* New York: Doubleday.

Kets de Vries, M. (2005) *Global Executive Leadership Inventory: Facilitator's guide.* San Francisco, CA: Pfeiffer.

Kets de Vries, M. F. R. with Florent-Treacy, E. (1999) *The new global leaders.* San Francisco: Jossey-Bass.

Kets de Vries, M. with Florent-Treacy, E. (2002) "Global leadership from A to Z: Creating high commitment organizations." *Organizational Dynamics*, 295(309): 1–16.

Kets de Vries, M. and Mead, C. (1992) "The development of the global leader within the multinational corporation." In V. Pucik, N. M. Tichy, and C. K. Barnett (eds.) *Globalizing management: Creating and leading the competitive organization.* New York: John Wiley.

Kets de Vries, M. F. R., Vrignaud, P., and Florent-Treacy, E. (2004). "Global Executive Leadership Inventory: Development and psychometric properties of a 360-degree feedback instrument." *International Journal of Human Resource Management*, 15, 3: 475–492.

Kidd, J. B. and Teramoto, Y. (1995) "The learning organization: The case of the Japanese RHQs in Europe." *Management International Review*, 35(2, special issue): 39–56.

Kluckhohn, F. and Strodtbeck, F. L. (1961) *Variations in value orientations.* Evanston, IL: Row, Peterson.

Kochan, T., Batt, R., and Dyer, R. (1992) "International human resource studies: A framework for future research." In D. Lewin, O. S. Mitchell and P. D. Sherer (eds.) *Research frontiers in industrial relations and human resources.* Madison, WI: Industrial Relations Research Association.

Kodama, M. (2005a) "How two Japanese high-tech companies achieved rapid innovation via strategic community networks." *Strategy and Leadership*, 33(6): 39–47.

Kodama, M. (2005b) "Technological innovation through networked strategic communities: A study on a high tech company in Japan." *SAM Advanced Management Journal*, 70(Winter): 21–35.

Kotter, J. P. (1990a) "a force for change: How leadership differs from management/review." *CA Magazine*, 123(10): 22.

Kotter, J. P. (1990b) "What leaders really do." *Harvard Business Review*, 68(3): 103.

Kotter, J. (1990c) *A force for change: How leadership differs from management.* New York: Free Press.

Kotter, J. and Cohen, D. (2002) *The heart of change: Real-life stories about how people change their organizations.* Cambridge, MA: Harvard Business School Press.

Koudal, P. and Coleman, G. C. (2005) "Coordinating operations to enhance innovation in the global corporation." *Strategy and Leadership*, 33(4): 20–32.

Kozai Group, Inc. (2002) *The Global Competencies Inventory.* St. Louis, MO: Kozai.

Lane, H. W., Maznevski, M. L., and Mendenhall, M. E. (2004a). "Hercules meets Buddha."

In H. W. Lane, M. Maznevski, M. E. Mendenhall, and J. McNett (eds.) *The handbook of global management: A guide to managing complexity.* Oxford: Blackwell: 3–25.

Lane, H. W., Maznevski, M. L., Mendenhall, M. E., and McNett, J. (2004b) *The Blackwell handbook of global management: A guide to managing complexity.* Oxford: Blackwell.

Lau, D. C. and Murnighan, J. K. (1998) "Demographic diversity and faultlines: The compositional dynamics of organizational groups." *Academy of Management Review*, 23: 325–340.

Lawson, E. and Price, C. (2003) "The psychology of change management." *McKinsey Quarterly*, Special Edition: The Value in Organization: 31–41

Lazarova, M. and Tarique, I. (2005) "Knowledge transfer upon repatriation." *Journal of World Business*, 40(4): 361–373.

Leavitt, H. J. (2003) "Why hierarchies thrive." *Harvard Business Review*, 81(3): 96–102.

Leiba-O'Sullivan, S. (1999) "The distinction between stable and dynamic cross-cultural competencies: Implications for expatriate trainability." *Journal of International Business Studies*, 30(4): 709–725.

Leslie, J. B., Dalton, M., Ernst, C., and Deal, J. (2002) *Managerial effectiveness in a global context.* A Center for Creative Leadership Report. Greensboro, NC: CCL Press.

Levy, O., Beechler, S., Taylor, S., and Boyacigiller, N. (2007) "What do we talk about when we talk about 'global mindset'? Managerial cognition in multinational corporations." *Journal of International Business Studies*, 38: 231–258.

Lewin, K. (1947) "Frontiers in group dynamics." *Human Relations*, 1: 5–41.

Loewe, P. and Dominiquini, J. (2006) "Overcoming the barriers to effective innovation." *Strategy and Leadership*, 34(1): 24–30.

Louis, M. (1980a) "Career transitions: Varieties and commonalities." *Academy of Management Review*, 5(3): 329–340.

Louis, M. R. (1980b) "Surprise and sense making: What newcomers experience in entering unfamiliar organizational settings." *Administrative Science Quarterly*, 25: 226–251.

Lubatkin, M., Ndiaye, M., and Vengroff, R. (1997a) "The nature of managerial work in developing countries: A limited test of the universalist hypothesis." *Journal of International Business Studies*, 28(4): 711–733.

Lubatkin, M., Ndiaye, M., and Vengroff, R. (1997b) "Assessing managerial work in Senegal: Do Western models apply?" *Gestión Internacional*, 1(1): 67–76.

Lustig, M. W. and Koester, J. (2003). *Intercultural competence: Interpersonal communication across cultures*, 4th edn. Boston, MA: Allyn and Bacon.

McBer and Co. (1995) "Mastering global leadership: Hay/McBer international CEO leadership study." Boston, MA: Hay/McBer Worldwide Resource Center.

McCall, M. W. Jr. (1998) *High flyers: Developing the next generation of leaders.* Boston, MA: Harvard Business School Press.

McCall, M. W. Jr. and Hollenbeck, G. P. (2002) *Developing global executives: The lessons of international experience.* Boston, MA: Harvard Business School Press.

McClelland, D. C. (1973) "Testing for competence rather than for intelligence." *American Psychologist*, 28: 1–14.

McCrae, R. R. and Costa, P. T. (1990) *Personality in adulthood.* New York: Guilford Press.

McFarland, L. J., Senn, L. E., and Childress, J. R. (1993) *21st century leadership: Dialogues with 100 top leaders.* New York: Leadership Press.

McGarvey, R. J. (2006) "Assembling the leader: Meet the new breed CEOs." In *Global talent: An anthology of human capital strategies for today's borderless enterprise.* Washington, DC: Human Capital Institute.

McKinsey and Co. (1998) "The war for talent." *McKinsey Quarterly*, (3): 44–58.

Madsen, S. R. and Hammond, S. (2005) "Where have all the leaders gone? An interview with Margaret J. Wheatley about life-affirming leadership." *Journal of Management Inquiry*, 14(1): 71–77.

Management Issues News (2006) "Women still rare in Europe's boardrooms" (June 20). http://www.management-issues.com/2006/8/24/research/women-still-rare-in-europes-boardrooms.asp (accessed December 26, 2006).

Marquardt, M. J. and Berger, N. O. (2000) *Global Leaders for the 21st Century.* Albany, NY: State University of New York Press.

Maruca, R. F. (1994) "The right way to go global: An interview with Whirlpool CEO David Whitwam." *Harvard Business Review*, 72(2): 134.

Masuda, T. and Nisbett, R. E. (2006) "Culture and change blindness." *Cognitive Science*, 30: 381–399.

Maznevski, M. L. (1994) "Understanding our differences: Performance in decision-making groups with diverse members." *Human Relations*, 47: 531–552.

Maznevski, M. L. and Athanassiou, N. A. (2006) "Bringing the outside in: Learning and knowledge management through external networks." In I. Nonaka and K. Ichijo (eds.) *Knowledge creation and management: New challenges for managers*. Oxford: Oxford University Press.

Maznevski, M. L. and Chudoba, K. M. (2000) "Bridging space over time: Global virtual team dynamics and effectiveness." *Organization Science*, 11(5): 473–492.

Maznevski, M. L. and DiStefano, J. J. (1995) "Measuring culture in international management: The cultural perspectives questionnaire." *The University of Western Ontario Working Paper Series*, 95-39.

Maznevski, M. L. and Jonsen, K. (2006) "The value of different perspectives." *Financial Times Mastering Management: Managing Uncertainty*, March 24.

Maznevski, M. L., Canney Davidson, S., and Jonsen, K. (2006) "Global virtual teams dynamics and effectiveness." In G. K. Stahl and I. Björkman (eds.) *Handbook of research in international human resource management*, Cheltenham, UK: Edward Elgar.

Mendenhall, M. (1999) "On the need for paradigmatic integration in international human resource management." *Management International Review*, 39(3): 65–87.

Mendenhall, M. (2001a) "New perspectives on expatriate adjustment and its relationship to global leadership development." In M. Mendenhall, T. Kühlmann, and G. Stahl (2001) *Developing global business leaders: Policies, processes and innovations*. Westport, CT: Quorum Books: 1–16.

Mendenhall, M. E. (2001b) "Global assignments, global leaders: Leveraging global assignments as leadership development programs." Paper presented at the Research Colloquium on Expatriate Management, Cranfield Business School, Cranfield, UK, March 15, 2001.

Mendenhall, M. (2006) "The elusive, yet critical challenge of developing global leaders." *European Management Journal*, 24(6): 422–429.

Mendenhall, M. and Oddou, G. (1985) "The dimensions of expatriate acculturation: A review." *Academy of Management Review*, 10(1): 39–47.

Mendenhall, M. and Osland, J. S. (2002) "An overview of the extant global leadership research." Symposium presentation, Academy of International Business, Puerto Rico, June.

Mendenhall, M. and Stahl, G. K. (2000) "Expatriate training and development: Where do we go from here?" *Human Resource Management*, 39(2/3): 251–265.

Mendenhall, M., Kühlmann, T., and Stahl, G. (2001) *Developing global business leaders: Policies, processes and innovations*. Westport, CT: Quorum Books.

Mendenhall, M., Kühlmann, T., Stahl, G., and Osland, J. S. (2002) "Employee development and expatriate assignments." In M. J. Gannon and K. L. Newman (eds.) *The Blackwell handbook of cross-cultural management*. Malden, MA: Blackwell: 155–183.

Mendenhall, M., Jensen, R., Black, J. S., and Gregersen, H. (2003) "Seeing the elephant: HRM challenges in the age of globalization." *Organizational Dynamics*, 32(3): 261–274.

Mercer Delta (2006) "The global leadership imperative." Presentation to the Human Resource Planning Society, March 8.

Meyer, J. P. and Allen, N. J. (1997) *Commitment in the Workplace: Theory, Research and Application*, Thousand Oaks, CA: Sage.

Meyer, S. E. and Kelly, J. E. (1992) *The Cross-Cultural Adaptability Inventory workbook.* Yarmouth, ME: Intercultural Press.

Miller, E. L. (1973) "The international selection decision: A study of some dimensions of managerial behavior in the selection decision process." *Academy of Management Journal*, 16: 239–252.

Millikin, J. P. and Fu, D. (2005) "The global leadership of Carlos Ghosn at Nissan." *Thunderbird International Business Review*, 47(1): 121–137.

Minbaeva, D. B. (2005) "HRM practices and MNC knowledge transfer." *Personnel Review*, 34(1): 125–144.

Mintzberg, H. (1973) *The nature of managerial work.* New York: Harper and Row.

Mobley, W. H. and Dorfman, P. W. (2003) *Advances in global leadership*, vol. 3. JAI Press.

Mobley, W. H. and McCall, M. W. (2001) *Advances in global leadership*, vol. 2, JAI Press.

Mobley, W. H. and Weldon, E. (2006) *Advances in global leadership*, vol. 4. Stamford, CT: JAI Press.

Mobley, W. H., Gessner, M. J., and Arnold, V. (1999) *Advances in global leadership*, vol. 1. Stamford, CT: JAI Press.

Mol, S. T., Van Oudenhoven, J. P., and Van der Zee, K. I. (2001) Validation of the Multicultural Personality Questionnaire among an internationally oriented student population in Taiwan." In F. Salili and R. Hoosain (eds.) *Multicultural education: Issues, policies, and practices.* Greenwich, CT: IAP: 167–186.

Monge, P. and Fulk, J. (1999) "Communication technology for global network organizations." In G. DeSanctis and J. Fulk (eds.) *Shaping organization form: Communication, connection and community.* Thousand Oaks, CA: Sage: 71–100.

Moran, R. T. and Riesenberger, J. R. (1994) *The global challenge: Building the new worldwide enterprise.* London: McGraw-Hill.

Moro Bueno, C. and Tubbs, S. (2004) "Identifying global leadership competencies: An exploratory study." *Journal of American Academy of Business*, 5(1/2): 80–87.

Morrison, A. J. (2000) "Developing a global leadership model." *Human Resource Management*, 39: 117–127.

Morrison, A. (2006) "Ethical standards and global leadership." In W. H. Mobley and E. Weldon (eds.) *Advances in Global Leadership*, 4: 165–179.

Mount, M. K. and Barrick, M. R. (1998) "Five reasons why the 'Big Five' article has been frequently cited." *Personnel Psychology*, 51: 849–857.

Mudrack, P. E. (1989) "Group cohesiveness and productivity: a closer look." *Human Relations*, 42: 771–785.

Mullen, B. and Copper, C. (1994) "The relation between group cohesiveness and performance: An integration." *Psychological Bulletin*, 115: 210–227.

Naumann, E. (1992) "A conceptual model of expatriate turnover." *Journal of International Business Studies*, 23(3): 499–531.

Nisbett, R. E. (2003) *The geography of thought: How Asians and Westerners think differently . . . and why.* New York: The Free Press.

Nonaka, I. (1990) "Managing innovation as a knowledge-creation process: A new model for a knowledge-creating organization." Paper presented at New York University, Stern School of Business, International Business Colloquium.

Nonaka, I. (1991a) "Managing the firm as an information creation process." *Advances in Information Processing in Organizations*, 4: 239–275. Greenwich, CT: JAI Press.

Nonaka, I. (1991b) "The knowledge-creating company." *Harvard Business Review*, 69(6): 96–104.

Nonaka, I. (1994) "A dynamic theory of organizational knowledge creation." *Organization Science*, 5: 14–37.

Nonaka, I. and Kenney, M. (1991) "Towards a new theory of innovation management: A case study comparing Canon, Inc. and Apple Computer, Inc." *Journal of Engineering and Technology Management*, 8(1): 67–83.

Nurasimha, S. (2000) "Organizational knowledge, human resource management and sustained competitive advantage: Toward a framework." *Competitiveness Review*, 10: 123–135.

Oddou, G. R. (2002) "Repatriate assets and firm performance: Toward a model." Paper presented at the annual meeting of the Academy of Management, Denver.

Oddou, G. and Mendenhall, M. (1988) "The overseas assignment: A practical look." *Business Horizons*, 31(5): 78–84.

Oddou, G. and Mendenhall, M. (1991) "Succession planning in the 21st century: How well are we grooming our future business leaders?" *Business Horizons*, January–February, 34(1): 26–34.

Oddou, G. and Osland, J. (2003) "The transfer of repatriate assets: Variables influencing the knowledge transfer." Paper given at the Seventh International Human Resource Management Congress, Limerick, Ireland, June.

Oddou, G., Gregersen, H., Derr, B., and Black, J. S. (2000a) "Internationalizing human resources: Strategy differences among European, Japanese and U.S. multinationals." In M. Mendenhall, T., Kühlmann, and G. Stahl (eds.) *Developing global business leaders: Policies, processes, and innovations*. Westport, CT: Quorum Books: 99–116.

Oddou, G., Mendenhall, M. E., and Ritchie, J. B. (2000b) "Leveraging travel as a tool for global leadership development." *Human Resource Management*, 39(2–3): 159–172.

Oddou, G., Osland, J. and Blakeney, R. (in press) "Repatriating knowledge: Variables influencing the 'transfer' process." *Journal of International Business Studies*.

Ones, D. S. and Viswesvaran, C. (1999) "Relative importance of personality dimensions for expatriate selection: A policy capturing study." *Human Performance*, 12(3–4): 275–294.

O'Reilly, C. A., Williams, K. Y., and Barsade, S. (1998) "Group demography and innovation: Does diversity help?" *Research on Managing Groups and Teams*, 1: 183–207.

Osland, J. S. (1991) "A replication of Mintzberg's managerial roles study." Unpublished working paper, Alajuela, Costa Rica: INCAE.

Osland, J. (1995) *The adventure of working abroad: Hero tales from the global frontier*. San Francisco: Jossey-Bass.

Osland, A. (1996) "The role of leadership and cultural contingencies in TQM in Central America." *Journal of Business and Management*, 3: 64–80.

Osland, J. S. (2000) "The journey inward: Expatriate hero tales and paradoxes." *Human Resource Management*, 39(2–3): 227–238.

Osland, J. S. (2001) "The quest for transformation: The process of global leadership development." In M. Mendenhall, T. Kühlmann, and G. Stahl (eds.) *Developing global business leaders: Policies, processes and innovations*. Westport, CT: Quorum Books: 137–156.

Osland, J. S. (2004) "Building community through change." In H. W. Lane, M. Maznevski, M. E. Mendenhall, and J. McNett (eds.) *The Blackwell handbook of global management: A guide to managing complexity*. Malden, MA: Blackwell: 134–151.

Osland, J. S. and Bird, A. (2000) "Beyond sophisticated stereotyping: Cultural sensemaking in context." *Academy of Management Executive*, 14(1): 65–76.

Osland, J. S. and Bird, A. (2006) "Global leaders as experts." In W. Mobley and E. Weldon (eds.) *Advances in Global Leadership*, vol. 4. Stamford, CT: JAI Press: 123–142.

Osland, A. and Osland, J. S. (2007) "Aracruz Celulose: Best practices icon but still at risk." *International Journal of Manpower*, 28(5): 435–450.

Osland, J. S., Adler, N. J., and Brody, L.W. (2002) "Developing global leadership in women: Lessons and sense making from an organizational change effort." In R. Burke and D. Nelson (eds.) *Advancing Women's Careers*. Oxford: Blackwell: 15–36.

Osland, J. S., Oddou, G., and Blakeley, R. (2005) "Getting the 'goods' back home: Variables influencing repatriate knowledge transfer." Paper presented at the Western Academy of Management. Las Vegas, Nevada, April 2005.

Osland, J., Bird, A., Mendenhall, M. E., and Osland, A. (2006) "Developing global leadership capabilities and global mindset: A review." In G. K. Stahl and I. Björkman (eds.) *Handbook of research in international human resource management*. Cheltenham, UK: Edward Elgar: 197–222.

Osland, J., Bird, A., Osland, A., and Oddou, G. (2007a) "Expert cognition in high technology global leaders." Paper presented at NDM8, Eighth Naturalistic Decision Making Conference, Monterey, CA, June.

Osland, J. S., Kolb, D., Rubin, I., and Turner, M. (2007b) *Organizational behavior: An experimental approach*. Upper Saddle River, NJ: Prentice Hall.

Paige, R. M. (ed.) (1993) *Education for the intercultural experience*. Yarmouth, ME: Intercultural Press.

Paige, R. M., Jacobs-Cassuto, M., Yershova, Y. A., and DeJaeghere, J. (2003) "Assessing intercultural sensitivity: An empirical analysis of the Hammer and Bennett Intercultural Development Inventory." *International Journal of Intercultural Relations*, 27(4): 467–486.

Pandya, M. and Shell, R. (2005) *Lasting leadership*. Upper Saddle River, NJ: Pearson Education publishing as Wharton School Publishing.

Parsons, T. and Shils, E. (1951) *Toward a general theory of action*. Cambridge, MA: Harvard University Press.

Pascale, R. (1998) "Grassroots leadership – Royal Dutch/Shell." *Fast Company* 14: 110. http://www.fastcompany.com/online/14/grassroots.html (accessed February, 4 2007).

Pascale, R. T. (1999) "Surfing the edge of chaos." *Sloan Management Review*, 40: 83–94.

Pascale, R.T. and Athos, A. G. (1981) *The art of Japanese management*. New York: Simon and Schuster.

Pedersen, P. (1994) *A handbook for developing multicultural awareness*, 2nd edn. Alexandria, VA: American Counseling Association.

Pederson, P. (1995) *The five stages of culture shock*. London: Greenwood.

Petrick, J. A., Scherer, R. F., Brodzinski, J. D., Quinn, J. F., and Fall Ainina, M. (1999) "Global leadership skills and reputational capital: Intangible resources for sustainable competitive advantage." *Academy of Management Executive*, 13(1): 58–69.

Pfeffer, J. (1995) "Producing sustainable competitive advantage through the effective management of people." *Academy of Management Executive*, 9(1): 55.

Polanyi, M. (1966) *The tacit dimension*. London: Routledge.

Politis, J. (2001) "The relationship of various leadership styles to knowledge management." *Leadership and Organization Development Journal*, 22(8): 354–364.

Prahalad, C. K. (1990) "Globalization: The intellectual and managerial challenges." *Human Resource Management*, 29(1): 27–37.

Prahalad, C. K. and Hamel, G. (1994) "Strategy as a field of study: Why search for a new paradigm?" *Strategic Management Journal*, 15: 5–16.

Price Waterhouse (1997) *International Assignments: European Policy and Practice*. London: Price Waterhouse Europe.

Prokesch, S. E. (2000) "Unleashing the power of learning: An interview with British Petroleum's John Browne." In J. E. Garten (ed.) *World view: Global strategies for the new economy*. Cambridge, MA: Harvard Business Review Book: 287–312.

Pusch, M. (1994) "The chameleon capacity." In R. D. Lambert (ed.), *Educational exchange and global competence*. New York: Council on International Educational Exchange: 205–210.

Quinn, R. and Cameron, K. (1988) *Paradox and transformation*. Cambridge, MA: Ballinger.

Redding, S. G. (1997) "The comparative management theory zoo: Getting the elephants and ostriches and even dinosaurs from the jungle into the iron cages." In B. Toyne and D. Nigh (eds.) *International business: An emerging vision*. Columbia, SC: University of South Carolina Press: 416–439.

Rhinesmith, S. (1993; 1996) *A manager's guide to globalization: Six skills for success in a changing world*, 1st and 2nd edns. New York: McGraw-Hill.

Rhinesmith, S. (2003) "Basic components of a global mindset. In M. Goldsmith, V. Govindarajan, B. and A. Vicere (eds.) *The many facets of leadership*. Upper Saddle River, NJ: Financial Times Prentice Hall.

Richard, O. C. and Johnson, N. B. (2001). "Understanding the impact of human resource diversity practices on firm performance." *Journal of Managerial Issues*, 13: 177–195.

Robert, C., Probst, T. M., Martocchio, J. J., Drasgow, F., and Lawler, J. J. (2000) "Empowerment and continuous improvement in the United States, Mexico, Poland and India: Predicting fit on the basis of the dimensions of power distance and individualism." *Journal of Applied Psychology*, 85: 643–58.

Roddick, A. (1991) *Body and Soul*. New York: Crown.

Rosen, R., Digh, P., Singer, M., and Philips, C. (2000) *Global literacies: Lessons on business leadership and national cultures*. New York: Simon and Schuster.

Rost, J. C. (1993) *Leadership for the twenty-first century*. Westport, CT: Praeger.

Rotter, J. B. (1966) "Generalized expectancies for internal vs. external control of reinforcement." *Psychological Monograph*, 80: 1–28.

Ruben, B. D. (1989) "The study of cross-cultural competence: Traditions and contemporary issues." *International Journal of Intercultural Relations*, 13: 229–239.

Saulsman, L. M. and Page, A. C. (2004) "The five-factor model and personality disorder empirical literature: A meta-analytic review." *Clinical Psychology Review*, 23: 1055–1085.

Saxe, J. G. (1878) "The blind men and the elephant." In W. J. Linton (ed.) *Poetry of America: Selections from one hundred American poets from 1776–1876*. London: George Bell: 150–152.

Schein, E. H. (1996) "Career anchors revisited: Implications for career development in the 21st century." *Academy of Management Executive*, 10(4): 80–88.

Schneider, S. C. and Barsoux, J. L. (2003). *Managing across cultures*, 2nd edn. Harlow, UK: Financial Times Prentice Hall.

Schollhammer, H. (1969) "The comparative management theory jungle." *Academy of Management Journal*, 12: 81–97.

Schwartz, S. H. (1994) "Beyond individualism/collectivism: New cultural dimensions of values." In U. Kim, H. C. Triandis, C. Katgitcibasi, S. Choi, and G. Yoon (eds.) *Individualism and collectivism: Theory, method and applications*. Thousand Oaks, CA: Sage: 85–119.

Shaffer, M. A., Harrison, D. A., and Gilley, K. M. (1999) "Dimensions, determinants and differences in the expatriate adjustment process." *Journal of International Business Studies*, 30: 557–581.

Shaffer, M. A., Harrison, D. A., Gregersen, H., Black, J. S., and Ferzandi, L. A. (2006) "You can take it with you: Individual differences and expatriate effectiveness." *Journal of Applied Psychology*, 9(1): 109–125.

Shalley, C. E. and Gilson, L. L. (2004) "What leaders need to know: A review of social and contextual factors that can foster or hinder creativity." *Leadership Quarterly*, 15: 33–53.

Shannon, C. E. and Weaver, W. (1949) *The mathematical theory of communication*, Urbana: University of Illinois Press.

Shih, S., Wang, J. T., and Yeung, A. (2006) "Building global competitiveness in a turbulent environment: Acer's journey of transformation." In W. Mobley and E. Weldon (eds.) *Advances in Global Leadership*, vol. 4. Stamford, CT: JAI Press: 201–217.

Simons, J. (2003) "Is it too late to save Schering? CNNMoney.Com. http://money.cnn.com/magazines/fortune/fortune_archive/2003/09/15/349150/index.htm (accessed January 20, 2007).

Sinangil, H. K. and Ones, D. S. (1995) *"Turkiye'de calisan yabanci yoneticilerin kisilik ozellikleri ve bunlarin kriter gecerligi"* [Personality characteristics of expatriates working in Turkey and the criterion-related validities of these constructs]. Unpublished paper, Marmara University, Istanbul, Turkey.

Sinangil, H. K. and Ones, D. S. (1997). "Empirical investigations of the host country perspective in expatriate management." In D. M. Saunders (series ed.) and Z. Aycan (vol. ed.) *New approaches to employee management*, vol. 4, *Expatriate management theory and research*. Greenwich, CT: JAI.

Smith, P. B. and Peterson, M. F. (1988) *Leadership, organizations and culture: An event management model*. London: Sage.

Spreitzer, G. M., McCall, M. W. Jr., and Mahoney, J. D. (1997) "Early identification of international executive potential." *Journal of Applied Psychology*, 82(1): 6–29.

Stephens, G. K., Bird, A., and Mendenhall, M. E. (2002) "International careers as repositories of knowledge: A new look at expatriation." In D. C. Feldman (ed.) *Work careers: A developmental perspective*. San Francisco: Jossey-Bass: 294–320.

Stevens, M., Furuya, N., Oddou, G., Bird, A., and Mendenhall, M. (2006) "HR factors affecting repatriate job satisfaction and job attachment for Japanese managers." *International Journal of Human Resource Management*, 17: 831–841.

Stogdill, R. M. (1974) *Handbook of leadership: A survey of the literature*. New York: Free Press.

Straffon, D. A. (2003) "Assessing the intercultural sensitivity of high school students attending an international school." *International Journal of Intercultural Relations*, 27: 421–445.

Stroh, L. K. (1995) "Predicting turnover among repatriates: Can organizations affect retention rates?" *International Journal of Human Resource Management*, 6: 443–456.

Stroh, L. K. and Caligiuri, P. M. (1997) *Increasing global competitiveness through effective people management*. San Diego, CA: Global Leadership Institute.

Stroh, L., Gregersen, H., and Black, J. S. (1998) "Closing the gap: Expectations versus reality among repatriates." *Journal of World Business*, 33(2): 111–124.

Stroh, L., Black, J. S., Mendenhall, M. E., and Gregersen, H. (2005) *Global leaders, global assignments: An integration of research and practice*. London: Lawrence Erlbaum.

Stuart, D. (2007) *Assessment instruments for the global workforce*. White paper. Alexandria, VA: Society for Human Resource Management.

Sutton, R. I. (2001) "The weird rules of creativity." *Harvard Business Review*, 79(8): 8.

Suutari, V. (2002) "Global leadership development: An emerging research agenda." *Career Development International*, 7(4): 218–233.

Suutari, V. and Taka, M. (2004) "Career anchors of managers with global careers." *Journal of Management Development*, 23(9): 833–847.

Takeuchi, R., Yun, S., and Tesluk, P. E. (2002) "An examination of crossover and spillover effects of spousal and expatriate cross-cultural adjustment on expatriate outcomes." *Journal of Applied Psychology*, 87(4): 655–666.

Tallman, S. and Fladmoe-Lindquist, K. (2002) "Internationalization, globalization and capability-based strategy." *California Management Review*, 45(1): 116–135.

Taras, V. (2006a) "Instruments for measuring acculturation." Unpublished manuscript, University of Calgary.

Taras, V. (2006b) "Instruments for measuring cultural values and behaviors." Unpublished manuscript, University of Calgary.

Tenkasi, R. V. and Mohrman S. A. (1999) "Global change as contextual collaborative knowledge creation." In D. Cooperrider and J. E. Dutton (eds.) *Organizational dimensions of global change: No limits to cooperation*. Thousand Oaks, CA: Sage: 114–136.

Tetlock, P. E. (1983) "Accountability and complexity of thought." *Journal of Personality and Social Psychology*, 45: 74–83.

Thaler-Carter, R. (2000) "Whither global leaders?" *HRMagazine*, 45(5): 82–88.

Thich, N. H. (1991) *Peace is every step: The path of mindfulness in everyday life*. New York: Bantam Books.

Thomas, D. C. (1999). "Cultural diversity and work group effectiveness." *Journal of Cross-Cultural Psychology*, 30: 242–263.

Thomas, D. C. and Lazarova, M. (2006) "Expatriate adjustment and performance: A critical review." In G. Stahl and I. Bjorkman (eds.) *Handbook of research in international human resource management*. Cheltenham, UK: Edward Elgar: 247–264.

Thomas, D. C., Ravlin, E. C., and Wallace, A. W. (1996) "Effect of cultural diversity in work groups." *Research in the Sociology of Organizations*, 14: 1–33.

Tichy, N. and Charan, R. (1995) "The CEO as coach: An interview with Allied Signal's Lawrence A. Bossidy." *Harvard Business Review*, March–April: 68–78.

Tichy, N. M. and Devanna, M. A. (1986) *The Transformational Leader*. John Wiley and Sons.

Tichy, N., Brimm, M., Charan, R., and Takeuchi, H. (1992) "Leadership development as a lever for global transformation." In V. Pucik, N. Tichy, and C. K. Barnett (eds.) *Globalizing management: Creating and leading the competitive organization*. New York: John Wiley: 47–60.

Ting-Toomey, S. (ed.) (1999) *Communicating across cultures*. New York: The Guilford Press.

Tjosvold, D. (1986) *Working together to get things done: Managing for organizational productivity*. Lexington, MA: Lexington Books.

Toyne, B. and Nigh, D. (1997) "Foundations of an emerging paradigm." In B. Toyne and D. Nigh (eds.) *International business: An emerging vision*. Columbia, SC: University of South Carolina Press: 3–26.

*Tribune, La* (2006) "Des conseils d'administration peu féminisées" (June 14). http://www.egonzehnderknowledge.com/knowledge/content/misc/news/index.php?month=JUNE+2006 (accessed December 26, 2006).

Trompenaars, F. and Hampden-Turner, C. (1993) *The seven cultures of capitalism*. New York: Doubleday.

Tsang, E. (1999) "Internationalization as a learning process: Singapore MNCs in China." *Academy of Management Executive*, 13(1): 91–101.

Tsui, A. S. and O'Reilly, C. A. III (1989) "Beyond simple demographic effects: The importance of relational demography in superior–subordinate dyads." *Academy of Management Journal*, 32: 402–424.

Tucker, R. (2002) *Driving growth through innovation: How leading firms are transforming their futures*. San Francisco: Berrett-Koehler.

Tushman, M. L. and O'Reilly, C. A. (1996) "Ambidextrous organizations: Managing evolutionary and revolutionary change." *California Management Review*, 38(4): 11.

Tye, K. (1990) *Global education: School-based strategies*. Orange, CA: Interdependence Press.

Van der Zee, K. and Brinkmann, U. (2004). "Construct validity evidence for the Intercultural Readiness Check against the Multicultural Personality Questionnaire." *International Journal of Selection and Assessment*, 12(3): 285–290.

Van der Zee, K. and Van Oudenhoven, J.-P. (2000) "The Multicultural Personality Questionnaire: A multidimensional instrument of multicultural effectiveness." *European Journal of Personality*, 14: 291–309.

Van der Zee, K. and Van Oudenhoven, J.-P. (2001) "The Multicultural Personality Questionnaire: Reliability and validity of self- and other ratings of multicultural effectiveness." *Journal of Research in Personality*, 35(3): 278–288.

Van Oudenhoven, J.-P. and Van der Zee, K. (2002) "Predicting multicultural effectiveness of international students: The Multicultural Personality Questionnaire." *International Journal of Intercultural Relations*, 26(6): 679–694.

Van Oudenhoven, J.-P., Mol, S., and Van der Zee, K. (2003) "Study of the adjustment of western expatriates in Taiwan ROC with the Multicultural Personality Questionnaire." *Asian Journal of Social Psychology*, 6: 159–170.

Von Glinow, M. A. (2001) "Future issues in global leadership development." In M. E. Mendenhall, T. M. Kühlmann, and G.K. Stahl (eds.) *Developing global leaders: Policies, processes and innovations.* Westport, CT: Quorum Books: 264–271.

Weber, M. (1946) *From Max Weber: Essays in sociology,* ed. Hans H. Gerth and C. Wright Mills. New York: Oxford University Press.

Weber, M. (1947) *The theory of social and economic organization,* ed. A. Henderson and T. Parsons. Glencoe, IL: Free Press.

Weber, W., Festing, M., Dowling, P. J., and Schuler, R. S. (1998) *Internationales Personalmanagement.* Wiesbaden: Gabler Verlag.

Weeks, D. (1992) *Recruiting and selecting international managers.* Report number R-998. New York: The Conference Board.

Weick, K. (1996) *Sensemaking in organizations.* Beverly Hills, CA: Sage.

Weick, K. E. and Quinn, R. E. (1999) "Organizational change and development." *Annual Review of Psychology,* 50: 361–386.

Welch, D. (1994) "Determinants of international human resource management approaches and activities: A suggested framework." *Journal of Management Studies,* 31(2): 139–163.

Wellsfry, L. W. (1993) "Global leadership: A hermeneutic perspective on the transnationalizing of organizations." Unpublished dissertation, University of San Francisco.

Welsh, D. H. B., Luthans, F., and Sommer, S. M. (1993) "Managing Russian factory workers: The impact of U.S.-based behavioral and participative techniques." *Academy of Management Journal,* 36(1): 58–80.

Wheatley, M. (2006) *Leadership and the new science: Discovering order in a chaotic world,* 3rd edn. San Francisco: Berrett-Koehler Publishers.

Whittington, R., Pettigrew, A., Peck, S., Fenton, E., and Conyon, M. (1998) "Change and complementarities in the new competitive landscape: A European panel study, 1992–1996." *Organization Science,* 10(5): 583–600.

Wilbur, K. (1983) *A Sociable God.* New York: McGraw-Hill.

Wills, S. and Barham, K. (1994) "Being an international manager." *European Management Journal,* 12(1): 49–58.

Winograd, T. and Flores, F. (1986) *Understanding Computers and Cognition.* Reading, MA: Addison-Wesley.

Wolfensohn, J., O'Reilly, D., Campbell, K., Shui-Bian, C., and Arbour, L. (2003) "In their own words: Leaders speak out." *Harvard International Review,* 25(3): 50–67.

Wood, J. T. (1997) *Communication in our lives.* New York: Wadsworth.

Yamazaki, Y. and Kayes, D. C. (2004) "An experiential approach to cross-cultural learning: A review and integration of competencies of successful expatriate adaptation." *Academy of Management Learning and Education,* 3(4): 362–379.

Yeung, A. K. and Ready, D. A. (1995) "Developing leadership capabilities of global corporations: A comparative study in eight nations." *Human Resource Management,* 34(4): 529–547.

Yukl, G. (2002) *Leadership in organizations,* 5th edn. Upper Saddle River, NJ: Pearson Prentice Hall.

Yukl, G. (2006) *Leadership in organizations,* 6th edn. Upper Saddle River, NJ: Pearson Prentice Hall.

Zahra, S. and George, G. (2002) "Absorptive capacity: A review and extension." *Academy of Management Review,* 27(2): 185–203.

Zander, U. and Kogut, B. (1995) "Knowledge and the speed of the transfer and imitati organizational capabilities." *Organization Science,* 6(1): 76–92.

# Index

Note: *italic* page numbers denote references to Figures/Tables.